The European Tour
Yearbook 2014

OFFICIAL PUBLICATION

FONDÉ ★ EN 1743

MOËT & CHANDON
CHAMPAGNE

★

TRIANON, MAISON MOËT & CHANDON, ÉPERNAY FRANCE

CONTENTS

The introduction of the Final Series, four tournaments embracing China, Turkey and Dubai, provided a fascinating finale to the fifth edition of The Race to Dubai.

A total of 46 tournaments were played on The European Tour International Schedule in 28 different destinations with players from no fewer than 18 countries capturing titles before Henrik Stenson emulated Lee Westwood, Martin Kaymer, Luke Donald and Rory McIlroy in winning the Harry Vardon Trophy. Henrik's unique, dominating performance in achieving the 'double-double' of Tour Championship and FedEx Cup then the DP World Tour Championship, Dubai and The Race to Dubai followed Justin Rose's truly outstanding victory in the US Open. Now we eagerly anticipate hosting in 2014 Tom Watson's United States Team at The Gleneagles Hotel in Scotland where Paul McGinley will captain The European Team in their defence of The Ryder Cup. We look forward to the future while also remembering the superb achievements of all our Members chronicled again in this special 26th edition of The European Tour Yearbook.

George O'Grady CBE
Chief Executive, The European Tour

ACKNOWLEDGEMENTS

Executive Editor
Mitchell Platts
Deputy Executive Editor
Scott Crockett
Production Editor
Frances Jennings
Editorial Consultant
Chris Plumridge
Picture Editors
Andrew Redington, Rob Harborne
Statistician
Steve Doughty

Art Direction
Tim Leney, Andrew Wright
TC Communications Ltd
Print Managed by
Peter Dane
Mark Baldwin
The Print House Ltd

The European Tour Yearbook 2014
is published by The European Tour, Wentworth Drive, Virginia Water, Surrey GU25 4LX.
© The European Tour.

Thriving on Loyalty

Paul McGinley, 2014 European Ryder Cup Captain, with (left) George O'Grady, Chief Executive, The European Tour, (right) Jean-Noël Bioul, Rolex Communication Strategic Advisor and Rolex Ambassadors Nicolas Colsaerts, Luke Donald, Paul Casey, Martin Kaymer and Matteo Manassero at the historic announcement of the extended partnership between Rolex and The European Tour to 2022

The relentless pursuit of fresh opportunities across new frontiers is crucial in a changing, developing world although, importantly, loyalty remains an essential component in the bond that exists between The European Tour and those tournaments which formed the foundation on which today's International Schedule continues to thrive.

It is perhaps no coincidence that in a year when players from the continent, led by Henrik Stenson winning The Race to Dubai, enjoyed widespread success so France, Italy, The Netherlands, Spain and Switzerland all hosted outstanding tournaments which have been in place since the Tour began in 1972. Moreover Stenson's win was the 95th by a Swedish golfer on The European Tour on which his country has hosted tournaments since 1973 beginning with the Scandinavian Enterprise Open and now the Nordea Masters.

John Jacobs, the founding father of The European Tour, observed when the Tour was born: "It is my opinion that any further advancement of professional golf here in Britain is fairly limited due to the fact that we are a small country. I am therefore convinced that any major advancement in golf tournament promotion, and therefore substantial increasing in prize money, must

be done through our getting more involved in Continental Europe."

In France they say it is not only important to make history but also to write history. There will be few more monumental sporting milestones in that country's heritage than the playing of The Ryder Cup in the shadow of the Eiffel Tower in 2018. Even so the contribution that France made in 2013 both in hosting competition and supplying a record-equalling four champions in a single season on The European Tour International Schedule provided meaningful evidence of how golf is flourishing in that country.

Le Golf National, part of European Tour Property's network of world class venues and where The 2018 Ryder Cup will unfold, has since 1991 challenged the best golfers in the world and 2010 US Open Champion Graeme McDowell became the latest winner of the Alstom Open de France – a Championship which started life in 1906 and

which in 2014 will be played for the 43rd time on The European Tour.

Then came the playing of the Seve Trophy by Golf+ at Saint-Nom-La-Bretèche, another fabulous course on the outskirts of Paris familiar to European Tour Members, when for the first time since the year 2000 Continental Europe, led by the 2012 winning Ryder Cup captain José María Olazábal, triumphed over Great Britain and Ireland.

Moreover Grégory Bourdy wrote his own slice of history when the man from Bordeaux became the first player in the history of the match to win five points out of five. Only one month earlier Bourdy had by winning the ISPS Handa Wales Open added his name to a roll call of French champions in 2013 which reached four when, following the victories Raphaël Jacquelin (Open de España) and Julien Quesne (70° OPEN D'ITALIA LINDT), Victor Dubuisson (Turkish Airlines Open by the Ministry of Culture and

L-R: Jean-Lou Charon, President of the French Golf Federation, Pascal Grizot, Chairman of The Ryder Cup 2018 Committee, Valérie Fourneyron, Ministry of Sport and Youth, France and George O'Grady, Chief Executive of The European Tour at the Alstom Open de France

Seve Ballesteros at the Spanish Open, 1991

Tourism) posted the 30th French victory on The European Tour in the third leg of the inaugural Final Series on The Race to Dubai.

In all France, which also in 2013 played host to the French Riviera Masters on the European Senior Tour, the Najeti Hotels et Golfs Open presented by Neuflize OBC on The European Tour and the Le Vaudreuil Golf Challenge on the European Challenge Tour, has hosted Tour competition on more than 200 occasions although the first shot ever struck on The European Tour was on

April 12, 1972, when the Open de España, similarly steeped in history as it first took place in 1912, was played at Pals.

Antonio Garrido won that first event since when his Spanish compatriots headed by the incomparable Seve Ballesteros's 50 victories have racked-up a total of 167 wins – only English players with 283 have recorded more – and the playing of the 2013 Open de España at Parador de El Saler, Valencia, started a new cycle in the Championship's history following the

centenary celebrations which took place one year earlier.

Then in the height of the 2013 season three tournaments with similar historical significance took place in successive weeks with first Denmark's Thomas Björn winning the Omega European Masters at Crans-sur-Sierre, Crans Montana, Switzerland, then Holland's Joost Luiten followed his earlier win in the Lyoness Open powered by Greenfinity with a "home" triumph in the KLM Open at Kennemer Golf & Country

L-R: Scott Kelly, Gaston Barras, the driving force behind the Omega European Masters, Angel Gallardo, Christian Barras, George O'Grady, Yves Mittaz, Stephen Urquhart and David Probyn celebrating the tournament's proud history and on-going success at Crans-sur-Sierre

Club, Zandvoort, The Netherlands, and finally Quesne raised the French Tricolour at Golf Club Torino, Turin, with his success in the 70° OPEN D'ITALIA LINDT.

It is perhaps fitting that Björn, Chairman of The European Tour's Tournament Committee, will be the defending champion in 2014 when the Omega European Masters, which started life in 1923 as the Swiss Open, will be played for the 80th time 5000 feet high in the Alps at Crans Montana where Gaston Barras, supported now for many years by his son, Christian, has been the driving force on the 42 occasions that European Tour Members have visited this iconic setting.

In that time many scoring records have been set and eclipsed on the spectacular Crans-sur-Sierre course and another special moment was celebrated when Miguel Angel Jiménez made his 25th successive appearance in an event which he won in 2010. The Spaniard, who became the oldest winner aged 48 years and 318 days on The European Tour when he won the 2012 UBS Hong Kong Open, had already made history earlier in the year when he made his 600th European Tour appearance in the BMW PGA Championship.

KLM were title sponsors of The Dutch Open from 1981 to 1990, during which time the rich heritage of the tournament started in 1912 was enhanced by the victories of Bernhard Langer, Ballesteros

and Olazábal, three men who all became winning Ryder Cup captains, and there was much to celebrate again in 2013 with Luiten winning the KLM Open on home soil and in so doing becoming the first Dutchman to record multiple wins in a single season. In fact Luiten shared with four other players the accolade of winning twice on The 2013 European Tour International Schedule with Brett Rumford (Ballantine's Championship; Volvo China Open), Phil Mickelson (Aberdeen Asset Management Scottish Open; The 142nd Open Championship), Tiger Woods (WGC - Cadillac Championship; WGC - Bridgestone

Invitational) and McDowell (Volvo World Match Play Championship; Alstom Open de France) emulating him.

The Anniversary 70th edition of the Open D'Italia – first played in 1925 – provided the opportunity to recall how the foundation of the "Roll Call of Honour" for Italian golfers on The European Tour was laid during an amazing 23 day spell in 1976. Then Baldovino Dassu won first the Dunlop Masters then the Italian Open with four years later Rome's Massimo Mannelli claiming his national title. By the end of 2013 it was again a case of looking to the

Joost Luiten, winner KLM Open 2013

ALWAYS DRIVEN

1970 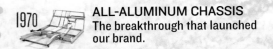 **ALL-ALUMINUM CHASSIS**
The breakthrough that launched our brand.

1981  **DS**
Showed the world, and the competition, what a golf car could be.

1983  **RACK AND PINION STEERING**
Ours was the first car that handled like one.

Innovate, Follow or
Get Out of the Way.

1994  **POWERDRIVE SYSTEM 48™**
A clean, efficient power plant to give gasoline a run for its money.

2004  **PRECEDENT®**
Player-centric design and engineering in a golf car. Finally.

2010  **VISAGE™**
Golf's groundbreaking mobile information system.

The Professional Golfers' Association
Partner

2

 OFFICIAL SPONSOR

The culture of innovation that permeates Club Car® began on day one in 1958. Since then, virtually every advance in the industry originated at Club Car. You know where to look for the next one.

www.clubcar.com   www.clubcar.tv   +44 7771 805463

L-R: George O'Grady, Chief Executive of The European Tour, The Right Honourable Alex Salmond MSP, First Minister of Scotland, Roger Cornick, Chairman of Aberdeen Asset Management and Martin Gilbert, Founder & Chief Executive of Aberdeen Asset Management

L-R: Francesco Molinari, Matteo Manassero and Edoardo Molinari

future after 24-year-old Andrea Pavan followed Edoardo Molinari (2009) as European Challenge Tour Number One.

The growth of the popularity of the game in Italy has accelerated with Edoardo and Francesco Molinari, apart from being European Tour champions and successful Ryder Cup winners, steering Italy in 2009 to World Cup glory and the emergence of Matteo Manassero, who celebrates his 21st birthday in April, 2014. Born 21 years after The European Tour started, he became the first teenager to win three events on The European Tour then at the age of 20 years and 37 days the youngest winner of the BMW PGA Championship – won by compatriot Costantino Rocca in 1996 – in an event which, like those national Opens in France, Spain, Switzerland, Holland and Italy, has been part of The European Tour along with the World Match Play Championship and Scottish Open since 1972.

The loyalty of sponsors and promoters is naturally vital to the Tour and in 2013 the BMW International Open celebrated its 25th birthday and Ernie Els provided the icing on the cake by "winning a tournament I've been trying to win for a long time" while the BMW Masters presented by SRE Group, won by Spain's Gonzalo Fernandez-Castaño, brought the curtain up on the inaugural Final Series in which Dustin Johnson (WGC – HSBC Champions), Dubuisson and Stenson (DP World Tour Championship, Dubai) were also victors. In all BMW have title-sponsored 40 tournaments on The European Tour and in 2014 the German automobile company will have more to rejoice with the BMW PGA Championship being played for the 60th time - the tenth with BMW as title sponsors – and for the 34th time at Wentworth Club.

Similarly Volvo have been long-term sponsors and in 2013 the playing of the Volvo Golf Champions, won by Louis Oosthuizen, Volvo China Open and Volvo World Match Play Championship took to 79 the number of tournaments they have title sponsored – with the 80th set to be the Volvo Golf Champions when it returns to the Durban Country Club in January, 2014.

Moreover the Alfred Dunhill Championship won by Charl Schwartzel in his native South Africa at Leopard Creek Country Club and the Alfred Dunhill Links Championship which England's David Howell claimed on the Old Course at St Andrews took to 55 the number of events title sponsored by the Alfred Dunhill brand.

L-R: Tony Jacklin, Sir Michael Parkinson, Peter Alliss, Bernard Gallacher and George O'Grady at the Gala Dinner to celebrate the 60th anniversary of The Ryder Cup being staged at Wentworth Club

L-R: Ukranian footballer Andriy Shevchenko, Conor Mallaghan, Owner and Managing Partner of Carton House, Rory McIlroy, Lee Mallaghan, Owner and President of Carton House and George O'Grady, Chief Executive of The European Tour, at the Irish Open

George O'Grady with guests from the Golf Channel at the International Media Dinner, Augusta Country Club; Jon Litner, Mike McCarley, Molly Solomon and Chris Murvin

The fifth edition of The Race to Dubai began with Glasgow's Scott Jamieson, a graduate of the 2010 Challenge Tour, claiming his maiden win in the Nelson Mandela Championship presented by ISPS Handa at Royal Durban and in all visited 28 destinations among those being Morocco where Germany's Marcel Siem won the Trophée Hassan II and Russia where the M2M Russian Open enabled Michael Hoey to give Northern Ireland their 49th European Tour win.

Jamieson was one of 12 first time winners on The European Tour in 2013 –England's Chris Wood (Commercial Bank Qatar Masters), American Matt Kuchar (WGC – Accenture Match Play Championship), South Africa's Dawie Van der Walt (Tshwane Open), Thailand's Kiradech Aphibarnrat (Maybank Malaysian Open), American Peter Uihlein (Madeira Islands Open –

Portugal – BPI), Ireland's Simon Thornton (Najeti Hotels et Golfs Open presented by Neuflize OBC), American Jason Dufner (US PGA Championship), England's Tommy Fleetwood (Johnnie Walker Championship at Gleneagles), Korea's Jin Jeong (ISPS HANDA Perth International), Johnson and Dubuisson also all recorded maiden victories. Uihlein, who finished 14th on The Race to Dubai, was named Sir Henry Cotton Rookie of the Year.

There were also a number of players warmly welcomed back as champions. Scotland's Stephen Gallacher completed the now traditional "Desert Swing" of Abu Dhabi HSBC Golf Championship, won by Welshman Jamie Donaldson, Commercial Bank Qatar Masters and Omega Dubai Desert Classic by winning the latter at the Emirates Golf Club so that he will be the defending champion when the 25th

edition of this event takes place in 2014. Richard Sterne, who missed most of the 2010 and 2011 season through injury, won the Joburg Open – one of six tournaments played in his native South Africa – and Darren Fichardt (Africa Open) and Thomas Aitken (Avantha Masters) took the number of tournaments won on The European Tour by his compatriots in 2013 to seven. David Lynn's victory in the Portugal Masters was his first since 2004 and provided a sixth English success with Paul Casey claiming the Irish Open at Carton House and pride of place, of course, going to Justin Rose with his magnificent US Open triumph. Rose became the first Englishman since Tony Jacklin in 1970 to return with this magnificent trophy and in so doing cemented his place in the record books alongside the other Major Championship winners in 2013 – Australia's Adam Scott (Masters Tournament), Mickelson and Dufner – and notched the 46th Major Championship win by a European Tour Member since Ballesteros won The Open Championship in 1979.

In creating history with his back to back wins, Mickelson's success in the Aberdeen Asset Management Scottish Open was also ground breaking. Not only was the future four years of the Championship confirmed that week but also the event became the first to be aired on a major United States TV broadcast network as it was shown by the Golf Channel on NBC. Two months later The European Tour signed a new ten year deal with the Golf Channel. Mike McCarley, Golf Channel President, said: "The European Tour is the first partner the Golf Channel ever had. It will be 20 years next year and this current deal takes it to three decades." O'Grady explained that the ten year extension showed the broad appeal of The European Tour with "immense talent

George O'Grady and Britain's Olympic heptathlon champion Jessica Ennis-Hill at the SJA British Sports Awards where O'Grady collected the Sports Team of the Year Award on behalf of Europe's winning Ryder Cup Team

being discovered in all the countries where our tournaments take place."

The global influence of The European Tour is well recognised. With Bulgaria and Turkey staging tournaments in 2013, no fewer than 41 countries – 69 when the Challenge and Senior Tours are included – have now hosted European Tour events and in all no fewer than 420 different players from 35 countries have been crowned European Tour champions. Rolex has been encouraging the development, organisation and promotion of golf worldwide throughout the Tour's lifetime, in addition to being the proud partner and Official Timekeeper of The European Tour since 1997, and on November 13, 2013, their long-standing partnership was further enhanced by a decade-long extension running until 2022 and including Rolex's partnership with The Ryder Cup.

George O'Grady, Chief Executive of The European Tour, said: "Rolex's commitment to the game of golf is unparalleled. They have been a valued partner of the Tour over many years, supporting us in every aspect of our mission to deliver golf worldwide. Rolex support us right across the board of all our Tours, including the Senior Tour, the Challenge Tour, The Ryder Cup and The European Tour itself. Rolex's partnership with us is unique and exceptional and together we look forward to creating a stage for tomorrow's golfers and working to shape the future of The European Tour."

The Ryder Cup, of course, has a treasured history which was celebrated at Wentworth Club, adjacent to the Tour's Headquarters,

Tom Watson, 2014 US Ryder Cup Captain, was presented with Honorary Life Membership of The European Tour by George O'Grady in 2010

towards the end of 2013 when the 60th Anniversary of the staging of the biennial match at the club in Surrey, England, was celebrated with Peter Alliss, the sole living survivor of the 1953 home team, joining Ryder Cup captains Tony Jacklin and Bernard Gallacher, happily fully recovered from suffering "sudden death syndrome," and O'Grady in being interviewed by Sir Michael Parkinson. Recent years have seen a transformation in Europe's fortunes, with Seve Ballesteros, Sam Torrance, Bernhard Langer, Ian Woosnam, Colin Montgomerie and José María Olazábal joining Jacklin and Gallacher as winning captains with Europe having won seven out of the last nine

matches heading to the 40th edition at The Gleneagles Hotel, Scotland, in September, 2014, when Paul McGinley and Tom Watson will captain Europe and the United States respectively.

Even so the old adage that if you don't respect the past then you'll find it hard to build the future remains true. As O'Grady said on that night at Wentworth: "It is a vital task of The European Tour to build and improve on the foundations set by the great stars of the game. That is our heritage and our duty."

Mitchell Platts

The 24 man field for the 2013 Volvo World Match Play Championship at Thracian Cliffs Golf & Beach Resort, Bulgaria

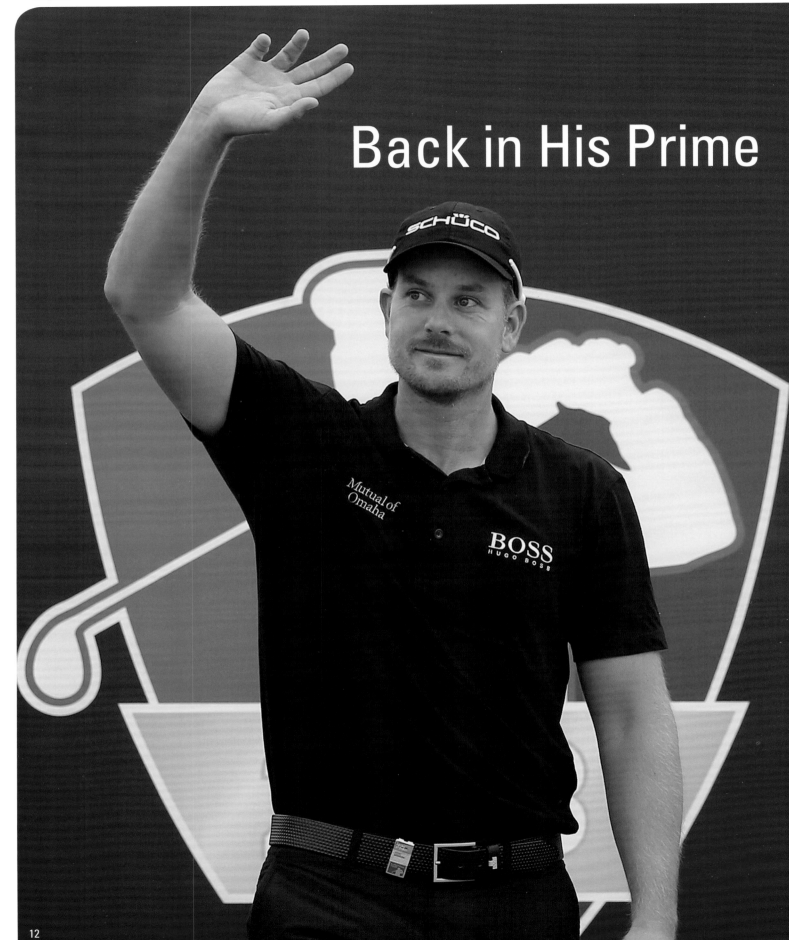

Back in His Prime

SOMETIMES life just isn't fair. Sometimes the stuff a man has been able to accomplish with ease becomes difficult and challenging. Sometimes a professional golfer begins to slide towards oblivion for no obvious reason.

So it has been on two occasions for Henrik Stenson. Eleven years ago the Swede with the hard, staring eyes found himself floundering just a couple of seasons into his European Tour career. Despite a victory in the Benson & Hedges International in 2001 to endorse his talent, just a year later he seemed to be heading for a very big door cruelly marked Exit.

Of course he recovered his balance, reignited his game and began an upward curve that took him into the 2006 and 2008 Ryder Cup teams. All was well in Henrik's world.

And then once again with the alarming abruptness of an unexpected thunderstorm, the man from Gothenburg lost whatever he had rediscovered. Confused, probably frightened, he began to slide. From fourth in the world rankings he moved to outside the top fifty. Then he lost his grip entirely. By the time 2012 dawned he was not even in the top 200. Few expected to see him

recover. Surely it was simply too far a plunge too swiftly.

After all he had not only lost his way as a golfer he had lost his go-to money, the reassuring treasure chest he had built up over several years of high-octane success. A victim of fraud his problems were big and apparently getting bigger. Time, clearly, for those of us who pay close attention to the old game to review with regret a career that had imploded.

The money loss did not help of course but it was a series of niggling injuries on top of a dramatic loss of confidence that contributed most to his problems. Yet while the rest of the world idly wondered where he was and then forgot about him, Stenson began to work even harder than before. Boosted by the support of his wife Emma and the ongoing encouragement of his swing coach Pete Cowen he grafted on the practice range.

Swedish national newspaper Dagens Nyheter:
"Brilliant Stenson - now only a Major remains"

Henrik celebrates with his family

Those hard eyes may have been focussed on a suddenly very distant horizon but as his work progressed so too did Stenson's belief that within him he still had the seeds of greatness. Golf may be contrary but Henrik Stenson is stubborn. Something had to give and eventually it was the game that gave way to a man who simply refused to accept his apparent fate.

He signalled his refurbished intent the week before The Open Championship with third place at the Aberdeen Asset Management Scottish Open at Castle Stuart. A week later those of us listening for it, heard his trumpet loud and clear again at Muirfield where he finished second.

From Scotland he flew back to America and another second place, this time in the WGC-Bridgestone. He followed this up with third in the US PGA Championship. By now the trumpet had turned into a full-blown horn section backed by a couple of drummers.

You had to be very deaf indeed not to hear the sound of something extraordinarily special happening for Stenson.

The man who had found himself nowhere was suddenly somewhere again.

And so it went on. Relentless doesn't quite capture how this golfer has performed since those reassuringly emphatic days of high summer in Scotland. He won twice in the United States, dominated their Fedex Cup play-offs and more than filled that treasure chest again. He returned to The European Tour and stomped his authority all over The Race to Dubai. Elsewhere you may read the detail of his final, pulsating victory at the DP World Tour Championship, Dubai and his elevation to European Number One as well as third in the World Rankings. Suffice to say here that his play over this climactic week was breathtaking in its considered intent and clinical execution.

Henrik with caddie Gareth Lord

Runner-up in the 142nd Open Championship at Muirfield

Henrik with wife Emma at The 2008 Ryder Cup Gala Dinner

"His ball-striking has been as good as anyone I've ever seen, " said Luke Donald. "Probably as good as Tiger in his prime." Ian Poulter, meanwhile, chipped in with "he is the best player on the planet right now."

These references endorse what has been the golfing comeback of my lifetime. Not bad for a chap who did not even really know golf existed until he was 12 years old and a friend invited him along to a practice range. Until then Stenson's passions had been football and badminton but there was something about this other strange game that intrigued him.

Hooked, he began to caress a lifetime habit by practising diligently every day. It turned out he had an instinctive ability but there were many other Swedish teenagers far

ahead of him and no-one really took a lot of notice of this late starter. He was pushing eighteen before he made scratch. Few outside his immediate family paid much attention to this achievement although one coach was sufficiently impressed by his powerful ability to drive the ball long and straight to offer a compliment. "That girl is really strong, " he told onlookers. Stenson admits he had very long hair at the time.

So he cut his hair, made the Swedish national team and decided he wanted to play golf for a living. By 2000 he was on the European Challenge Tour. It's a tough circuit and it swiftly tells a young man if he has got what it takes to take the next step. Three victories that year and the Number One ranking endorsed Stenson's credentials

and secured his place on The European Tour. He was off and very soon running with that first B&H win. Then he stumbled.

"I never really doubted my ability but obviously it can be frustrating when you go through long periods where you don't perform the way you know you can. But when you don't deliver the only recipe is hard work and trying to make things simple," he has said. "When you feel you are struggling then it's no fun. You're travelling halfway across the world and feel like you're going into a Formula One race and you've only got second gear. It's like how much fun is it going to be to fight it out like crazy for thirtieth place?

"When you've been out here as long as I have and have won a number of

A first European Tour title - the 2001 Benson & Hedges International Open

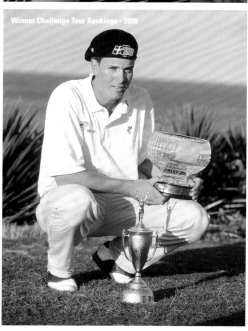

Winner Challenge Tour Rankings - 2000

Celebrating Europe's winning putt in The 2006 Ryder Cup at The K Club

tournaments then that's the buzz you're looking for – of being in contention. You know you're never going to win all the time but you want to feel you've got that chance."

This is an eloquent description of the task facing all players and further evidence that Stenson is a man who considers properly not just golf but life itself. At thirty-seven he is back in his prime. He is also a father, his son Karl toddling out to greet him on the final green in Dubai, his daughter Lisa waving happily from the side.

Naturally, he says he finds it hard to leave this family for long stretches but he also admits that he remains something of a child himself at times. His reputation as a practical joker is, if anything, even bigger than as a professional golfer. It's silly stuff... pens that give their holders an electric shock, practice balls that are super-glued together, that sort of thing. Like many Swedes he goes through much of life seeing the potential humour in a discarded banana skin. Maybe it is all those long, dark nights they endure in Scandinavia. "You never grow up – you just learn how to act in public, " he smiles by way of explanation.

He can often look remote and eerily cocooned in his own mysterious bubble when he is playing but away from the cut and thrust of high competition he is by instinct an amiable and approachable man, someone who enjoys removing this mask

of concentration and joining in the banter that helps everyone survive the rigours of a travelling life.

His home town of Gothenburg has long since been left behind. For ten years he lived in Dubai before moving to Florida in 2012 but each winter he returns to his Swedish cabin with his family to play in the snow. "We have a large extended family with siblings, parents and cousins that often come to see us wherever we are in the world. The house is always full of family, friends and coaches. It's a family affair," he enthuses.

Now as he carefully digests the enormity of his achievements in 2013, as he savours a glittering return to the game's high table and relishes participation once more in The Ryder Cup in 2014, he can turn his formidable mind to the next big task. "It has been an incredible summer for me, a dream season. A major next year would be the icing on the cake. How did I do it this year? I succeeded in staying in the moment and it just turned out to be a very long moment."

There is much more to Stenson's success than this explanation, of course but for now it will have to do. Sometimes it seems that a man has to move a very long way back before suddenly making huge strides forward.

Bill Elliott
Golf Monthly

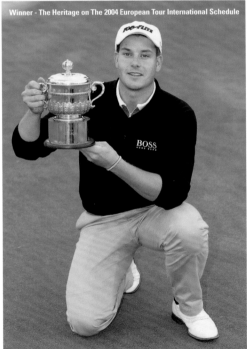

Winner - The Heritage on The 2004 European Tour International Schedule

Enjoying Europe's 2006 Ryder Cup triumph

HENRIK STENSON - FACTS AND ACHIEVEMENTS

Became European Tour Number One for the first time.

Follows compatriot Robert Karlsson (2008) in becoming the second Swede to finish European Tour Number One.

First golfer to complete DP World Tour Championship, Dubai and The Race to Dubai / TOUR Championship and FedExCup double.

Fifth Continental European to be European Number One following Seve Ballesteros (1976, 1977, 1978, 1986, 1988, 1991), Bernhard Langer (1981, 1984), Robert Karlsson (2008) and Martin Kaymer (2010).

First player in European Tour history to win the Challenge Tour Rankings (2000) and be crowned European Tour Number One (2013).

THE 2013 RACE TO DUBAI FINAL STANDINGS

			Points
1	**HENRIK STENSON**		**4,103,796**
2	Ian Poulter		3,172,729
3	Justin Rose		2,665,376
4	Graeme McDowell		2,420,306
5	Jamie Donaldson		2,181,113
6	Victor Dubuisson		2,031,675
7	Gonzalo Fernandez-Castaño		1,767,156
8	Richard Sterne		1,687,014
9	Thongchai Jaidee		1,585,521
10	Thomas Björn		1,546,736

1	**SCOTT JAMIESON**		66	57	**123**	**-7**
2	Eduardo De La Riva		62	61	123	-7
	Steve Webster		63	60	123	-7
4	Tim Clark		60	64	124	-6
	Maximilian Kieffer		62	62	124	-6
	Morten Ørum Madsen		60	64	124	-6
	Matthew Nixon		63	61	124	-6
8	Björn Åkesson		63	62	125	-5
	Sam Little		62	63	125	-5
	Colin Nel		62	63	125	-5
	Julien Quesne		62	63	125	-5
	Matthew Southgate		62	63	125	-5
	Jaco Van Zyl		68	57	125	-5

Total Prize Fund €1,000,000   **First Prize** €118,875

Scott Jamieson and Dr Haruhisa Handa

"To get your name on any European Tour trophy is a fantastic achievement, but it's a little more special when it is for someone like Nelson Mandela"

Scott Jamieson

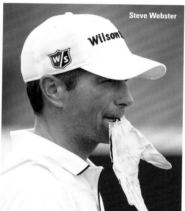

Steve Webster

Breaking with Tradition

Scott Jamieson launched the fifth edition of The Race to Dubai by becoming not only the first Scot to win the opening tournament of the season since the challenge for the Harry Vardon Trophy was renamed in 2009, but also the first Scot to win the opening tournament of any European Tour season since Stephen McAllister in 1990.

Furthermore the 29 year old from Glasgow gained his maiden win on The European Tour International Schedule in his 65th event and did so the hard way in a play-off in which he overcame Eduardo De La Riva – bidding to revive a Spanish tradition as Sergio Garcia (2009) and Pablo Martin Benavides (2010 and 2011) had captured season-opening Race to Dubai tournaments – and England's Steve Webster.

What made it all the more special for Jamieson was that not only did he come from six shots behind but he did so with an extraordinary 57, albeit that the Royal Durban course had been significantly shortened with a modified par of 65 after heavy rain washed out the first two days reducing the tournament to 36 holes.

Jamieson, however, produced a quite spectacular performance – De La Riva and Webster having set the clubhouse benchmark with scores of 61 and 60 respectively for seven under par totals of 123 – and then outlasted his rivals in the play-off with two par fours at the 18th as firstly De La Riva and then Webster made bogey five.

Eduardo De La Riva

Matthew Nixon

EUROPEAN TOUR
RACE TO
DUBAI

1	**CHARL SCHWARTZEL**		67	64	64	69	264	-24
2	Kristoffer Broberg		70	69	67	70	276	-12
3	Grégory Bourdy		66	65	74	72	277	-11
	Scott Jamieson		70	68	71	68	277	-11
	Garth Mulroy		71	68	70	68	277	-11
	Andy Sullivan		73	71	64	69	277	-11
7	Keith Horne		70	69	68	71	278	-10
	Richard Sterne		70	68	70	70	278	-10
	Steve Webster		67	69	70	72	278	-10
10	Richard Bland		67	73	71	68	279	-9
	George Coetzee		71	70	73	65	279	-9

Total Prize Fund €1,500,000   **First Prize** €237,750

Charl Schwartzel and Gaynor Rupert, wife of Johann Rupert, Executive Chairman and CEO Richemont

"Leopard Creek has always been a
special place for me. It's where my
career started with my first win,
and it's certainly close to my heart"

Charl Schwartzel

Kristoffer Broberg

Andy Sullivan

18
541 yds 495 mtrs
Par 5

ALFRED DUNHILL
CHAMPIONSHIP

dunhill
LONDON

Garth Mulroy

Grégory Bourdy

From Here to Eternity

For Charl Schwartzel the wait for his next victory following his magnificent success in the 2011 Masters Tournament had seemed like an eternity but he strode centre-stage once again with not one but two spectacular wins in eight days – first by 11 shots in the Thailand Golf Championship and then by 12 for this, his eighth triumph on The European Tour.

Not that there should have been any surprise about his win at Leopard Creek. Familiar territory has a habit of breeding success as Schwartzel's first European Tour triumph arrived at this venue in 2005. Moreover he was in a rich vein of form with this 24 under par performance taking him to a staggering 84 under par for his last five tournaments.

Grégory Bourdy initially took command with an opening 66 but Schwartzel joined him in the halfway lead after six birdies and an eagle in a 64. Then another equally stunning 64 swept him into an emphatic ten shot third round lead.

Second place eventually went to Kristoffer Broberg, who started his first full European Tour season in style despite being 12 shots adrift of the eventual champion at the end. Elsewhere, Keith Horne had a tournament to remember as he holed in one at the 192 yard 12th hole on both Friday and Saturday, the first player in history to achieve such a feat.

EUROPEAN TOUR
RACE TO
DUBAI

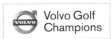

Minister Toko Xasa – Deputy Minister for Tourism, National Government; Madame First Lady Tobeka Zuma – First Lady of South Africa; Per Ericsson – President, Volvo Event Management-Golf; Louis Oosthuizen; Collins Chabane - Minister in The Presidency: Performance, Monitoring and Evaluation as well as Administration; Michael Mabuyakhulu – MEC for Economic Development and Tourism, KwaZulu-Natal Provincial Government and Minister Zoliswa Kota-Fredericks – Deputy Minister, Human Settlements, National Government

1	LOUIS OOSTHUIZEN		68	64	74	66	272	-16
2	Scott Jamieson		69	64	68	72	273	-15
3	Thongchai Jaidee		65	68	73	68	274	-14
4	Padraig Harrington		70	71	67	68	276	-12
5	Julien Quesne		72	67	67	71	277	-11
	Danny Willett		69	70	70	68	277	-11
7	Branden Grace		75	67	69	67	278	-10
	Paul Lawrie		69	70	70	69	278	-10
9	Thomas Björn		69	70	72	68	279	-9
	Rafa Cabrera-Bello		72	69	70	68	279	-9
	Nicolas Colsaerts		73	67	71	68	279	-9
	Shane Lowry		70	69	70	70	279	-9
	Matteo Manassero		75	69	66	69	279	-9
	Francesco Molinari		70	70	68	71	279	-9
	Richie Ramsay		69	73	70	67	279	-9

Total Prize Fund €2,000,000   **First Prize** €350,000

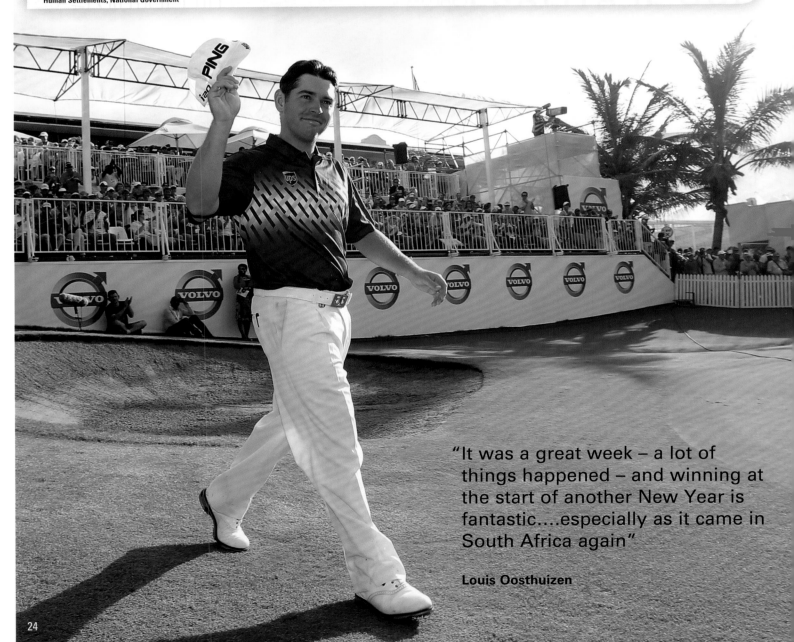

"It was a great week – a lot of things happened – and winning at the start of another New Year is fantastic....especially as it came in South Africa again"

Louis Oosthuizen

Thongchai Jaidee

Padraig Harrington

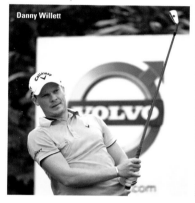
Danny Willett

Julien Quesne

Happy New Year

No player ushers in a New Year quite like Louis Oosthuizen. Successive victories in the Africa Open enabled him to launch both 2011 and 2012 with victories on The European Tour International Schedule, and the only difference in 2013 was the tournament title – the South African again being successful in his native country, this time in the Volvo Golf Champions.

Neither was it a surprise that a South African should win at Durban Country Club since that has been the case in every European Tour event hosted by the club – Ernie Els and Tim Clark each having won the South African Open there twice while Wayne Westner captured the FNB Players Championship.

Oosthuizen added his name to that list in style, elevating himself to a career high fourth place in the Official World Golf Ranking, as he swooped from five behind with a closing 66. Scott Jamieson, who led after a third round 68, was bidding for a second win in Durban in six weeks and came within a whisker of forcing a play-off when his

eagle chip at the 18th stopped two inches short of the hole, although the resulting birdie did secure the Scot second place on his own ahead of first round leader Thongchai Jaidee.

What delighted Oosthuizen almost as much as winning, however, was being presented with a Volvo Compact Excavator EC55 – a digger rather than a car – for his part in the winning Pro-Am team on the Wednesday.

volvoingolf.com

188 yds 172 mtrs
Par 3

2

Kwa-Zulu Natal Province

Scott Jamieson

Volvo Golf Champions

EUROPEAN TOUR
RACE TO
DUBAI

Jamie Donaldson and HH Sheikh Sultan Bin Tahnoon Al Nahyan – Chairman Abu Dhabi Tourism and Culture Authority

"I said to my Pro-Am partners that a top ten finish would be a miracle as the course was tough – so this is mad! I'm chuffed – you just never know what is going to happen in this game"

Jamie Donaldson

1	**JAMIE DONALDSON**		67	70	69	68	274	-14
2	Thorbjørn Olesen		68	69	69	69	275	-13
	Justin Rose		67	69	68	71	275	-13
4	Ricardo Santos		71	72	66	68	277	-11
5	Branden Grace		71	69	73	65	278	-10
6	David Howell		69	71	68	71	279	-9
	Martin Kaymer		71	69	70	69	279	-9
	Joost Luiten		70	69	73	67	279	-9
9	Jorge Campillo		74	68	69	69	280	-8
	George Coetzee		69	71	71	69	280	-8
	Jason Dufner		71	69	72	68	280	-8
	Gonzalo Fernandez-Castaño		70	67	71	72	280	-8
	Anders Hansen		71	71	69	69	280	-8
	Peter Hanson		73	72	66	69	280	-8
	Thongchai Jaidee		70	71	66	73	280	-8
	Jbe Kruger		72	69	69	70	280	-8

Total Prize Fund $2,700,000   **First Prize** €336,726

Ricardo Santos

Justin Rose

Branden Grace

Back to the Future

In the dark days when he fought a chronic back condition which might well have brought his career to a premature end, Jamie Donaldson could only dream of that first European Tour win. That it came after 255 tournaments in the 2012 Irish Open was a victory for perseverance.

Then again, winning breeds confidence so it was perhaps no surprise that his second win arrived just 13 events later and once again in a stellar field that included Rory McIlroy and Tiger Woods.

Donaldson set out purposefully – following the announcement made earlier in the week that Paul McGinley would captain Europe's 2014 Ryder Cup Team – with an opening 67 to sit alongside Justin Rose in pole position.

A last hole birdie gave Rose the halfway lead by one from Gonzalo Fernandez-Castaño, Thorbjørn Olesen and Donaldson while the Englishman, out in 32 in the third round, led by two from Donaldson and Olesen.

Rose was in the form of his life. Donaldson, however, was in a similar vein and he applied the pressure with five birdies in an excellent closing 68. The outcome was that both Olesen and Rose needed to hole birdie putts at the last to force a play-off. Olesen went close and Rose's attempt lipped out, meaning it was Donaldson's day.

Thorbjørn Olesen

Chris Wood and Andy Stevens, Group CEO Commercial Bank of Qatar

1	**CHRIS WOOD**		67	70	64	69	270	**-18**
2	George Coetzee		69	67	70	65	271	-17
	Sergio Garcia		69	66	70	66	271	-17
4	Alex Noren		71	67	66	71	275	-13
	Steve Webster		69	71	67	68	275	-13
6	Branden Grace		70	68	67	71	276	-12
	Simon Khan		67	73	64	72	276	-12
	Anthony Wall		66	71	70	69	276	-12
9	Felipe Aguilar		69	67	73	68	277	-11
	Victor Dubuisson		68	72	68	69	277	-11
	Jason Dufner		71	70	67	69	277	-11
	Mikko Ilonen		71	69	68	69	277	-11
	Thongchai Jaidee		70	69	70	68	277	-11
	Martin Kaymer		68	67	72	70	277	-11
	Andy Sullivan		67	71	74	65	277	-11

Total Prize Fund $2,500,000   **First Prize** €310,917

"I've seen a few of my mates pick up trophies on Tour in recent years; it feels such an honour to join them"

Chris Wood

Sergio Garcia

Steve Webster

Martin Kaymer

George Coetzee

EUROPEAN TOUR
RACE TO
DUBAI

Alex Noren

Sink or Swim

With the famous Mother of Pearl trophy in his sights it was a case of sink or swim. Chris Wood was aware, as he played the 72nd hole, that this was the time to remain calm if he was to rescue a famous win from the jaws of defeat. The Englishman had started the final round with a comfortable three shot lead before falling behind, only to resurface at the par five 18th requiring a birdie to tie George Coetzee and Sergio Garcia.

After a booming drive, a towering 202 yard six iron second over water changed his focus, leaving him, as it did, with an eagle putt from ten feet to take the title outright.

When the ball disappeared the celebrations began. After three runners-up finishes and 19 top tens on The European Tour, Wood had finally confirmed the potential he first displayed when he finished fifth as an amateur in the 2008 Open Championship and 12 months later missed the play-off at Turnberry by a solitary shot.

Ricardo Santos, the 2012 Sir Henry Cotton Rookie of the Year, claimed first round honours, watched by members of the Manchester United squad who were at a training camp in Doha, and he shared the halfway lead with Marcus Fraser, Martin Kaymer and Garcia. Then Wood, after a thundering third round 64, edged ahead before taking the applause he deserved.

Anthony Wall

Manchester United players Jonny Evans, Michael Carrick, Ryan Giggs, Paul Scholes and Wayne Rooney take a break from their Doha training camp to watch the golf

Simon Khan

OMEGA DUBAI DESERT CLASSIC
Emirates GC (Majlis Course), Dubai, UAE January 31-February 3, 2013

بطولة أوميغا دبي دزرت كلاسيك

1	**STEPHEN GALLACHER**		63	70	62	71	**266**	**-22**
2	Richard Sterne		62	70	66	71	269	-19
3	Felipe Aguilar		68	68	66	69	271	-17
	Thorbjørn Olesen		67	66	67	71	271	-17
5	Marcus Fraser		67	69	69	67	272	-16
	Lee Westwood		67	71	66	68	272	-16
7	Robert Rock		70	68	67	68	273	-15
	Ricardo Santos		66	71	69	67	273	-15
	Steve Webster		69	69	65	70	273	-15
10	Tommy Fleetwood		65	68	69	72	274	-14
	Jeev Milkha Singh		68	67	67	72	274	-14

Total Prize Fund $2,500,000   **First Prize** €309,233

Stephen Gallacher and HH Sheikh Majid bin Mohammed bin Rashid Al Maktoum

"Five eagles and a 62 – not a bad week all in all! The standard on Tour is so good now if you don't come up with some sort of magic like that then you don't win"

Stephen Gallacher

Richard Sterne

Where Eagles Dare

Five eagles over the course of the week and his lowest score in more than 1000 rounds of European Tour competition contributed to Stephen Gallacher's stunning victory. That Richard Sterne threatened to spoil the party, surging past Gallacher early in the final round, only served to illustrate the strength of character and skill that the Scot possesses as he regained control.

Sterne led with ten birdies in a first round 62 with Gallacher one behind courtesy of a holing a seven iron for a two at the 495 yard sixth before notching another eagle three at the 13th. Gallacher, still trailing by one at halfway, again eagled the 13th in a

career-low third round 62, climaxed with a 40 yard bunker shot for a three at the par five 18th.

Gallacher started the final day three ahead, bogeyed the first two holes and Sterne swept past him. The Scot, one behind with eight to play, was, however, oozing confidence after a brilliant recovery shot from the right rough at the ninth yielded an unlikely birdie. That shot was the catalyst for him to dig deep on the back nine – the 110 yard wedge he holed from the rough at the 16th being a stroke of genius that gave him a nap hand of eagles as well as the famous coffee pot trophy.

Thorbjørn Olesen

Felipe Aguilar

Lee Westwood

JOBURG OPEN
Royal Johannesburg & Kensington GC (East & West Courses), Johannesburg, South Africa February 7-10, 2013

1	**RICHARD STERNE**		63	65	68	64	260	-27
2	Charl Schwartzel		68	65	68	66	267	-20
3	Felipe Aguilar		67	66	68	67	268	-19
	George Coetzee		67	64	70	67	268	-19
	Ricardo Santos		70	65	69	64	268	-19
6	Thomas Aiken		67	70	66	66	269	-18
	Trevor Fisher Jnr		66	62	68	73	269	-18
	Keith Horne		67	66	71	65	269	-18
9	Lorenzo Gagli		67	68	68	67	270	-17
	Garth Mulroy		70	68	65	67	270	-17

Total Prize Fund €1,300,000   First Prize €206,050

L-R: Mpho Parks Tau, Executive Mayor of Johannesburg, Richard Sterne and George O'Grady, Chief Executive of The European Tour

"The only thing that kept
me going when my back
stopped me playing was
watching all the other
South Africans winning...
...I believed if they could
do it then I could again"

Richard Sterne

Ricardo Santos

George Coetzee

Simply Sublime

Richard Sterne, champion in 2008, completed a wire to wire win in the most emphatic manner. His first European Tour win in four years, following a career threatening back injury caused by bulging discs and arthritis, was secured with a tournament record 27 under par 260. In four rounds he carded only one bogey and his seven shot win eclipsed Charl Schwartzel's victory margin in 2010 by one.

Sterne book-ended his resurgence with two outstanding rounds. He opened with a 63 on the West Course to share the lead with 2012 Challenge Tour graduate Max Kieffer and ended with a 64 on the more demanding East Course, a round he nominated as probably the finest of

his career with birdies at the first and second, three more in a row from the sixth, another at the 13th and two more at the 17th and 18th.

A second round 65 gave him a share of the lead on 128 with Trevor Fisher Jnr, who shot 62, and the two shared the honour of posting the lowest halfway total in the tournament's history. Both men then scored third round 68s to stretch their overall tournament lead to five shots before Sterne showed his class in the final round to stride away from the field.

In the end, the 2011 Masters Tournament winner Charl Schwartzel took second with Felipe Aguilar, George Coetzee and Ricardo Santos sharing third.

Charl Schwartzel

Darren Fichardt and Zukiswa Ncitha, Mayor of Buffalo City Metropolitan Municipality

1	**DARREN FICHARDT**		69	67	65	71	**272**	**-16**
2	Grégory Bourdy		70	67	67	70	274	-14
	Jaco Van Zyl		66	67	68	73	274	-14
4	Garth Mulroy		72	67	69	67	275	-13
5	Desvonde Botes		74	67	66	70	277	-11
	Andy Sullivan		70	70	69	68	277	-11
	Mark Tullo		69	69	68	71	277	-11
	Tjaart Van Der Walt		70	68	68	71	277	-11
9	Andrew Curlewis		69	73	69	67	278	-10
	Emiliano Grillo		70	71	64	73	278	-10
	Ricardo Santos		71	66	70	71	278	-10

Total Prize Fund €1,000,000   **First Prize** €158,500

"To have my name on a trophy alongside Retief Goosen, Louis Oosthuizen and Charl Schwartzel makes winning here in Buffalo City so very special – I just love playing this course"

Darren Fichardt

Andy Sullivan

Grégory Bourdy

Mark Tullo

Garth Mulroy

Tjaart Van Der Walt

Jaco Van Zyl

Synchronised Success

Darren Fichardt has earned a reputation for being a strong front-runner. Indeed, he owned a 100 per cent record of winning on The European Tour when leading or sharing the lead entering the final round. So it came as little surprise that he claimed his fourth European Tour win, and 13th Sunshine Tour title, by a two shot margin in this co-sanctioned event after starting the last day alongside good friend and regular practice round partner Jaco Van Zyl.

Both Fichardt and Van Zyl had synchronised their own scoring to reach that point. Fichardt opened with scores of 69 and 67 then added a 65 in which he bagged seven birdies and one eagle. Van Zyl moved in a different direction with scores of 66-67-68 although six birdies in his third round underlined his scoring potential.

Adilson da Silva had emphasised the course could be attacked, setting a furious pace with five birdies in his first six holes in an opening ten under par 62, and led by three at halfway after adding a 68. Blustery conditions, however, made scoring more challenging on the final day and Fichardt's steady 71 guided him home although Grégory Bourdy swooped with a 70 to share second place with Van Zyl, while Garth Mulroy birdied the 14th, 16th and 18th for an equal best of the day 67 and fourth spot.

CHAMPION	MATT KUCHAR	
Runner-Up	Hunter Mahan	
Third	Jason Day	
Fourth	Ian Poulter	
Semi-Finals:	Matt Kuchar beat Jason Day 4 and 3	
	Hunter Mahan beat Ian Poulter 4 and 3	
Final:	Kuchar beat Mahan 2 and 1	
Consolation Match:	Day beat Poulter 1 up	

Total Prize Fund $8,750,000   **First Prize** €1,114,637

Matt Kuchar and Tim Finchem, PGA TOUR Commissioner

"I find match play such an amazing and unique format – it is so much fun to play with so much pressure and so much intensity"

Matt Kuchar

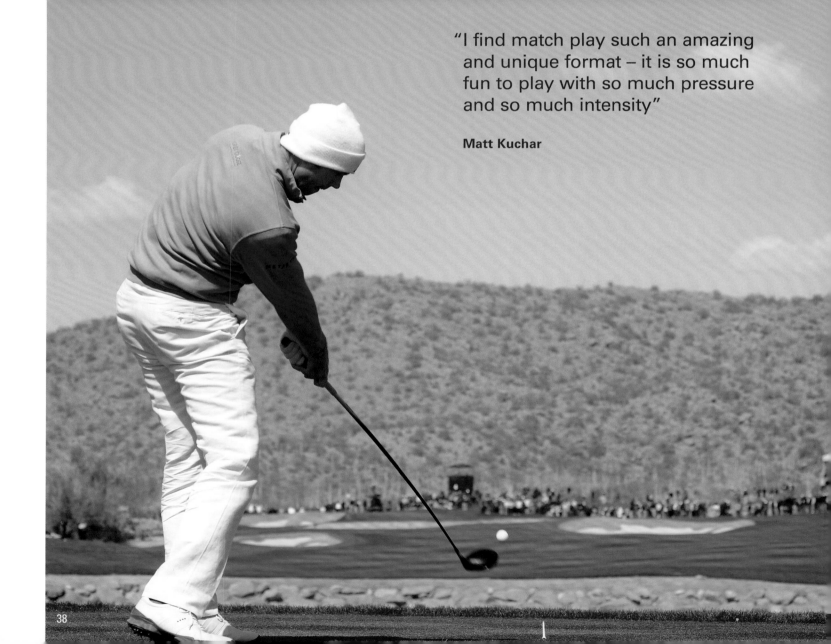

Ian Poulter

Shane Lowry and Graeme McDowell

Hunter Mahan

Winter's Tale

From the moment a freak snowstorm created a winter wonderland – play being suspended on day one by mid-morning – this was always destined to be an intriguing week and no sooner had the white stuff disappeared then so had the Number One and Two seeds with Rory McIlroy and Tiger Woods being beaten by Shane Lowry and Charles Howell III respectively.

Lowry then skied past Carl Pettersson 6 and 5 before his winter's tale was ended by Graeme

McDowell. When McDowell departed in the quarter-finals, defeated on the last green by Jason Day, it left Ian Poulter carrying the European flag in the semi-finals.

Poulter, of course, was the hero of The 2012 Ryder Cup and the 2010 winner of this title in addition to the 2011 Volvo World Match Play Championship.

The Englishman had arrived in Tucson following a six-week self-imposed sabbatical, but his attempt

to return in triumph was thwarted by Hunter Mahan at the last four stage.

That pitched two Americans together for the final and Matt Kuchar, who had proved his match play credentials early in his career when he captured the 1997 US Amateur Championship, claimed the honours in a wind-chilled final to become the third first time winner on The 2013 European Tour International Schedule after Scott Jamieson and Chris Wood.

EUROPEAN TOUR
RACE TO DUBAI

Kgosientso Ramokgopa, Executive Mayor of Tshwane and Dawie Van Der Walt

1	**DAWIE VAN DER WALT**		68	65	67	67	**267**	**-21**
2	Darren Fichardt		65	71	64	69	269	-19
3	Louis De Jager		71	65	65	69	270	-18
4	Peter Uihlein		68	66	68	69	271	-17
5	Björn Åkesson		66	75	66	65	272	-16
	Charl Coetzee		67	65	68	72	272	-16
	Danny Willett		68	68	70	66	272	-16
8	Morten Ørum Madsen		70	67	69	67	273	-15
	Graham Van Der Merwe		70	66	68	69	273	-15
10	Desvonde Botes		69	70	71	64	274	-14
	Vaughn Groenewald		68	70	70	66	274	-14
	David Howell		67	69	67	71	274	-14
	Hennie Otto		71	68	68	67	274	-14
	Jake Roos		69	67	69	69	274	-14
	Romain Wattel		70	66	71	67	274	-14

Total Prize Fund €1,500,000   **First Prize** €237,750

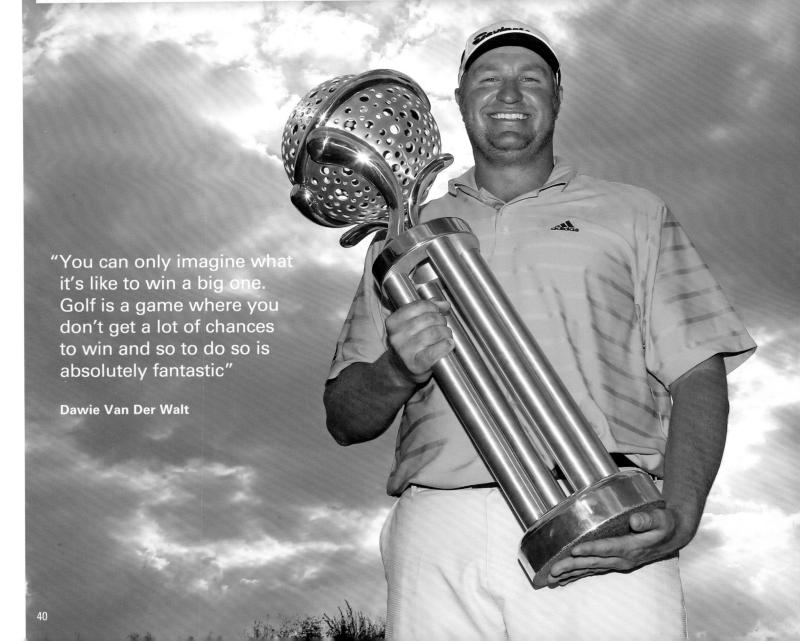

"You can only imagine what it's like to win a big one. Golf is a game where you don't get a lot of chances to win and so to do so is absolutely fantastic"

Dawie Van Der Walt

Charl Coetzee

Peter Uihlein

Epic Triumph

Björn Åkesson

Louis De Jager

Fast starts in final rounds are inevitably the foundation for glory so when Darren Fichardt, recognised as one of the best front runners in the game, began with three birdies in his first five holes, a second win in three weeks appeared the most likely conclusion.

Dawie Van Der Walt, however, challenged Fichardt by following an eagle at the fourth with birdies at the sixth and seventh to edge one ahead and, despite recording his only bogey in 72 holes at the tenth, squeezed further birdies out of the 12th and 15th to gain his maiden win on The European Tour International Schedule.

Fichardt had shown a clear pair of heels to his rivals with eight birdies in an opening 65; Charl Coetzee matched that 65 on the second day to climb to the top of the leaderboard; and Fichardt brilliantly closed his third round 64 with three straight birdies to tie Mark Tullo, Coetzee and Van Der Walt.

Twenty four hours later Van Der Walt was celebrating an epic triumph as Louis De Jager, who plays out of The Els Club Copperleaf, showed the benefit of local knowledge by finishing third with former world number one amateur Peter Uihlein fourth.

Darren Fichardt

EUROPEAN TOUR RACE TO DUBAI

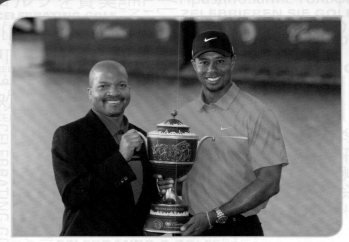

Don Butler, Vice President of Marketing for Cadillac and Tiger Woods

1	**TIGER WOODS**		66	65	67	71	269	-19
2	Steve Stricker		67	67	69	68	271	-17
3	Sergio Garcia		66	72	67	69	274	-14
	Graeme McDowell		66	67	69	72	274	-14
	Phil Mickelson		67	67	69	71	274	-14
	Adam Scott		72	70	68	64	274	-14
7	Keegan Bradley		68	68	69	71	276	-12
8	Peter Hanson		67	71	70	70	278	-10
	Rory McIlroy		73	69	71	65	278	-10
	Justin Rose		68	72	70	68	278	-10
	Michael Thompson		69	69	67	73	278	-10

Total Prize Fund $8,750,000   **First Prize** €1,139,523

"I feel like my game's becoming more efficient, and it's more consistent day-in and day-out"

Tiger Woods

Sergio Garcia

Seventh Heaven

If ever there was an appropriate moment for Tiger Woods to return to seventh heaven then this was that time. Woods, aged 37, competing in his 17th full season on the US PGA Tour, won his seventh WGC-Cadillac Championship, equalling his achievement of capturing seven WGC-Bridgestone Invitationals, and for good measure this was his 17th WGC success in 41 individual events in addition to being his 76th US PGA Tour triumph.

The figure seven also featured heavily in his playing statistics as he racked up 27 birdies in 72 holes and with a closing 71 claimed the title by two shots from Steve Stricker from whom he received a putting tip prior to the start

of the tournament. Stricker generously conceded that Woods might have putted just as well without that tip, albeit that Woods required only a career-record 100 putts.

This was also Woods's 39th win on The European Tour International Schedule in his 120th European Tour event and his 98th victory worldwide. Graeme McDowell pushed the World Number Two most of the way, eventually finishing tied third with Sergio Garcia, Phil Mickelson and Adam Scott, while Rory McIlroy climbed from tied 50th at the end of the first day to finish tied eighth with a closing 65.

Graeme McDowell

Steve Stricker

Rory McIlroy

1	**THOMAS AIKEN**		67	69	62	67	265	-23
2	Gaganjeet Bhullar		68	69	67	64	268	-20
3	Liang Wen-chong		66	66	69	69	270	-18
4	Kiradech Aphibarnrat		68	68	66	69	271	-17
5	Seuk-hyun Baek		68	68	70	66	272	-16
6	David Drysdale		67	67	68	71	273	-15
	Scott Hend		67	68	68	70	273	-15
	David Horsey		72	68	66	67	273	-15
9	Victor Dubuisson		69	68	70	67	274	-14
	Tommy Fleetwood		69	65	69	71	274	-14
	Julien Quesne		69	66	69	70	274	-14
	Himmat Rai		70	71	68	65	274	-14

Total Prize Fund €1,800,000   **First Prize €300,000**

Gautam Thapar, Chairman and Chief Executive Officer, Avantha Group and President of the PGTI and Thomas Aiken

"From the time my wife Kate, to whom I dedicate this win, and I arrived the people were great, so happy and always smiling. Therefore winning was the perfect end to a fantastic week"

Thomas Aiken

Liang Wen-chong

Scott Hend

Joy of Six

The European Tour's six tournament sector in South Africa might have concluded two weeks previously but Thomas Aiken ensured the continuing dominance of players from that nation by becoming the sixth South African champion in 12 events in 2013. In so doing Aiken foiled a potential home celebration as he held off the challenge of India's Gaganjeet Bhullar, emphasising his dominance with a birdie putt of 20 feet at the last.

Bhullar's closing 64 maintained a week of serious scoring – Aiken's 23 under par total was the lowest winning score in the tournament's history – which started in the first round with Chinnarat Phadungsil who built a five shot lead coming home in 28, including seven straight birdies from the tenth for an 11 under par 61 which fell just one shot shy of The European Tour record.

Chapchai Nirat notched seven birdies and Liang Wen-chong eight to be among the scoring heroes on day two, both recording 66s to share the lead. In round three, Aiken overshadowed the field with eight birdies and an eagle in a flawless 62 to move three ahead of Liang whose last day challenge, similar to that of Bhullar, emphasised again the strength of Asian golf even if, ultimately, they could not take the shine off the Rainbow Nation.

David Horsey

David Drysdale

Gaganjeet Bhullar

EUROPEAN TOUR
RACE TO DUBAI

L-R: Tan Sri Dato' Megat Zaharuddin Megat Mohd Nor, Chairman of Maybank, Yang Amat Berhormat Tan Sri Muhyiddin bin Yassin, Deputy Prime Minister of Malaysia, Kiradech Aphibarnrat and Tan Sri Dato' Mohd Anwar Mohd Nor, President of the MGA

1	**KIRADECH APHIBARNRAT**		65	68	70	203	-13
2	Edoardo Molinari		66	71	67	204	-12
3	Anders Hansen		66	73	66	205	-11
4	Victor Dubuisson		67	69	70	206	-10
	Charl Schwartzel		67	68	71	206	-10
6	Mark Foster		69	69	69	207	-9
	Padraig Harrington		69	68	70	207	-9
	David Howell		69	68	70	207	-9
	Pablo Larrazábal		69	70	68	207	-9
	Alex Noren		69	68	70	207	-9

Total Prize Fund $2,750,000   **First Prize** €350,411

"I just play for fun. I don't have any routine. I'm happy with the name John Daly of Asia. He won Majors and I'm proud people call me that"

Kiradech Aphibarnrat

Charl Schwartzel

Victor Dubuisson

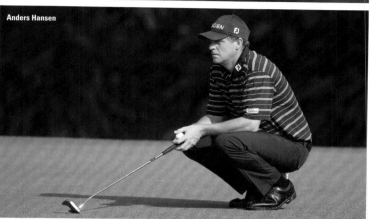

Anders Hansen

Exclusive Club

Kiradech Aphibarnrat earned membership of an exclusive club by becoming only the fourth player from Thailand to win on The European Tour International Schedule – following in the footsteps of Thongchai Jaidee, a five time champion, Chapchai Nirat and Thaworn Wiratchant, despite the demands of being compelled to wait for two hours with only three holes remaining when play was halted because of bad weather.

Aphibarnrat was on the 16th hole when, with the tournament reduced to 54 holes following storms on each of the first three days, he was forced off the course by lightning in the knowledge that he held a one shot advantage but that his closest pursuer Edoardo Molinari, back to his best after wrist surgery, was in the sanctuary of the clubhouse having shot a closing 67. Aphibarnrat, aged 23, was too excited to eat during the suspension!

Nevertheless the former junior world champion, dubbed Asia's John Daly because of his physique allied to his grip-it-and-rip-it style of play, returned to the course, nervelessly struck his approach to three feet for a birdie at the 16th, saved par at the next with a 15 foot putt and claimed a famous wire-to-wire triumph having held off the challenges of, among others, Anders Hansen, Padraig Harrington and Charl Schwartzel.

Edoardo Molinari

EUROPEAN TOUR
RACE TO DUBAI

TROPHÉE HASSAN II
Golf du Palais Royal, Agadir, Morocco March 28-31, 2013

L-R: HRH Princess Lalla Meryem, Marcel Siem, HRH Prince Moulay Rachid, Crown Prince of Morocco and M Mohammed Ouzzine Minister of Youth and Sports

1	**MARCEL SIEM**		64	68	69	70	271	-17
2	David Horsey		68	67	70	69	274	-14
	Mikko Ilonen		69	66	70	69	274	-14
4	Pablo Larrazábal		72	64	69	71	276	-12
5	Matthew Baldwin		72	70	68	69	279	-9
	Alvaro Velasco		67	74	69	69	279	-9
	Bernd Wiesberger		72	66	69	72	279	-9
8	David Howell		71	70	72	68	281	-7
9	Craig Lee		69	69	70	74	282	-6
	Julien Quesne		71	72	71	68	282	-6

Total Prize Fund €1,500,000   **First Prize** €250,000

"It was a big day for me and there was a lot of pressure out there. I'm happy I stayed cool and calm"

Marcel Siem

Golf

IN MOROCC

WWW.VISI MOROCCO.C

Mikko Ilonen

Alvaro Velasco

Pablo Larrazábal

Sweet and Sour

Wire to wire wins do not come much sweeter than this although for Marcel Siem there was a bitter pill to swallow. A few hours after savouring his third European Tour victory, he learned he had missed out on a Masters Tournament debut via the Official World Golf Ranking as, by the merest 0.03 of a point, he had failed to make the top 50.

Coincidentally, Siem had spoken with two time Masters champion and fellow German Bernhard Langer on the eve of the final round — seeking advice on how best to defend a four shot lead.

Langer offered many words of wisdom including the thought that his young compatriot should not look at the leaderboards on the front nine but then do so coming home.

Siem's name was top of the leaderboard after a brilliant opening 64 which included an eagle-birdie finish. He stayed three ahead with seven birdies in a second round 68, stretched that lead by one with a 69 before repelling challengers David Horsey and Mikko Ilonen and receiving the jewel encrusted gold dagger.

David Horsey

MASTERS TOURNAMENT
Augusta National GC, Augusta, Georgia, USA April 11-14, 2013

50

1	ADAM SCOTT		69	72	69	69	279	-9
2	Angel Cabrera		71	69	69	70	279	-9
3	Jason Day		70	68	73	70	281	-7
4	Marc Leishman		66	73	72	72	283	-5
	Tiger Woods		70	73	70	70	283	-5
6	Thorbjørn Olesen		78	70	68	68	284	-4
	Brandt Snedeker		70	70	69	75	284	-4
8	Sergio Garcia		66	76	73	70	285	-3
	Matt Kuchar		68	75	69	73	285	-3
	Lee Westwood		70	71	73	71	285	-3

Total Prize Fund $8,000,000   **First Prize** €1,104,379

Adam Scott receives the coveted Green Jacket from Bubba Watson, the 2012 Champion

Resolve and Redemption

"Australia is a proud sporting nation and this was one notch on the belt that we'd never got. But there was one guy that inspired us and that's Greg Norman. He's been incredible to me and all the young golfers in Australia and part of this definitely belongs to him"

Adam Scott

The 77th Masters Tournament will go down in the annals for a Sunday afternoon duel that really did have everything. It drew the second largest US television audience for the tournament in 12 years despite the fact no American, when it came to the closing holes, had a chance to win.

Patriotic loyalty was far from a requirement owing to the quality of the drama and the tales of human intrigue of those involved. If you did happen to have taken Monday morning off work to be watching in Australia, or delayed your Sunday evening meal in Argentina, this was one of those nerve-shredding occasions where the hand covers the face and you can only watch through the gaps in your fingers.

For fate had decided to play its most bewitching card. Two friends who had forged bonds of golfing brotherhood whilst playing together in the Presidents Cup had been picked for an epic game of who blinks first.

From Down Under, we had Adam Scott, the man who had always appeared the golfer most likely to end the jinx and become the first Aussie to win the Masters. The 32 year old was also trying

to atone for missing out on winning The Open the previous year, when he had bogeyed the last four holes at Royal Lytham & St Annes to hand the Claret Jug to Ernie Els.

From Argentina came Angel Cabrera, the 43 year old from Cordoba's poorest barrio, mentored by Roberto de Vicenzo and who just happened to be trying to win the Masters on the occasion of the great man's 90th birthday.

Jason Day

Angel Cabrera

Tian-lang Guan

Tiger Woods

Literally half a lifetime ago the most feted of all South American golfers had missed out on a play-off for the 1968 Masters by a stroke after signing for a four at the 17th when he had actually made a birdie three, and the higher score stood. One way or the other, then, this was all about resolve and redemption.

Before the smoke had cleared to reveal these two, however, there had been another Aussie, Jason Day, who had actually led the Masters with three holes to play. A brilliant young talent, on this day the 25 year old from Victoria was also cursed with a young man's mistakes as he bogeyed the 16th and 17th holes. We had also enjoyed the wonderful performance of 23 year old Dane Thorbjørn Olesen, who opened with a 78 on his Masters debut but who showed his exciting qualities to bounce back and finish in the top ten. Sandy Lyle completed all four rounds on the 25th anniversary of becoming the first British player to win the Masters, while 55 year old Bernhard Langer,

20 years on from the second of his victories, birdied each of the first three holes on Sunday to get within one of the lead before time's arrow pierced him on the back nine.

Most prominent of all, among the supporting cast, was the remarkable 14 year old Chinese Tian-lang Guan, who seemed to have written his own fairytale simply to make it to Augusta to become its youngest participant. Let's be honest, what were our best predictions for him – a couple of rounds in the early 80s? There would have been no shame in that. Instead, he opened with an astounding 73 and went on to make the halfway cut with an extraordinary display of composure to claim the Silver Cup as the leading amateur.

Striding up the 18th, though, there were only two men who held fate in their hands. Scott had once been allowed to stay off school to watch the conclusion of the 1996 Masters, the day when Greg Norman held a six stroke lead with a round

to play. The 15 year old had ended up in tears as Norman was caught by Sir Nick Faldo and vowed not only to play in the Masters himself one day, but win it.

Now, just for a moment, as his 15ft birdie putt trickled down the shelf in the middle of the 18th green before turning into the hole, he pictured himself in the Green Jacket. 'C'mon Aussie!' he screamed in rapture. Back down the fairway, Cabrera now had to make a birdie of his own to force extra holes.

The Argentine doesn't do nerves. Taking dead aim, his stupendous eight iron touched down next to the hole. All Australia must have been thinking: will this curse ever end?

At the first extra hole, the 18th, Cabrera's birdie try grazed the edge of the hole while Scott's

also stayed above ground. At the second, the tenth, both men finished within 20 feet of the flag in two. Again, Cabrera's attempt finished agonisingly on the edge.

Now Scott had a 15 foot putt to win. 'Now is the time to show how much you want this,' he told himself. Back home, a nation held its breath. On it went, the putt of destiny, the putt of redemption, before falling into the hole.

New Zealander Craig Heatley, chairman of Augusta's media committee, would sum up the moment beautifully: "When I heard that cheer on the tenth," he said, "I heard about 30 million people cheering in Australia and New Zealand as well."

Derek Lawrenson
Daily Mail

Marc Leishman

L-R: Honorary Starters Gary Player, Arnold Palmer and Jack Nicklaus

Thorbjørn Olesen

Lee Westwood

Sergio Garcia

1	**RAPHAËL JACQUELIN**		73	66	73	71	283	-5
2	Felipe Aguilar		68	71	74	70	283	-5
	Maximilian Kieffer		75	68	69	71	283	-5
4	Magnus A Carlsson		70	75	68	71	284	-4
	David Horsey		71	74	66	73	284	-4
	Paul Waring		71	71	69	73	284	-4
	Marc Warren		70	70	68	76	284	-4
8	Matteo Delpodio		73	69	73	70	285	-3
	Espen Kofstad		71	72	70	72	285	-3
	Eddie Pepperell		70	70	73	72	285	-3
	Peter Uihlein		70	68	74	73	285	-3

Total Prize Fund €1,500,000   **First Prize** €250,000

L-R: Gonzaga Escauriaza, Presidente Real Federación Española de Golf, Raphaël Jacquelin and Ignacio Mariscal, Director General de Reale Seguros

"I'm very happy to win at El Saler because the last time I played here in 2003 was with Seve Ballesteros as Continental Europe's Captain in the Vivendi Seve Trophy, and that means a lot to me"

Raphaël Jacquelin

Paul Waring

Marathon Man

Maybe it was simply a coincidence, with the London Marathon having been run earlier that day, but the Open de España most certainly evolved into a test of endurance with a record equalling nine hole play-off required before Raphaël Jacquelin brought closure with a five foot birdie putt against Maximilian Kieffer after Felipe Aguilar, who shared the first round lead with Morten Ørum Madsen and Gary Stal, exited at the third extra hole.

Jacquelin indicated his intentions with an outstanding second round 66 in tricky conditions to move alongside Rikard Karlberg and Aguilar, one behind halfway leader Peter Uihlein, before Marc Warren swooped ahead with a third round 68 – leading by two from Craig Lee with Jacquelin and Kieffer among those four behind and Aguilar five back.

The much revered course refused to submit to low scoring but Jacquelin's two birdies in the last four holes for a 71 enabled him to advance into the play-off with Aguilar (70) and Kieffer (71).

Nevertheless, for the Frenchman to gain his fourth European Tour triumph it needed another two hours of intense golf. The nine hole long distance contest equalled the 1989 Dutch Open play-off in which José María Olazábal beat Roger Chapman and Ronan Rafferty; Jacquelin eventually closing the deal with a wedge to five feet as they played the 18th hole for the tenth time that day. Sudden-death finish? Not quite!

Felipe Aguilar

Magnus A Carlsson

Marc Warren

BALLANTINE'S CHAMPIONSHIP
Blackstone GC (West & North Courses), Icheon, Seoul, South Korea April 25-28, 2013

Brett Rumford and James Maxwell, Regional Director Chivas Brothers Asia

1	**BRETT RUMFORD**		73	67	69	68	277	-11
2	Marcus Fraser		70	70	69	68	277	-11
	Peter Whiteford		70	69	69	69	277	-11
4	Romain Wattel		70	69	71	69	279	-9
5	Louis Oosthuizen		69	71	71	69	280	-8
6	Stephen Gallacher		70	68	75	68	281	-7
	Thongchai Jaidee		71	72	73	65	281	-7
	Hyung-sung Kim		71	69	74	67	281	-7
	Pablo Larrazábal		70	70	68	73	281	-7
	Alex Noren		71	67	69	74	281	-7

Total Prize Fund €2,205,000   **First Prize** €367,500

"It was an absolute rollercoaster ride of emotions – and a real honour to win the Ballantine's Championship"

Brett Rumford

Louis Oosthuizen

Romain Wattel

Peter Whiteford

Ticket to Ride

Brett Rumford will not easily forget the 18th hole – a 543 yard par five – where, after courageously holing an eight foot putt to save par in normal time, he struck a beautiful drive, a brilliant five iron approach to five feet then boldly holed for an eagle to beat compatriot Marcus Fraser and Peter Whiteford at the first extra hole.

Rumford gave credit for his first European Tour win since 2007 to swing coach Pete Cowen, with whom he had worked on taming a disobedient driver, although his prospects of success appeared minimal after an opening 73 left him sharing 75th place as Matthew Baldwin, Johan Edfors, Jean-Baptiste Gonnet, Gi-whan Kim and Kieran Pratt led the way with 67s.

Kiradech Aphibarnrat notched three late birdies in a 66 to share the halfway lead with Wade Ormsby and Arnond Vongvanij, as Rumford climbed 62 places with a 67, before Alex Noren's third round 69 took him one ahead of Pablo Larrazábal and Whiteford with Rumford, after finishing with five successive birdies, now joint fourth alongside Fraser.

Rumford continued like an express train on the last day with a stunning outward 30, moving two ahead, then digested the disappointment of a double bogey at the 17th – which enabled Fraser and Whiteford to draw level – by finding his ticket to ride with the eagle three that abruptly stopped his rivals in their tracks.

Marcus Fraser

EUROPEAN TOUR
RACE TO DUBAI

1	**BRETT RUMFORD**		68	67	69	68	272	-16
2	Mikko Ilonen		69	63	73	71	276	-12
3	Victor Dubuisson		71	72	66	68	277	-11
4	Robert-Jan Derksen		66	70	73	69	278	-10
5	Pablo Larrazábal		71	66	69	73	279	-9
	Ricardo Santos		70	72	68	69	279	-9
7	Andreas Hartø		72	71	70	67	280	-8
8	Felipe Aguilar		71	73	68	69	281	-7
	Thomas Björn		70	73	68	70	281	-7
	Paul Casey		71	68	72	70	281	-7
	Joost Luiten		73	67	68	73	281	-7

Total Prize Fund RMB20,000,000   **First Prize** €407,906

Brett Rumford and Li Hao, President of Binhai Lake Golf Club

"It's the first time I've played the week after a win – it's hard to get my head around what's happened at the moment"

Brett Rumford

Victor Dubuisson

Robert-Jan Derksen

Pablo Larrazábal

The Wizard of Oz

They might come to be known as the Wizards of Oz. Initially Adam Scott became the first Australian to win the Masters Tournament then, within a heartbeat, Brett Rumford claimed European Tour titles in successive weeks. This was no fantasy adventure for Rumford; this was a truly wonderful eight days in his career as he played beautifully to move to the top of The Race to Dubai.

The opening two days saw history made, firstly by Ye Wo-cheng who, at 12 years and 242 days became the youngest player to tee-up on The European Tour although he was outscored by Chinese compatriot

Dou Ze-cheng (16 years and 101 days), who shot 70. Subsequently, Dou went on to become the seventh youngest player to make the halfway cut on The European Tour as Mikko Ilonen with a nine-birdie 63 swept three ahead of Kiradech Aphibarnrat and Rumford, who birdied his last four holes in a 67. Blustery conditions did not deter Rumford on Saturday as, with three successive birdies from the sixth, he shot 69 to move to 12 under — one ahead of Ilonen, with Pablo Larrazábal one shot further back.

The Wizard, however, was in no mood to allow his rivals to upstage him. He put daylight between himself and Ilonen with three successive birdies from the 12th to become only the 31st different player in European Tour history to record back to back wins. As he celebrated so did young Dou, who finished 72-73 for a share of 33rd place.

420 yds 384 mtrs
Par 4
5

volvoingolf.com

Mikko Ilonen

EUROPEAN TOUR
RACE TO DUBAI

CHAMPION	GRAEME MCDOWELL
Runner-Up	Thongchai Jaidee
Third	Thomas Aiken
	Branden Grace
Semi-Finals:	Jaidee bt Aiken 3 & 2
	McDowell bt Grace 3 & 2
Final:	McDowell bt Jaidee 2 & 1

Total Prize Fund €3,000,000*   **First Prize** €800,000*
* Capped for The Race to Dubai €2,126,032 / €499,999

Per Ericsson, President, Volvo Event Management-Golf and Graeme McDowell

"A stunning course – intimidating, fast, fiery and one hundred per cent perfect for match play...and a special moment to have my name on this trophy with so many legends of the game"

Graeme McDowell

Thomas Aiken

Branden Grace

382 yds 349 mtrs
Par 4
6
Thracian Cliffs, Bulgaria

Volvo World Match Play Championship

Thongchai Jaidee

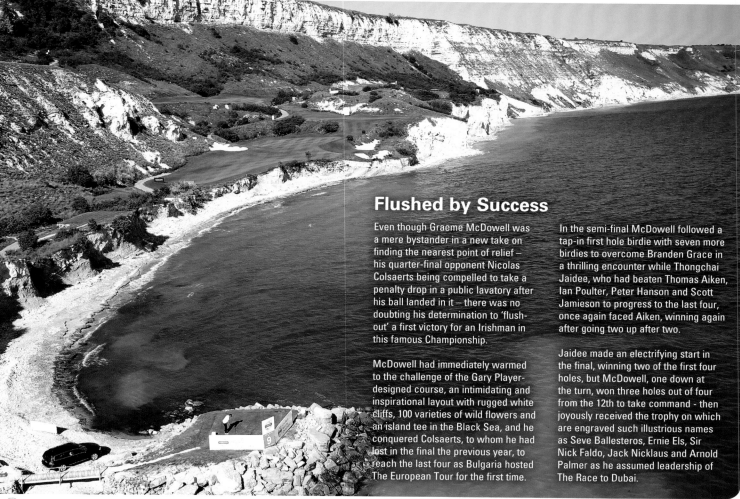

Flushed by Success

Even though Graeme McDowell was a mere bystander in a new take on finding the nearest point of relief – his quarter-final opponent Nicolas Colsaerts being compelled to take a penalty drop in a public lavatory after his ball landed in it – there was no doubting his determination to 'flush-out' a first victory for an Irishman in this famous Championship.

McDowell had immediately warmed to the challenge of the Gary Player-designed course, an intimidating and inspirational layout with rugged white cliffs, 100 varieties of wild flowers and an island tee in the Black Sea, and he conquered Colsaerts, to whom he had lost in the final the previous year, to reach the last four as Bulgaria hosted The European Tour for the first time.

In the semi-final McDowell followed a tap-in first hole birdie with seven more birdies to overcome Branden Grace in a thrilling encounter while Thongchai Jaidee, who had beaten Thomas Aiken, Ian Poulter, Peter Hanson and Scott Jamieson to progress to the last four, once again faced Aiken, winning again after going two up after two.

Jaidee made an electrifying start in the final, winning two of the first four holes, but McDowell, one down at the turn, won three holes out of four from the 12th to take command - then joyously received the trophy on which are engraved such illustrious names as Seve Ballesteros, Ernie Els, Sir Nick Faldo, Jack Nicklaus and Arnold Palmer as he assumed leadership of The Race to Dubai.

MADEIRA ISLANDS OPEN - PORTUGAL - BPI
Clube de Golf do Santo da Serra, Madeira, Portugal May 16-19, 2013

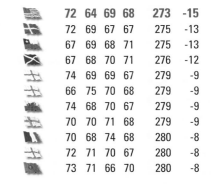

1	**PETER UIHLEIN**		72	64	69	68	**273**	**-15**
2	Morten Ørum Madsen		72	69	67	67	275	-13
	Mark Tullo		67	69	68	71	275	-13
4	Craig Lee		67	68	70	71	276	-12
5	Seve Benson		74	69	69	67	279	-9
	Richard Bland		66	75	70	68	279	-9
	Rhys Davies		74	68	70	67	279	-9
	Roope Kakko		70	70	71	68	279	-9
9	Christophe Brazillier		70	68	74	68	280	-8
	Jamie Elson		72	71	70	67	280	-8
	José-Filipe Lima		73	71	66	70	280	-8

Total Prize Fund €600,000   **First Prize** €100,000

Peter Uihlein and Alberto João Jardim, President of the Regional Government of Madeira

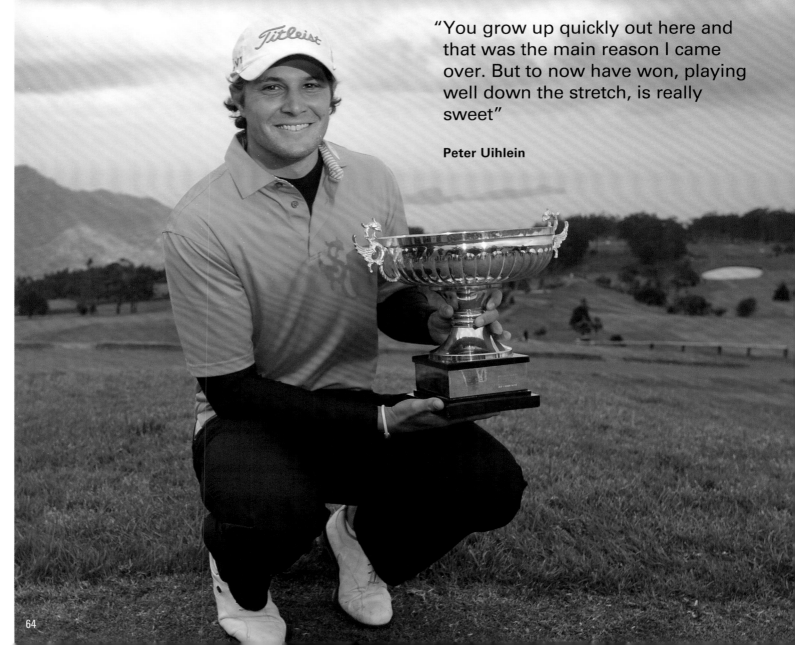

"You grow up quickly out here and that was the main reason I came over. But to now have won, playing well down the stretch, is really sweet"

Peter Uihlein

Sweet Sixteen

Peter Uihlein climbed new heights, claiming his maiden European Tour win on the mountain-top course, by calmly compiling a closing 68 despite seeing playing partner Mark Tullo hole in one and Morten Ørum Madsen launch a pulsating attack with eight birdies.

Tullo's ace with an eight iron at the 201 yard fourth edged him clear but Uihlein, the 2010 US Amateur champion, blitzed the back nine with four birdies – three in a row from the 11th – to overhaul Tullo before celebrating as Madsen's enterprising challenge came up a couple of shots shy.

Uihlein's second round 64 – he threatened to break 60 after negotiating the first 12 in ten under – took him from eight shots off the lead to sharing second place with Tullo one behind halfway leader Craig Lee after Lloyd Saltman had set the first round pace also with a 64.

Tullo holed from ten feet at the 17th for his fifth birdie in a 68 to move one ahead of Lee and Uihlein but Uihlein, advised by father Walter – CEO of major golf apparel and equipment manufacturer Acushnet – to launch his professional career on the Challenge Tour and The European Tour, made it a sweet 16th appearance.

Richard Bland

Mark Tullo

Craig Lee

Morten Ørum Madsen

Charm and Determination

"I feel unbelievable, really emotional. It's been an amazing week. I have always felt something really special about this place and this tournament. Everything has come together this week"

Matteo Manassero

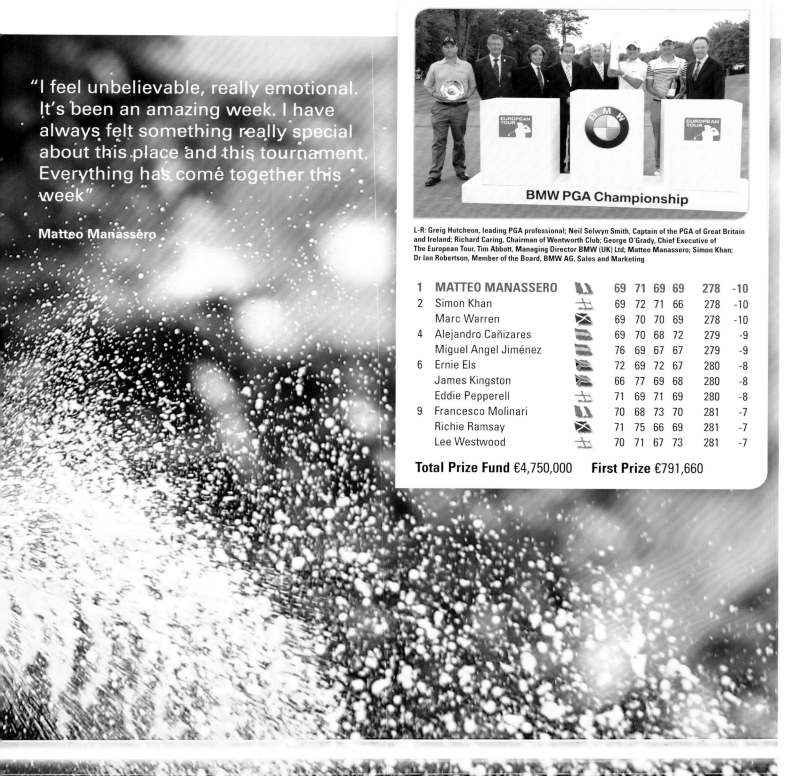

BMW PGA Championship

L-R: Greig Hutcheon, leading PGA professional; Neil Selwyn Smith, Captain of the PGA of Great Britain and Ireland; Richard Caring, Chairman of Wentworth Club; George O'Grady, Chief Executive of The European Tour; Tim Abbott, Managing Director BMW (UK) Ltd; Matteo Manassero; Simon Khan; Dr Ian Robertson, Member of the Board, BMW AG, Sales and Marketing

1	MATTEO MANASSERO		69	71	69	69	278	-10
2	Simon Khan		69	72	71	66	278	-10
	Marc Warren		69	70	70	69	278	-10
4	Alejandro Cañizares		69	70	68	72	279	-9
	Miguel Angel Jiménez		76	69	67	67	279	-9
6	Ernie Els		72	69	72	67	280	-8
	James Kingston		66	77	69	68	280	-8
	Eddie Pepperell		71	69	71	69	280	-8
9	Francesco Molinari		70	68	73	70	281	-7
	Richie Ramsay		71	75	66	69	281	-7
	Lee Westwood		70	71	67	73	281	-7

Total Prize Fund €4,750,000   **First Prize** €791,660

Matteo Manassero and Simon Khan

There occasionally comes a moment in a young golfer's life when the future is unveiled for all to see Such a moment arrived for Matteo Manassero early on a sun-speckled Sunday evening in May.

Three times he and Simon Khan had replayed the revamped 18th hole on Wentworth's West Course as each tried to win the BMW PGA Championship. Three times their skill and ambition had cancelled each other out as the record crowd remained rooted to the spot and purred with appreciation at what had turned into a play-off masterclass.

Then as he was driven back to the tee a fourth time, his caddie Dave McNeilly clinging on the back of the buggy, the pair discussed a change in tactics. McNeilly was a good man to have at the centre of this chat for the Belfast veteran has worked with some of the keenest brains in the game, men like Sir Nick Faldo, Retief Goosen, Padraig Harrington and Nick Price.

For the three previous playings of this sharp dogleg, the 20 year old Italian had taken a three wood. By the time he and McNeilly got to the tee, however, the decision had been taken to go for broke. This time it was to be the driver. The young gentleman from Verona had decided, the older supporter had nodded his approval or, as Shakespeare had Antonio say in Two Gentleman Of Verona... "Muse not that I thus suddenly proceed, for what I will, I will and there's an end." Quite so.

What Manassero wanted was to slide his ball further round that dogleg and thus be able to hit in a shorter club, the ball gaining height and spin and so becoming more likely to stay on a green that by now had shrunk in the players' eyes to an ever smaller and more intimidating target. The risk was that if he hit it even slightly poorly that he might find the trees as Marc Warren had during the first

Marc Warren

Mikko Ilonen

Par 3
168m
184yds
10

www.bmw-golfsport.com

of these play-off holes, the Scotsman's vibrant challenge for this glittering title suddenly lost in a tangle of leaves and branches.

Manassero, however, made no such error, his ball zipping off the tee to end in the perfect position. Khan murmured his approval before going for the same shot. He had no choice and he was unlucky when he caught his drive slightly off-balance to end a significant twenty or so yards behind his younger rival.

No choice either but to go for the green and when his shallow approach came up inches short of perfection, thudding instead into the snaking canal that now guards this final hole, the game was up, Manassero's carefully considered blow to the safe side of the green confirming this thought.

It was the perfect end to a near-perfect weekend, a two-day burst of high-octane play

by a posse of players who celebrated the return of warmth and sunshine after earlier cold and rain with a rainbow of top-class golf.

Not just Manassero, Kahn and Warren but also the likes of Lee Westwood, Spaniards Alejandro Cañizares and Miguel Angel Jiménez – the latter making his 600th European Tour appearance – and the man who oversaw the dramatic changes to that final hole, Ernie Els. This flurry of shot-making on a course that demands intelligence as well as power, emphasised not only that we were witnessing bravado performances from The European Tour's established battalion of stars but also applauding the arrival of the next generation.

This scenario, of course, is at the core of this great championship. It is always terrific to welcome back to the Tour's home the biggest of European names and particularly pleasing in

Ernie Els

James Kingston

Lee Westwood and Alejandro Cañizares

HOLD YOUR BREATH AND

Beauty has a new form. Muscular and sporty, the new BMW 4 Series Coupé exudes power even when standing still. Feast your eyes on the perfectly honed body which injects new life into the classic coupé shape and feel your pulse quicken in anticipation of the surefooted BMW xDrive: intelligent all-wheel-drive system.* The driving pleasure begins before you even open the door. From £31,575 OTR.** Visit **www.bmw.co.uk/4seriescoupe** to find out more.

THE NEW BMW 4 SERIES COUPÉ.

The new BMW
4 Series Coupé

BMW

bmw.co.uk
0800 013 2191

The Ultimate
Driving Machine

M · MY 8455

COUNT TO FOUR.

(6.2 – 4.1 l/100km). Combined 34.9 – 61.4 mpg (8.1 – 4.6 l/100km). CO₂ emissions 189 – 121 g/km. *Selected models only. **On the road
12 months' road fund licence, vehicle first registration fee, delivery, number plates and VAT. Figures may vary depending on driving style and conditions.

2013 to see the men who made Ryder Cup history at Medinah trying to strut their stuff, some succeeding better than others. But while this celebration of the game is good it is also gratifying to say hello to the younger men who must still walk some of the hardest of yards on the Tour's International Schedule.

Good also to see the West Course in such wonderful condition and an early tribute to the new man in charge of groundwork at Wentworth Club, Kenny Mackay and his team. His supervision of the preparation of the battleground, despite a winter that oozed stubbornly into what was supposed to be spring, brought a swift round of applause from the man he succeeded, Chris Kennedy, who had returned from Scotland to cast an experienced eye over the week.

What is beyond dispute is that the old, if freshened up, layout that is the West Course remains one hell of a challenge. Straight, long driving, precise approaches and careful, studied putting

remain the templates of any success to be had in this leafy corner of Surrey.

Westwood will ruefully confirm this thought. The English yeoman returned from Florida looking fit and tanned and happily bragging about the sensational improvement in his short game. He was right too, Els complimenting him during their round together on becoming a "short game wizard". Gone suddenly was the old, tentative stroke, cast away was the edgy look in his eyes when he contemplated a 'feel' shot.

Yet golf remains the most contrary of sporting pursuits, a game designed to encourage disbelief and regret as much as it releases conviction and joy. Westwood found this out the hard way. Birdies at three early holes on that final Sunday took him into a two shot lead and the word whistled round that he had the title sewn up.

Instead, having unveiled his new short-game prowess,

Miguel Angel Jimenez

Eddie Pepperell

Westwood lost his main strength, his ability to drive the ball straight and long. It meant a back nine of 40 blows and an eventual share of ninth place with his Ryder Cup team-mate Francesco Molinari and Scotland's Richie Ramsay.

Meanwhile Khan, a quiet, studied and polite Englishman who had to battle his way into the top flight in 2002 at 30 years of age via the minor circuits but who made his own history when he won this title three years ago, shot a final round 66 to secure his play-off place. Despite losing he then pitched up the following day at Walton Heath to qualify for the US Open Championship in another remarkable performance.

Manassero, of course, had already qualified by moving into the world's top 50. He is the youngest ever BMW PGA champion and, at just 20, is now heir apparent to his hero Severiano Ballesteros not just in ability but in charm and determination.

McNeilly, asked to describe his player, did not hesitate. "The way he behaves, he is so mannerly and very courteous but he is also a fierce competitor, let me tell you. Fierce!"

The other good news is that he is also quick. See it, visualise it, hit it, that is his mantra. It is not just the Sunday green trousers that tie him to Seve, not by a long, long way. Grazie mille Seve indeed.

Grazie also to the tented village that burst into vibrant life as the sun broke through over this thrilling weekend. There was much to do here, much to eat, drink and to see and at the centre was a racetrack with radio-controlled BMW racing cars. This is where the kids gathered – some of them very big kids indeed – to play and to have fun.

But then, in the end, this BMW PGA Championship turned out to be all about youngsters of one kind or another having an awful lot of fun.

Bill Elliott
Golf Monthly

Rory McIlroy receives the 2012 Players' Player of the Year award from the 2011 recipient Luke Donald

Ricardo Santos receives the 2012 Sir Henry Cotton Rookie of the Year award from the 2011 recipient Tom Lewis

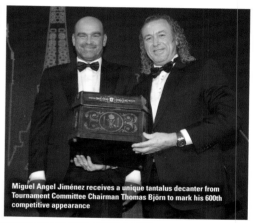
Miguel Angel Jiménez receives a unique tantalus decanter from Tournament Committee Chairman Thomas Björn to mark his 600th competitive appearance

The winning 2012 European Ryder Cup Team present Captain José Maria Olazábal with a framed picture

EUROPEAN TOUR RACE TO DUBAI

1	**MIKKO ILONEN**		70	63	65	69	**267**	**-21**
2	Jonas Blixt		70	66	66	68	270	-18
3	Bernd Wiesberger		69	72	64	66	271	-17
4	Thomas Björn		70	67	68	67	272	-16
	Rikard Karlberg		69	68	67	68	272	-16
	Matteo Manassero		66	65	71	70	272	-16
	Alex Noren		67	69	64	72	272	-16
8	Ross Fisher		72	67	70	64	273	-15
9	Felipe Aguilar		71	67	70	66	274	-14
	Julien Quesne		73	67	66	68	274	-14

Total Prize Fund €1,500,000   **First Prize** €250,000

HRH Prince Daniel, Duke of Västergötland and Mikko Ilonen

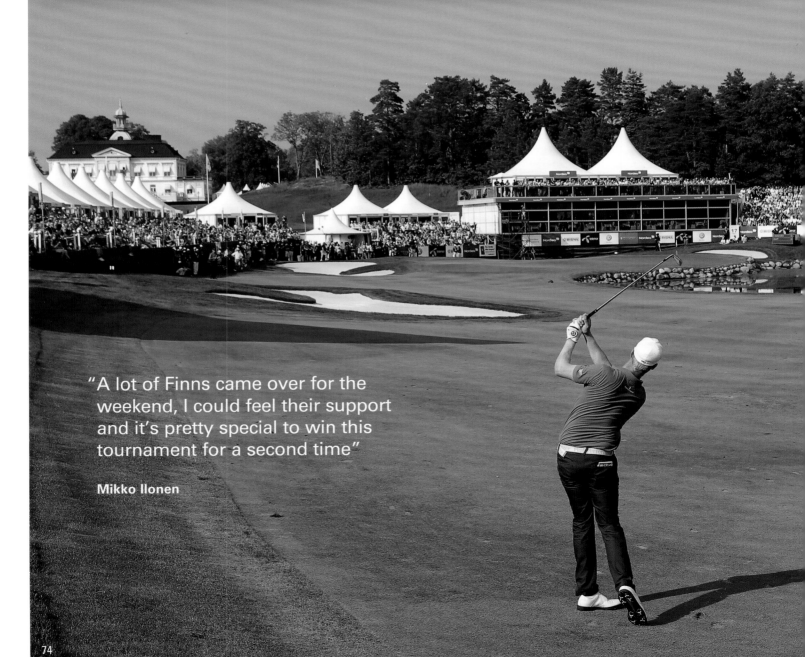

"A lot of Finns came over for the weekend, I could feel their support and it's pretty special to win this tournament for a second time"

Mikko Ilonen

Jonas Blixt

Bernd Wiesberger

Rikard Karlberg

Matteo Manassero

Thomas Björn and Alex Noren

Coronation Time

As coronations go, coinciding as it did with the 60th Anniversary of Queen Elizabeth II being crowned, this was pretty special for Mikko Ilonen as, suitably enough, he turned the final round into a victory procession before being presented with the beautiful crystal trophy by HRH Prince Daniel, Duke of Västergötland, the husband of HRH The Crown Princess Victoria of Sweden.

Given that Matteo Manassero had arrived in regal form, following his victory in The European Tour's flagship event the previous week, it was inevitable that he would command the early attention of the enthusiastic gallery and he did so by leading at halfway.

Ilonen, however, had announced himself by moving into second place, coming home in 30 for a second round 63, before sweeping ahead, holing with a pitching wedge for an eagle at the 15th in a third round 65 to continue the rich vein of form that had seen him post runner-up finishes in both China and Morocco earlier in the season.

Nevertheless it had been five years, 287 days and 126 tournaments since the Finn's last European Tour win, which just happened to be this title in 2007 in a year he won twice. Birdies at the second and third gave him the perfect start in a closing 69, enabling him to finish three shots ahead of Jonas Blixt and four in front of Bernd Wiesberger, who shot 64-66 on the weekend, with Manassero tied fourth alongside Thomas Björn, Rikard Karlberg and Alex Noren.

EUROPEAN TOUR
RACE TO DUBAI

LYONESS OPEN POWERED BY GREENFINITY
Diamond CC (Diamond Course), Atzenbrugg, Vienna, Austria June 6-9, 2013

1	**JOOST LUITEN**		65	68	67	71	271	-17
2	Thomas Björn		71	70	64	68	273	-15
3	Liang Wen-chong		67	72	69	66	274	-14
	Romain Wattel		68	68	69	69	274	-14
5	Jorge Campillo		70	67	66	72	275	-13
	Paul Waring		67	67	72	69	275	-13
7	Eduardo De La Riva		69	65	69	73	276	-12
8	Grégory Bourdy		70	68	70	69	277	-11
9	Lee Slattery		71	68	70	69	278	-10
10	Lorenzo Gagli		72	67	68	72	279	-9
	Shiv Kapur		68	72	71	68	279	-9
	Alexander Levy		66	75	68	70	279	-9
	Graeme Storm		66	74	71	68	279	-9

Total Prize Fund €1,000,000   **First Prize** €166,660

Mathias Vorbach, Director Communications International, Lyoness and Joost Luiten

"After a long time waiting it's special to claim my second win – the key was not making any silly mistakes in the last round"

Joost Luiten

Romain Wattel

Thomas Björn

Liang Wen-chong

Jorge Campillo

Call of The Siren

Joost Luiten could have been forgiven for wondering if this was not to be his day despite starting the final round three ahead. Firstly, playing partner Jorge Campillo birdied the opening hole as he bogeyed it, next Romain Wattel birdied four of his first six holes to also move within a shot, then Thomas Björn and Liang Wen-chong started snapping at his heels before finally, as he stood on the 14th tee, the siren called the players off the course due to lightning in the area.

Luiten, however, used the enforced one hour break to relax, returned to the course totally focused and at the 16th struck a marvellous approach which almost disappeared into the hole leaving him a simple tap-in birdie from where he moved on to gain his second European Tour win following his initial success in the Iskandar Johor Open in 2011.

Tom Lewis set the first round pace with nine birdies in a brilliant 63 but Luiten laid the foundations for his challenge with an excellent 65 before carding a second round 68 to edge one ahead of Callum Macaulay, Eduardo De La Riva and Paul Waring. Luiten's masterful third round 67 gave him that three shot advantage ahead of Campillo and De La Riva – Björn moved to within two with a sizzling 64 – and a closing 71 secured a two shot win for the 27 year old Dutchman.

Grégory Bourdy

Paul Waring

Eduardo De La Riva

NAJETI HOTELS ET GOLFS OPEN PRESENTED BY NEUFLIZE OBC
Aa St Omer GC, Lumbres, France June 13-16, 2013

Simon Thornton with the Najeti Hotels et Golfs Open presented by Neuflize OBC trophy

1	**SIMON THORNTON**		74	70	65	70	279	-5
2	Tjaart Van Der Walt		67	71	71	70	279	-5
3	Seve Benson		75	65	70	70	280	-4
4	Robert Dinwiddie		72	66	74	70	282	-2
5	Pelle Edberg		74	69	69	71	283	-1
	Chris Lloyd		73	68	70	72	283	-1
7	Agustin Domingo		74	71	68	71	284	0
	Jeppe Huldahl		73	67	73	71	284	0
	Victor Riu		68	71	72	73	284	0
10	Jamie Elson		75	69	68	73	285	+1
	Daniel Gaunt		70	70	75	70	285	+1
	Max Glauert		77	65	69	74	285	+1
	Brooks Koepka		75	70	68	72	285	+1
	Gary Orr		73	71	74	67	285	+1

Total Prize Fund €500,000   **First Prize** €83,330

"This is such a big win for me. My dad passed away three years ago, it still hurts, and so I dedicate this victory to him"

Simon Thornton

Seve Benson

Robert Dinwiddie

Tjaart Van Der Walt

Father's Day

Grandstand finishes in sport provide both participants and spectators with that never-to-be-forgotten moment to savour and Simon Thornton, unquestionably, will reminisce for many a year on his maiden European Tour triumph.

For not only did Thornton keep his hopes alive as he holed several important putts during a head to head final round battle of wills with playing partner Tjaart Van der Walt, he also saved the best for last as he rattled home a ten foot par putt on the 18th green to earn a play-off.

Just what it meant to the 36 year old Irishman became crystal clear when,

after two putts from 30 feet secured the title at the first extra hole, he dedicated the victory to his late father.

Quite a success then for Thornton as little more than a decade ago he was a seven handicap golfer playing for fun not funds. It looked unlikely to be his week after an opening 74 – seven behind pacesetter Van der Walt – but he followed a 70 with a 65, including a hole in one with a seven iron at the 206 yard 11th, before completing the first win by a Challenge Tour Member on The European Tour since Austria's Martin Wiegele in this event in 2010.

Pelle Edberg

Chris Lloyd

EUROPEAN TOUR
RACE TO DUBAI

1	JUSTIN ROSE		71	69	71	70	281	1
2	Jason Day		70	74	68	71	283	3
	Phil Mickelson		67	72	70	74	283	3
4	Jason Dufner		74	71	73	67	285	5
	Ernie Els		71	72	73	69	285	5
	Billy Horschel		72	67	72	74	285	5
	Hunter Mahan		72	69	69	75	285	5
8	Luke Donald		68	72	71	75	286	6
	Steve Stricker		71	69	70	76	286	6
10	Nicolas Colsaerts		69	72	74	72	287	7
	Gonzalo Fernandez-Castaño		71	72	72	72	287	7
	Rickie Fowler		70	76	67	74	287	7
	Hideki Matsuyama		71	75	74	67	287	7

Total Prize Fund $8,000,000   **First Prize** €1,101,397

Glen D Nager, USGA President, and Justin Rose

Heaven Sent

"The look up to the heavens was absolutely for my Dad.
Father's Day was not lost on me today. You don't have
many opportunities to really dedicate a win to someone
you love"

Justin Rose

IF all the worlds' a stage and all the men and women merely players, whoever scripted the closing scenes of the US Open Championship at Merion Golf Club surely must be awarded the Nobel Prize for Literature.

Justin Rose, of course, was author of his own destiny over 72 holes of a gruelling Championship, but the way in which the Englishman's final four shots melded with history, and the clouds suddenly parted over Ardmore, Pennsylvania, that Sunday evening, lent the occasion a mystical air.

It's a measure of Rose, the man, that even as he completed the greatest victory of his career, he grasped the full historic and spiritual significance of his achievement.

The dignity with which he spoke as he cradled the gleaming silver trophy was as impressive as the quality of the golf Rose had played at Merion. No doubt, the 2013 US Open got the great champion it deserved.

"I think a lot of us come from great men and we have the responsibility to our children to show them what a great man can be," said Rose, explaining why he'd paused after his final putt, gazed upwards and pointed towards heaven.

"I couldn't help but look to the heavens

and think that my old dad Ken had something to do with it," added the 32-year old, now a father himself. Rose and wife Kate have two children, Leo and Charlotte.

His gesture on that final green wasn't triumphal. Rose knew Phil Mickelson had two to play and a birdie by the American would force a play-off. Instead, the look in his averted eyes revealed how close Rose felt to his late father at that moment.

Win or lose, it didn't matter. He'd given his best on Father's Day and no proud dad could ask for more.

"The time we had together was quality not quantity," said Rose, who was 22 when his father succumbed to cancer at the age of 57 in September, 2002. "I can look back at our life together with a lot of fondness. Out there (in the final round), I felt I practised a lot of the lessons he taught me and conducted myself in a way he'd be proud of.

"I think my dad always believed I was capable of this. When he was close to

passing away, he told my mum 'Don't worry, Justin will be okay, he'll know what to do'. He kind of believed in me to be my own man. I took a lot of confidence from that."

The faith of his father was well founded. That Sunday at Merion, Justin Rose showed he knew precisely what to do and how, especially on the 18th, where he took up the gauntlet of history and played the shot of his life.

As Rose crested the hill on the final fairway, he saw his ball lying just yards from the plaque commemorating the most iconic stroke of all time.

The one iron approach Ben Hogan played into the 18th green on US Open Sunday in 1950 commands awe and reverence 63 years later. It set-up a pain-racked Hogan for the par he needed to reach a play-off and win for the first time in a Major since his near-fatal car crash 16 months earlier.

Many great champions were crowned at Merion. This is where amateur Bobby Jones completed his unique 'Grand

Ernie Els

84

Phil Mickelson

Slam' in 1930 … where Lee Trevino infamously tossed a rubber snake at Jack Nicklaus on the first tee before crushing him in the 1971 playoff.

Yet for those who revere Hogan as the father of modern professional golf, the opportunity to pay homage at his Merion memorial was worth the minor inconveniences caused to players and spectators alike by staging the 2013 US Open in the cramped, 126-acre confines of the East Course.

Naturally, that plaque posed a challenge to Rose.

"It's hard not to play Merion and envision yourself hitting the shot Hogan did," he agreed. "When I saw my drive sitting perfectly in mid-fairway, with the sun coming out, it was almost fitting.

"I've seen that Hogan photo a million times and I just stood over that shot and said to myself 'This is my time'. I felt at that point it was a good iron shot onto the green, two putts, like Hogan did, and possibly win."

If anything, Rose's four iron surpassed Hogan's, though it rolled 20 feet past the back pin into greenside rough. "I felt I did myself justice – probably put enough of a good swing where Ben Hogan might have thought it was a decent shot too."

From there, he expertly tapped a three wood off the long grass to inches, setting-up the par which effectively ended England's 17-year drought at the Majors and bridged the yawning 43-year gap to Tony Jacklin's 1970 US Open victory at Hazeltine.

A final round of even-par 70 left Rose on one-over, two ahead of Australia's Jason Day and the 'heartbroken' Mickelson, who'd led for three rounds but had to endure a sixth runner-up finish in 24 appearances at his national open.

Mickelson dominated the early agenda at Merion by returning in the early hours of Thursday morning from a trans-continental trip to his daughter Amanda's eighth grade graduation to take the first round lead with a 67.

Jason Dufner

Gonzalo Fernandez-Castaño

Jason Day

The Dorchester
The Beverly Hills Hotel
Le Meurice
Hôtel Plaza Athénée
Hotel Principe di Savoia
Hotel Bel-Air
Coworth Park
45 Park Lane
Le Richemond
Hotel Eden

London Paris Beverly Hills

Paris   Milan   Ascot   London

Rome   *Los Angeles*   Geneva

)(Dorchester *Collection*

ICONIC HOTELS IN ICONIC PLACES

He was one ahead of Luke Donald and Matt Goggin when the first round finished on Friday with just five players under par. Rose shot 71.

Mickelson shared the lead with Billy Horschel on one-under when 36 holes were completed on Saturday morning, with Rose (69), Donald (72) and Steve Stricker (69) one back

Mickelson was the only player below par through 54 holes, with Hunter Mahan, Charl Schwartzel and Stricker one back. Rose was two behind, tied fifth with Donald and Horschel on one-over.

With a frostbitten putter, Mickelson was slow getting into his stride in round four as double-bogeys at the gruelling par three third and par four fifth sandwiched a birdie at the long fourth.

Rose played those tortuous first five holes in one-over but seized the initiative with back-to-back birdies at six and seven.

Mickelson then set the Championship and the galleries alight with a pitch-in at the tenth. Rose, absorbing a three-putt bogey at 11 when he heard the roars from behind, responded superbly with crucial back-to-back birdies at 12 and 13.

Any hopes Mickelson harboured were dashed by dropped shots at the short 13th and difficult 15th holes, leaving him too much to do down the stretch.

The stage was set for Rose's soliloquy and this quintessential English gent delivered it with rare eloquence.

Karl MacGinty
Irish Independent

Nicolas Colsaerts

Billy Horschel

Hunter Mahan

Luke Donald

Ernie Els and Dr Friedrich Eichiner, Member of the Board of Management, BMW AG

#	Name		R1	R2	R3	R4	Total	Par
1	**ERNIE ELS**		**63**	**69**	**69**	**69**	**270**	**-18**
2	Thomas Björn		68	69	65	69	271	-17
3	Alexander Levy		65	68	68	71	272	-16
4	Martin Kaymer		64	71	69	69	273	-15
	Alex Noren		64	71	66	72	273	-15
	Bernd Wiesberger		66	68	71	68	273	-15
7	Darren Fichardt		70	66	69	69	274	-14
	Sergio Garcia		71	69	65	69	274	-14
	Wen-yi Huang		71	69	69	65	274	-14
10	Robert-Jan Derksen		64	72	70	69	275	-13
	Joost Luiten		69	68	67	71	275	-13
	John Parry		67	72	67	69	275	-13
	Marcel Siem		67	68	69	71	275	-13
	Henrik Stenson		68	69	71	67	275	-13
	Brandon Stone		66	71	67	71	275	-13
	Peter Uihlein		70	66	67	72	275	-13
	Paul Waring		66	73	67	69	275	-13

Total Prize Fund €2,000,000   **First Prize** €333,330

"I am proud to see my name on this beautiful trophy – I've been trying to win here for a long time and I'm delighted to have done it"

Ernie Els

Alexander Levy

Thomas Björn

Bernd Wiesberger

Alex Noren and Marcel Siem

As passionate about beer
as you are about golf.

PREMIUM GERMAN BEER
WITH A GLOBAL REPUTATION

- No. 1 Imported Premium Pilsner
  among the German private breweries[*]

- Enjoyed in more than 60 countries
  around the globe

EUROPEAN TOUR **OFFICIAL**
SUPPLIER

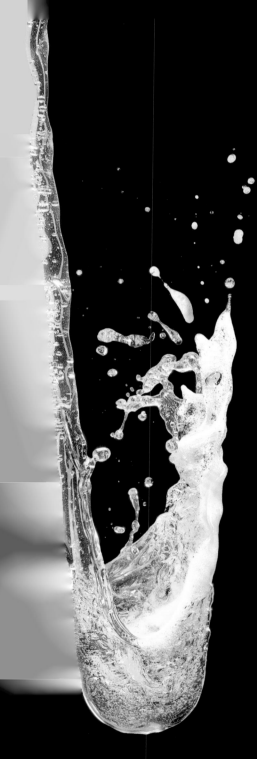

RSTEINER

UM GERMAN BEER · SINCE 1753

WARSTEINER
EINE KÖNIGIN UNTER DEN BIEREN
1753
WARSTEINER
PREMIUM VERUM

Crème de la Crème

Ernie Els brought a new meaning to the old adage that the cream always rises to the top when the four-time Major Champion captured his 28th European Tour title – and 68th as a professional – after launching the week by wearing lederhosen and winning a cow-milking contest with team mates Paul Casey and Sergio Garcia.

Els, one month shy of defending his Open Championship title, made this a very special Silver Anniversary edition of a tournament previously won by no fewer than four Major Champions – Paul Azinger (twice), Sandy Lyle, John Daly and Martin Kaymer – as he became, at 43, the oldest winner in its 25 year history.

The South African maestro was a wire-to-wire champion, following a superlative opening 63, although after back to back 69s he was joined at the top by Alexander Levy,

who practices at European Tour Property Terre Blanche, and Alex Noren. Then Thomas Björn birdied three holes in a row from the third in the final round, swooping ahead, before Els edged him out by one with Levy, making only his 14th European Tour start, third and local favourite Kaymer, cheered by 16,000 spectators, tied fourth with Bernd Wiesberger and Noren,

Dr Friedrich Eichiner, Member of the Board of Management of BMW AG, pointed out that "BMW's success story as an internationally valued partner of golf began 25 years ago at Golfclub München Eichenried – the way this tournament was embraced by the fans showed again that we are dead right with our extensive support of this captivating sport."

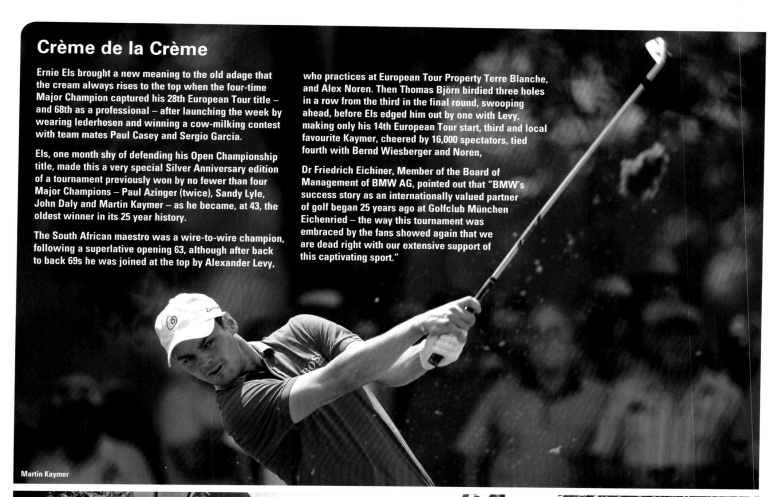

Martin Kaymer

Maximilian Kieffer of Germany sits on the BMW mountain bike that he won in a nearest to the pin competition

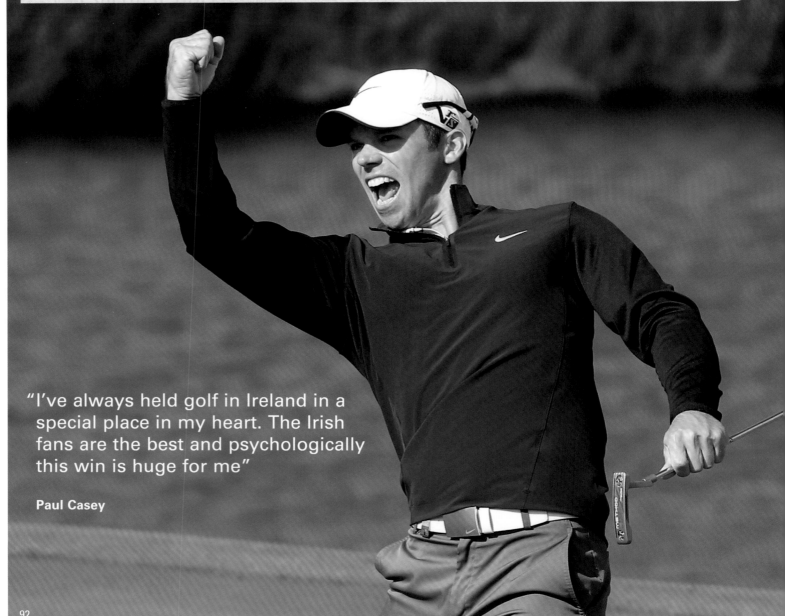

1	**PAUL CASEY**		68	72	67	67	274	-14
2	Joost Luiten		67	70	66	74	277	-11
	Robert Rock		69	66	71	71	277	-11
4	Pablo Larrazábal		69	69	66	75	279	-9
5	Rafa Cabrera-Bello		69	70	70	71	280	-8
	Shane Lowry		67	70	74	69	280	-8
	José María Olazábal		68	69	71	72	280	-8
	Alvaro Quiros		72	68	68	72	280	-8
	Gareth Shaw		73	68	70	69	280	-8
10	Alejandro Cañizares		71	69	69	72	281	-7
	Jamie Donaldson		69	71	69	72	281	-7
	Peter Lawrie		72	71	67	71	281	-7
	Peter Whiteford		71	68	69	73	281	-7
	Danny Willett		73	68	71	69	281	-7

Total Prize Fund €2,000,000   **First Prize** €333,330

L-R: Taoiseach Enda Kenny, Paul Casey and and George O'Grady, Chief Executive of The European Tour

"I've always held golf in Ireland in a special place in my heart. The Irish fans are the best and psychologically this win is huge for me"

Paul Casey

Shane Lowry

Pablo Larrazábal

Gareth Shaw

Jamie Donaldson

EUROPEAN TOUR
RACE TO
DUBAI

Golf must be about freedom.
The freedom to focus on the perfect stroke.
The freedom of golfing in any weather.
We give every golfer the ability to play golf
in its purest and most stripped-down form.
A form independent of weather, location,
situation or demands. If you ask us,
golf should only be about golfing.

That's what we call Freedom of Golf.
And that's why our partners trust abacus®

www.abacussportswear.com

FREEDOM OF GOLF
by abacus®

Richard S Johnson, abacus® ambassador at the Nordea Masters 2013

abacus partners

Robert Rock

Something in the Air

There must be something in the air in Ireland that inspires Paul Casey. When last seen at Carton House in 2006, he came within a whisker of winning the Irish Open and later that year he was unbeaten as Europe destroyed the United States in The Ryder Cup at The K Club.

Then misfortune struck. A rib injury was followed by a dislocated shoulder and a painful toe cartilage problem, meaning, not surprisingly, the trademark Casey swagger was seriously diluted. So the massive roar from an appreciative Irish crowd that greeted his 50 foot 18th green eagle putt disappearing was sweeter than sweet; confirming Casey's well-being as, on The European Tour International Schedule, he notched his 12th triumph, 29 months after his last.

Casey opened with a 68, two behind Oscar Floren, slipped back with a 72 as Robert Rock (66), who lost a play-off to Shane Lowry in the 2009 Irish Open, and Peter Uihlein led at halfway at nine under, then climbed back into a tie for fourth with a 67 – four behind Joost Luiten, who shot 66.

Pablo Larrazábal started the last day one back although Spanish compatriot José María Olazábal initially rolled back the years, sweeping ahead, but Casey spread-eagled the field with five birdies in six holes from the eighth, survived a couple of mishaps then with that grandstand finale sentenced Luiten and Rock to a share of second place.

Joost Luiten

EUROPEAN TOUR
RACE TO DUBAI

1	**GRAEME MCDOWELL**		69	69	70	67	**275**	**-9**
2	Richard Sterne		68	69	71	71	279	-5
3	Eduardo De La Riva		72	67	72	69	280	-4
	Graeme Storm		70	68	73	69	280	-4
5	Simon Dyson		70	68	72	71	281	-3
6	Jamie Donaldson		70	70	71	71	282	-2
	Richard Green		69	70	70	73	282	-2
8	Thomas Björn		68	69	74	72	283	-1
	Stephen Gallacher		68	70	75	70	283	-1
	David Howell		69	71	69	74	283	-1
	Søren Kjeldsen		69	68	73	73	283	-1
	Gareth Maybin		71	73	71	68	283	-1

Total Prize Fund €3,000,000   **First Prize** €500,000

L-R: Valerie Fourneyron, Ministry of Sport and Youth, Patrick Kron, Chairman & Chief Executive of Alstom and Graeme McDowell

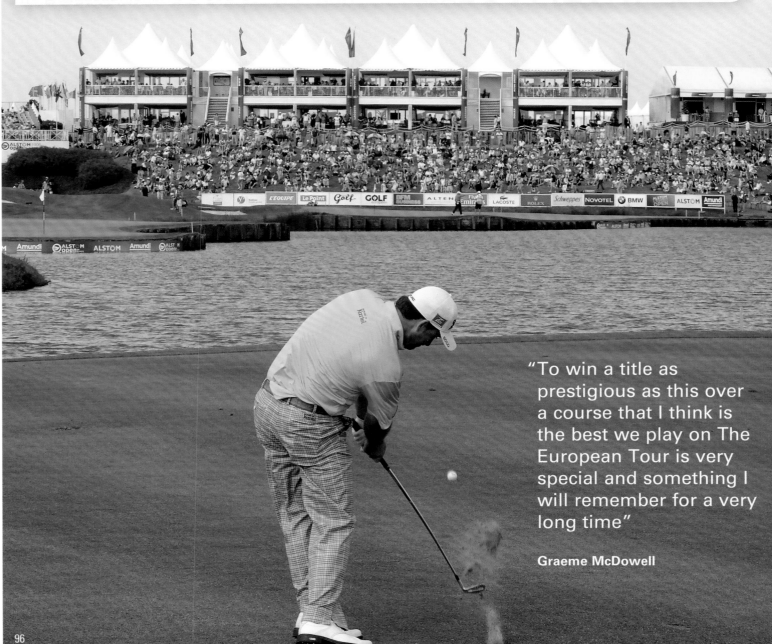

"To win a title as prestigious as this over a course that I think is the best we play on The European Tour is very special and something I will remember for a very long time"

Graeme McDowell

Victor Dubuisson

Richard Green

Graeme Storm

Richard Sterne

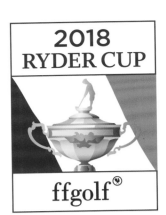

2018 RYDER CUP
ffgolf

legolfnational®

All golfers are already
dreaming of it.
So am I.

2018,
I'll be there

 SOCIETE GENERALE

 ROLEX

GENERALI
Solutions d'assurances
Génération responsable

BMW

LE FIGARO

 LACOSTE

NOVOTEL HOTELS

ALSTOM

L'EQUIPE
Partageons le sport.

SAINT QUENTIN en YVELINES
communauté d'agglomération
NATURELLEMENT GOLF

Bouygues Immobilier

OPEN GOLF CLUB
Hotel Golf Resorts

vivendi

CLUB DES PARTENAIRES FRANCE 2018

Jamie Donaldson

Simon Dyson

David Howell

Eduardo De La Riva

History Boys

The Great British summer of sport truly achieved lift-off on a weekend when the Lions claimed Series glory in Australia, Andy Murray ended 77 years of hurt at Wimbledon, Chris Froome extended his lead in the Tour de France and Graeme McDowell secured his second European Tour victory of 2013; one which propelled him to within touching distance of Justin Rose in The Race to Dubai.

Le Golf National, venue for The 2018 Ryder Cup, played its part by offering the magical and mystical amphitheatre that is the 'Final Four' – a 1,528 yard (1,398 metre) closing stretch which tantalises and teases, but one which McDowell, courtesy of a brilliant birdie at the 17th in the final round, played in level par over the four days.

Anders Hansen notched seven birdies to be the first round leader with a 66 – a score that went unequalled until Victor Dubuisson matched it on the final day to finish both inside the top 20 and as the leading French player.

Fabrizio Zanotti shot back to back 68s to lead at halfway, one ahead of Thomas Björn, Søren Kjeldsen and Richard Sterne, before McDowell's third round 68 tied him with Sterne. The South African held sway early in the final round then McDowell levelled with a nine-foot birdie at the tenth, edged ahead at the 12th and completed the 'Final Four' to become the first winner from Northern Ireland since the tournament began in 1906.

ABERDEEN ASSET MANAGEMENT SCOTTISH OPEN
Castle Stuart Golf Links, Inverness, Scotland July 11–14, 2013

1	**PHIL MICKELSON**		66	70	66	69	271	-17
2	Branden Grace		71	65	66	69	271	-17
3	JB Hansen		68	65	69	71	273	-15
	Henrik Stenson		70	64	66	73	273	-15
5	Martin Laird		68	69	69	68	274	-14
	Gareth Maybin		69	70	64	71	274	-14
	John Parry		64	72	66	72	274	-14
8	Nicolas Colsaerts		70	68	68	69	275	-13
	Raphaël Jacquelin		68	70	65	72	275	-13
10	Marcel Siem		67	69	72	69	277	-11
	Peter Uihlein		67	66	70	74	277	-11

Total Prize Fund £3,000,000   **First Prize** €579,080

L-R: Martin Gilbert, Founder & Chief Executive of Aberdeen Asset Management, Roger Cornick, Chairman of Aberdeen Asset Management, Phil Mickelson, The Right Honourable Alex Salmond MSP, First Minister of Scotland and George O'Grady, Chief Executive of The European Tour

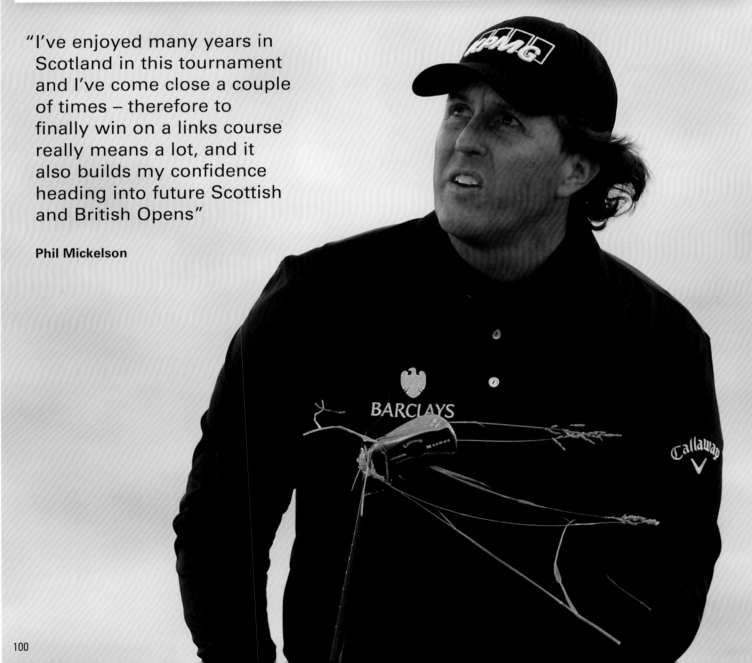

"I've enjoyed many years in Scotland in this tournament and I've come close a couple of times – therefore to finally win on a links course really means a lot, and it also builds my confidence heading into future Scottish and British Opens"

Phil Mickelson

Gareth Maybin

JB Hansen

John Parry

Henrik Stenson

MOUTON CADET

The finest red
now on the best greens

Branden Grace

L-R: Martin Gilbert, Founder & Chief Executive of Aberdeen Asset Management, The Right Honourable Alex Salmond MSP, First Minister of Scotland and Championship Director Peter Adams at a press conference announcing Aberdeen Asset Management and the Scottish Government's joint commitment to the tournament through to 2017

King of The Castle

Phil Mickelson not only captured his first title in the British Isles, he also did so in front of a 'new' audience, with his triumph being secured in the first regular European Tour event to be shown live on network television in the United States.

The left-hander thrilled NBC's viewers on a pulsating final day, firstly by opening the door to South African Branden Grace by taking six at the 72nd hole, before swiftly closing it at the first extra hole where he expertly nipped the ball off a tight lie and, from 45 yards, stopped it stone dead for a winning birdie four.

It completed a joyous weekend highlighted by a unique tri-party partnership between Aberdeen Asset Management, the Scottish Government and The European Tour

confirming the tournament's future with a strategy embracing a rota of leading venues, including a return to Castle Stuart Golf Links, and prize money rising to £3.5 million in 2017.

A sunshine week started with Chris Doak raising home hopes with back to back 66s for the halfway lead before Henrik Stenson followed a second round 64 with a 66 to move two clear of JB Hansen, John Parry, Grace and Mickelson. Sunday saw the wind arrive off the Moray Firth, providing the test that Mickelson has studiously sought to conquer and, after Hansen and Stenson had taken turns to lead, he gained the most satisfying of wins in the home of golf.

Chris Doak

The Big Chipping Challenge with ClubGolf Scotland

Martin Laird

Day to Cherish

"This is just an amazing feeling winning this great Championship and to play probably the best round of my career. I needed to bring my 'A' game here this week. And I did"

Phil Mickelson

1	PHIL MICKELSON		69	74	72	66	281	-3
2	Henrik Stenson		70	70	74	70	284	0
3	Ian Poulter		72	71	75	67	285	1
	Adam Scott		71	72	70	72	285	1
	Lee Westwood		72	68	70	75	285	1
6	Hideki Matsuyama		71	73	72	70	286	2
	Zach Johnson		66	75	73	72	286	2
	Tiger Woods		69	71	72	74	286	2
9	Hunter Mahan		72	72	68	75	287	3
	Francesco Molinari		69	74	72	72	287	3

Total Prize Fund £5,250,000   **First Prize** €1,097,570

Robin Dow, Captain of Muirfield and Phil Mickelson

In a British summer of outstanding sporting success, perhaps only one man could spoil the party so convincingly and yet become even more popular in the process.

Was this not meant to be Lee Westwood's moment to rejoice in company with Andy Murray and Chris Froome not to mention the British Lions and, of course, Justin Rose who, only four weeks earlier, memorably won the US Open. And what about Henrik Stenson trying to become Sweden's first male Major Champion; or Adam Scott, a Masters winner seeking Open redemption after his demise at Royal Lytham & St Annes in 2012; or World Number One Tiger Woods hoping for a first Major victory in five years?

That they were all overshadowed by the brilliance and panache of one man was wonderful to behold, and the admiration for Phil Mickelson's victory at the 142nd Open Championship was felt worldwide.

There was the manner in which he played, finding a way to magic birdies out of a treacherously hard and fast Muirfield links that challenged the finest golfers in the world. There was the manner of his victory, with a thrilling go-for-broke charge late on the final day that swept him past serious contenders such as Ian Poulter who launched a charge that raised England's expectations again. And there was the manner in which he

conducted himself by first acknowledging the genuine support of the enthusiastic spectators then leaving the 18th green with his arm round the shoulders of his faithful caddie, Jim "Bones" Mackay, his cheeks stained with tears of joy, and finally plunging into a group hug with wife Amy, daughters Amanda and Sophia, and son Evan.

That morning, with optimism that belied his recent US Open heartbreak after a sixth runner-up finish at Merion where Rose triumphed, Mickelson had told Amy: "I'm off to bring home the Claret Jug."

The American started the final round five strokes behind Westwood and was still four off the pace after a bogey at the tenth. It was his only falter although a reminder that on the sun-baked links of Muirfield, fearsome enough without the prevailing conditions, not a single player managed a bogey-free round throughout the Championship. Westwood set off in a positive frame of mind for that high octane final round; Scott birdied four out of five holes around the turn; Poulter produced an outrageous spurt of an eagle and three birdies from the ninth, rekindling memories of the Miracle at Medinah from The 2012 Ryder Cup.

Then Poulter stalled, Scott returned the shots he had stolen from the course, Westwood felt the dream beginning to fade and although Stenson remained hopeful it was suddenly all about one man.

At the short 13th, Mickelson hit a five iron to ten feet and holed a crucial putt. "It was a putt that was going to make the rest of the round go one way or the other," he said. "It was a nice momentum boost because it was so hard to make birdies out there." Yet another arrived at the next thanks to a putt from 20 feet and, after a vital par-save at the 16th, getting up and down from short of the green, he arrived at the 17th green in the lead.

Mickelson had found that green, tantalisingly out of reach to his rivals, with two swashbuckling three woods – he said his best two shots of the week - and he knew that two putts would put him in the lead by two. That accomplished, he then hit a six iron to the last and the ball

nudged off the shoulder of the left hand bunker and finished 12 feet away. He curled that in with a deft touch which suggested he had been playing links golf all his life.

Well, Mickelson had been *trying* to play links golf all his life. Not surprisingly, having grown up in southern California, it was a brand of the game alien to him. Mickelson, with the help of his coach Butch Harmon, had taken time to figure out how to temper his natural aggression and use the terrain and conditions to his advantage. Even the week before, he had bashed a putt so hard on the 18th green at Castle Stuart that he had to go to a playoff before winning the Aberdeen Asset Management Scottish Open. At Muirfield, on the 72nd green, the putt died into the hole with its last roll….. the final piece of the jigsaw had quite literally fallen into place and, similar to Darren Clarke two years earlier, at the 20th attempt, he brought home as he said he would the old Claret Jug.

Ian Poulter

Adam Scott

Matthew Fitzpatrick, winner of the Silver Medal as leading amateur

Henrik Stenson

The 2014 Ryder Cup.
Welcome home.

Scotland
The Home of Golf

Scotland is not only the Home of Golf, it is the home of great golf events and i 2014 we will welcome back The Ryder Cup. It has been more than 40 years sinc the prestigious tournament has been contested on Scottish soil, with Arnold Palme Jack Nicklaus and Lee Trevino all featuring in the successful US team at Muirfield i 1973. The stunning PGA Centenary Course at Gleneagles will host the historic matc in 2014, and preparations are well underway across the country to deliver what wi be an unforgettable Ryder Cup.

As part of our ongoing commitment to hosting golf tournaments in the lead u to The 2014 Ryder Cup and beyond, we are proud to support the Aberdeen Asse Management Scottish Open on the European Tour, as well as events across th Challenge, Senior and Ladies European Tour schedules in 2014.

Scotland is preparing. Are you?

RYDER CUP
2014

GLENEAGLES
SCOTLAND 2014

The PGA Centenary Course, Gleneagles

RyderCup2014.con

"I always wondered if I would develop the skills needed to win this Championship," Mickelson said. "It took me a while to figure it out but I putted these greens phenomenally, the best I've ever putted. To play the best round of my career, hit some of the best shots I've ever hit and to go out and get it the way I've always tried to do, this is just an amazing feeling to win this great Championship. It's a day I'll always cherish."

As well as emulating Ernie Els (2012) and Clarke, all Champions having turned 40, the 43-year-old left-hander – only Sir Bob Charles 50 years earlier had won The Open the 'wrong way round' – was the third successive winner who had played at Castle Stuart the week before. But Mickelson was the first ever to do the double of winning the Scottish Open and The Open in successive weeks, although he had also won the week before he won the 2006 Masters.

"It was a special week for me following Castle Stuart because I was playing so well," he added. "It was exactly what I needed to propel me into this Championship. Castle Stuart was very firm and fast, just like here at Muirfield, and it gave me some great links golf experience. And playing well on the final day in difficult conditions gave me the confidence that I could play some of my best golf in links conditions. Today was as good as I could play."

Muirfield's menu of Open Champions – Hilton, Vardon, Braid, Ray, Hagen, Perry, Cotton, Player, Nicklaus, Trevino, Watson, Faldo and Els – serves to show how on this course the cream inevitably rises to the top and with a closing 66, arguably the finest final Open round in the history of the Royal and Ancient game, Phil Mickelson deservedly became a member of that special Hall of Fame.

Andy Farrell

Miguel Angel Jiménez

Lee Westwood

Phil Mickelson with wife Amy, children Sophia, Evan and Amanda, Manager Steve Loy (back left), coach Butch Harmon and caddie Jim "Bones" Mackay (far right)

EUROPEAN TOUR RACE TO DUBAI

M2M RUSSIAN OPEN
Tseleevo Golf & Polo Club, Moscow Region, Russia July 25-28, 2013

1	**MICHAEL HOEY**		70	67	65	70	272	-16
2	Alexandre Kaleka		70	67	71	68	276	-12
	Matthew Nixon		69	70	68	69	276	-12
4	JB Hansen		72	70	67	68	277	-11
5	Mark Foster		69	69	72	68	278	-10
	Grégory Havret		72	70	70	66	278	-10
	Liang Wen-chong		67	70	75	66	278	-10
	James Morrison		68	71	70	69	278	-10
9	Simon Dyson		67	74	71	68	280	-8
10	Matthew Baldwin		68	69	73	72	282	-6
	Mikko Korhonen		69	70	70	73	282	-6
	Alexander Levy		72	72	71	67	282	-6

Total Prize Fund €1,000,000   **First Prize** €166,660

Andrey Vdovin, Chairman of the Board of M2M Private Bank / President of the Russian Golf Association and Michael Hoey

"I absolutely loved the Jack Nicklaus course and it's pretty amazing to think I've now won five European Tour titles"

Michael Hoey

Alexandre Kaleka

Grégory Havret

Hole #9
413 metres
452 yards
Par 4

JB Hansen

James Morrison

Spark of Life

Golf can be a challenging game at the best of times and when Michael Hoey, following seven missed cuts in his previous ten tournaments, began with a bogey on his first hole of the opening day he appeared to be facing another frustrating day at the office.

Then came that spark of life to transform Hoey's outlook, instantly repairing the damage on his scorecard and restoring his self-belief. Seven birdies in 12 holes enabled him to also digest the disappointment of a double bogey seven so although trailing first round leader Simon Dyson (67) by three shots he was convinced there was better to come.

So it proved as a second round 67 – only English amateur Jack Singh Brar (66) scored lower – moved him into a share of second place, two behind Rikard Karlberg, before a brilliant 65, including six birdies and an eagle, catapulted him five clear of nearest pursuers Matthew Nixon and Karlberg.

Hoey knew he could take nothing for granted with Liang Wen-chong's outward 31 and Grégory Havret's five birdies in the first six holes emphasising the scoring opportunities – both closed with 66s on the Jack Nicklaus layout to eventually tie fifth with Mark Foster and James Morrison.

However, the Northern Irishman stayed focused, birdied the seventh and eighth in an outward 34 and repelled the challenges of Alexandre Kaleka, five birdies in a 68, and Nixon (69), who tied second, and JB Hansen, seven birdies and an eagle in a 68, for a season-changing four shot victory.

Matthew Nixon

WGC - BRIDGESTONE INVITATIONAL
Firestone CC (South Course), Akron, Ohio, USA August 1-4, 2013

Masaaki Tsuya, CEO, Bridgestone Coporation and Tiger Woods

1	**TIGER WOODS**		66	61	68	70	265	-15
2	Keegan Bradley		66	68	71	67	272	-8
	Henrik Stenson		65	70	67	70	272	-8
4	Jason Dufner		67	69	67	71	274	-6
	Miguel Angel Jiménez		71	69	65	69	274	-6
	Zach Johnson		69	70	68	67	274	-6
7	Bill Haas		67	68	69	71	275	-5
	Chris Wood		66	68	70	71	275	-5
9	Luke Donald		67	69	68	72	276	-4
	Jim Furyk		67	69	72	68	276	-4
	Martin Kaymer		74	67	69	66	276	-4
	Richard Sterne		70	68	70	68	276	-4

Total Prize Fund $8,750,000   **First Prize** €1,139,341

"I'm very proud of how many World
Golf Championships I've won and
that I've won five times or more in
no fewer than ten seasons"

Tiger Woods

Miguel Angel Jiménez

Henrik Stenson

Chris Wood

Out of Sight

Keegan Bradley

A title virtually decided on the second day with Tiger Woods shooting a sensational 61, which might have been an historic 59 or even a 58, and left the question: "Who's going to come second." In fact Henrik Stenson claimed a share of the runners-up berth with Keegan Bradley and he, too, had good reason to celebrate as he moved to Number One in The 2013 Race to Dubai and to 11th place in the Official World Golf Ranking.

Stenson led by one with a first round 65 but Woods swept seven shots ahead at halfway by following an outward 30 with four birdies in succession from the tenth although he was unable to find the two birdies in his last five holes for that elusive 59. Woods maintained that advantage with a third round 68 as Stenson (67) became his closest pursuer with Luke Donald and Chris Wood among those tied fourth and Miguel Angel Jiménez making a forward move with six birdies in a 65.

Woods duly celebrated victory with a closing 70 and the record books will show this to be his eighth WGC-Bridgestone Invitational title, his 18th WGC career victory in 42 appearances and his 79th US PGA Tour triumph taking him to within three of Sam Snead's record of 82.

Stenson, too, shot 70, claiming that share of second place as Jiménez finished tied fourth and Wood tied seventh, and for the record the Swede climbed above Justin Rose and Graeme McDowell in The 2013 Race to Dubai by continuing a scintillating sequence following a tie for third in the Aberdeen Asset Management Scottish Open and a runners-up finish in The 142nd Open Championship.

Generation Game

"I just decided I was going to be confident, really put my best foot forward, play aggressive and try and win this thing. I'm happy to get the job done. It's a big step in my career"

Jason Dufner

1	**JASON DUFNER**		68	63	71	68	270	-10
2	Jim Furyk		65	68	68	71	272	-8
3	Henrik Stenson		68	66	69	70	273	-7
4	Jonas Blixt		68	70	66	70	274	-6
5	Scott Piercy		67	71	72	65	275	-5
	Adam Scott		65	68	72	70	275	-5
7	David Toms		71	69	69	67	276	-4
8	Jason Day		67	71	72	67	277	-3
	Dustin Johnson		72	71	65	69	277	-3
	Zach Johnson		69	70	70	68	277	-3
	Rory McIlroy		69	71	67	70	277	-3

Total Prize Fund $8,000,000   **First Prize** €1,095,693

Jason Dufner with the Wanamaker Trophy

Henrik Stenson

Golf's rich tapestry has been embellished by the stars of the game monopolising Major Championships so chronicling the history in cycles for others to challenge.

These golden ages can be traced from the origins of golf to specific eras being dominated either by individuals or groups of players inspired by their fairway rivalries.

The Great Triumvirate of Braid, Taylor and Vardon with 17 Majors and The Big Three of Nicklaus, Palmer and Player set a standard which few in their times could threaten. Walter Hagen and Bobby Jones won between them 18 Majors before The Masters began; Ben Hogan captured nine between 1946 and 1953; Tom Watson eight (1975-1983), Seve Ballesteros and Sir Nick Faldo together 11 before Tiger Woods launched his assault on the Nicklaus individual record of 18 by winning 14 between 1997 and 2008.

Quite what the historians will make of the current era is guesswork but when Jason Dufner

won the US PGA Championship he continued a fascinating trend by becoming the 15th first time Major winner in the last 21 played and the 19th different player to win during that stretch.

Rory McIlroy began his burgeoning career during that time with victories in the US Open (2011) and US PGA Championship (2012) and Phil Mickelson followed his 2010 Masters Tournament success by claiming The 142nd Open Championship to solidify his place in history with five Major titles so far.

Yet what the triumphs of Adam Scott (Masters Tournament), Justin Rose (US Open) and Dufner confirmed during 2013 is that the cast of players capable of claiming golf's most prized trophies is now greater than ever.

European Tour Members have played a significant role during

Jonas Blixt

Jim Furyk

this age, which goes back to Padraig Harrington winning the 2008 US PGA Championship, as emphasised by the phenomenon of Graeme McDowell (US Open), Louis Oosthuizen (The Open Championship), Martin Kaymer (US PGA Championship), Charl Schwartzel (Masters Tournament), McIlroy (US Open) and Darren Clarke (The Open Championship) completing six successive victories from the summer of 2010 in addition to wins by Angel Cabrera (Masters Tournament, 2009) and Ernie Els (The Open Championship, 2012).

The prospect of another European Tour Member closing the chapter on the Major Championships in 2013 with a success in the US PGA Championship initially dawned at Oak Hill when Lee Westwood made four birdies in a flawless 66 to be one behind Jim Furyk and Adam Scott. Westwood has played in eight successive Ryder Cups starting with the one following Europe's triumph in 1995 at Oak Hill so adding a touch of irony to his challenge whereas Scott was seeking to bookend the Major season following his

Masters success and five straight birdies in an outward 30 ignited his charge.

On Day Two Henrik Stenson and Rose, who played the course the wrong way round and shot a six under par 29 on the front nine, both followed opening 68s with 66s to be three off the pace as Dufner swept in front by threatening there and then to re-write the record books with a first ever 62 in Major Championship history in his sights.

Ultimately, Dufner came up one shy but his 63, the 26th such score in Major

Championships, sparked by holing a 105 yards wedge for an eagle two at the second, still broke the existing East course record held by Ben Hogan, Curtis Strange and Webb Simpson, who had compiled a 64 earlier in the day.

Dufner, with his tousled hair not dissimilar to that of lead singer Eric Burdon of rock band The Animals, has that laid-back approach of the "Swinging Sixties" as reflected by the internet craze christened "Dufnering" that he introduced to the world which involves

THE DIFFERENCE BETWEEN A GOLF BALL AND THE #1 BALL IN GOLF.

Excellence is a commitment. It requires passion, innovation and relentless attention to detail. Excellence is the result of over 1,200 associates designing and manufacturing every Titleist golf ball in Titleist owned and operated ball plants. Our operations team, with over 20,000 years of golf ball manufacturing experience, works every day to find new ways to make the best performing, most consistent golf balls in the game even better. Our goal is to help every player shoot lower scores. So when you place your trust in Titleist, you can be confident your golf ball will perform exactly the way you want it to, if you hit the shot the way you intended. And that's the difference between a golf ball and the #1 ball in golf. Visit titleist.co.uk to learn more.

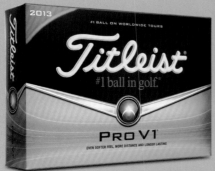

Titleist
#1 ball in golf.®

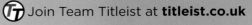
Join Team Titleist at **titleist.co.uk**

Rory McIlroy

rather weirdly lying slumped against a wall gazing, expressionless, straight ahead.

The 36-year-old America's relaxed manner was abundantly evident as, after leaving a 15 foot uphill putt for *that* 62 short of the hole, he declared: "It is tough when you're chasing history to be the first man to do something. I don't think I've been the first man to do anything in my life."

On Saturday the sun shone but not on those players wayward off the tee as many were snared by the gnarly rough that was almost growing before their very eyes following above average rainfall prior to the Championship. Then further rain during the first two rounds considerably softened the course and made it ripe for growth when the weather changed at the weekend. McIlroy found encouragement with closing birdies at 17 and 18 for a 67 as Mickelson, who played in The 1995 Ryder Cup, Rose and Woods backtracked, but out of all the carnage 43-year-old Furyk emerged one clear of Dufner courtesy of holing a 15 foot putt on the last green for a 68.

Furyk went seeking 24 hours later a second Major to attach to the US Open he won in 2003 but for Dufner this was to be his Day of Redemption. Two years earlier he had driven home to Auburn, Alabama, digesting the disappointment of self-destructing in the closing stages of the final round – he made three bogeys as good friend Keegan Bradley birdied two - of the US PGA Championship in Atlanta. "The drive took two hours and I was probably over 95 per cent of it by the time I got back home," Dufner said.

This time he flew back home from Rochester with the Wanamaker Trophy – "You could fit 43 beers in it," he quipped – after a master-class of golf took him into the outright lead at the eighth, where Dufner made his second tap-in birdie in four holes, and on to a two shot victory from Furyk. Stenson threatened especially after a two putt birdie at the 13th although misfortune struck at the driveable 14th where he laid up for safety only for the ball to finish in a divot from where he made bogey so that he eventually finished third ahead of Swedish compatriot Jonas Blixt.

Dufner celebrated with a muted fist pump, firmly shook Furyk's hand, received a bear-hug from good friend Bradley then cheekily pinched wife Amanda's behind before warmly embracing his bride of 14 months.

If success has brought acclaim for Chuck Cook, his 68-year-old instructor, then it has also revived memories of one of those golden eras since Dufner's hero is Hogan. Cook sees a similarity in their swings and comparisons can be made since his pre-shot routine involving waggling the golf club resembles that of Hogan even if it is a touch more exaggerated.

Not that Dufner's elevation to Major Championship status will faze him. He said: "It's definitely going to change my life but I'm determined it's not going to change me." With that he boarded the flight home with a sapling and some acorns acquired from the General Manager at Oak Hill with the intention of planting them on a 50 acre spread where he and Amanda are building their new home. The start, you could say, of another generation.

Mitchell Platts

JOHNNIE WALKER CHAMPIONSHIP AT GLENEAGLES
The Gleneagles Hotel (PGA Centenary Course), Perthshire, Scotland August 22–25, 2013

JOHNNIE WALKER®

1	**TOMMY FLEETWOOD**		68	65	67	70	270	-18
2	Stephen Gallacher		71	68	64	67	270	-18
	Ricardo Gonzalez		65	65	70	70	270	-18
4	Scott Henry		72	65	67	67	271	-17
	Bernd Wiesberger		65	66	72	68	271	-17
6	Emiliano Grillo		71	66	69	66	272	-16
	Brett Rumford		66	69	69	68	272	-16
	Paul Waring		75	63	67	67	272	-16
9	Thorbjørn Olesen		71	68	66	68	273	-15
10	David Drysdale		71	67	68	68	274	-14
	Mikko Korhonen		71	69	67	67	274	-14
	Shane Lowry		68	70	67	69	274	-14
	Richie Ramsay		69	68	69	68	274	-14

Total Prize Fund £1,400,000   **First Prize** €272,273

L-R: Patrick Elsmie, Managing Director of The Gleneagles Hotel, Lord Macfarlane of Bearsden, Tommy Fleetwood, Ian Wright, Corporate Relations Director, Diageo, Graeme Marchbank, Head of Global Sports Sponsorship, Diageo and Richard Hills, European Ryder Cup Director

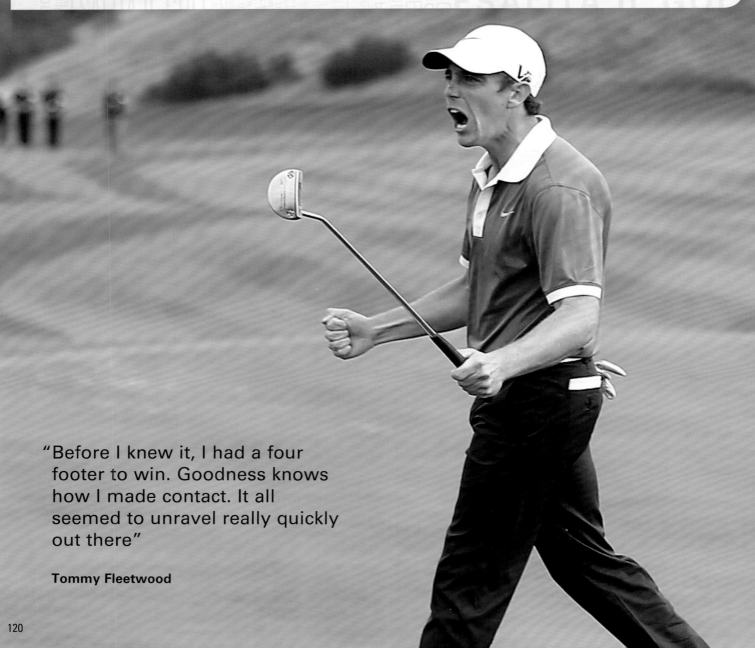

"Before I knew it, I had a four footer to win. Goodness knows how I made contact. It all seemed to unravel really quickly out there"

Tommy Fleetwood

Ricardo Gonzalez

Stephen Gallacher

Scott Henry

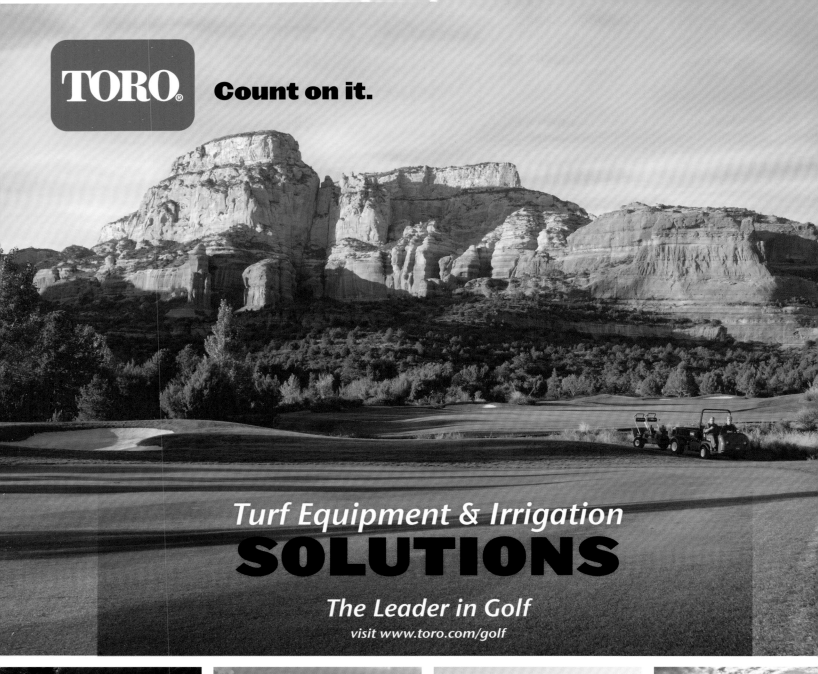

TORO. Count on it.

Turf Equipment & Irrigation
SOLUTIONS

The Leader in Golf

visit www.toro.com/golf

ST ANDREWS LINKS
the home of golf®
SUPPLIER

EUROPEAN TOUR
OFFICIAL SUPPLIER

EGCOA
EUROPEAN GOLF COURSE OWNERS ASSOCIATION
PREFERRED SUPPLIER

Bernd Wiesberger

Emiliano Grillo

Thorbjørn Olesen

Star of The Show

If the decibel level is likely to reach a crescendo when The Ryder Cup unfolds on the PGA Centenary Course in 2014, then as a dress rehearsal this provided a fascinating feast of roller-coaster excitement for the enthusiastic spectators.

Quite whether any one could have predicted the outcome is debatable as the risk and reward challenge created by Jack Nicklaus presented a stage on which fortunes fluctuated before Tommy Fleetwood became the star of the show.

Ricardo Gonzalez and Bernd Wiesberger notched seven birdies each to share the first round lead on 65; Gonzalez followed with seven birdies in eight holes for the halfway lead and stayed ahead entering the final round albeit tied with Fleetwood

with Scotland's hopes galvanised by Stephen Gallacher's sensational 64.

Then what drama! Gonzalez lost a ball at the first, Fleetwood fell behind and Gallacher advanced with three birdies and an eagle to lead at the turn. Gonzalez closed with a birdie at 16 then almost holed for an eagle at the last; Fleetwood fought back with an eagle at 16 and a birdie at 18; Gallacher's lead slipped with a triple bogey at 11, but he recovered with birdies at 14 and 16 and an eagle at 18.

So to the final curtain, a three way play-off and for Fleetwood a maiden European Tour win at the first extra hole and a chance to dream of a return to Gleneagles in twelve months time.

Brett Rumford

Paul Waring

L-R: George O'Grady, Chief Executive of The European Tour, Grégory Bourdy and Midori Miyasaki, ISPS Executive Director of International Affairs

1	**GRÉGORY BOURDY**		67	72	70	67	276	-8
2	Peter Uihlein		69	70	67	72	278	-6
3	Søren Kjeldsen		69	74	70	66	279	-5
4	Joost Luiten		73	68	69	71	281	-3
	John Parry		71	69	73	68	281	-3
6	Damien McGrane		70	71	70	71	282	-2
	Graeme Storm		72	67	72	71	282	-2
8	Seve Benson		76	70	69	68	283	-1
	Gonzalo Fernandez-Castaño		70	75	69	69	283	-1
	Anders Hansen		71	71	70	71	283	-1
	Mikko Korhonen		71	70	70	72	283	-1
	Paul McGinley		70	69	77	67	283	-1
	Brett Rumford		72	69	72	70	283	-1
	Simon Wakefield		70	74	70	69	283	-1

Total Prize Fund £1,800,000   **First Prize** €348,660

"I'm going to remember this for a long time. Lots of great moments took place on this course during The Ryder Cup and I'm so proud to win this trophy at Celtic Manor"

Grégory Bourdy

Damian McGrane

Liam Bond

Joost Luiten

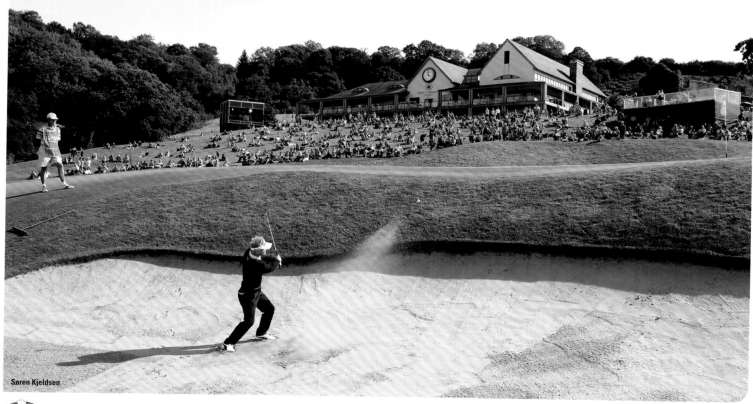

Søren Kjeldsen

Accidents can happen in unlikely places.

It's best to protect yourself against the unexpected.

Lifestyle Protection Insurance

Genworth Lifestyle Protection is a global specialist insurance provider, helping people maintain their credit obligations and lifestyle in the event of the unexpected – whether that is an accident, sickness, unemployment or loss of life. We partner with banks, car manufacturers and retailers to not only get our products to you, but to help them grow their businesses too.

Visit www.genworth.co.uk to find out more

Creditor | Living Expenses | GAP & Commercial | Life Protection Insurances

EUROPEAN TOUR OFFICIAL PARTNER

Genworth ®

Peter Uihlein

Ticker Tape Finish

Paul McGinley struck the opening shot, igniting the race for places in Europe's team for The 2014 Ryder Cup in Scotland, but, ironically, the eventual champion hailed from the country which will next host the contest when it returns to the continent in 2018.

Grégory Bourdy claimed his fourth European Tour title, and the 28th French win, with a finish that would not have been out of place when The 2010 Ryder Cup was staged on the Twenty Ten Course – three consecutive closing birdies enabling him to overhaul front-running Peter Uihlein.

Espen Kofstad, European Challenge Tour Number One in 2012 and John Parry, the 2012 European Tour Qualifying School winner, partnered McGinley on Day One. Kofstad would enjoy the early honours, claiming the first round lead with a stunning back nine 29 for a 64, although Parry finished the strongest for a share of fourth. Before that, Welshman Liam Bond, aged 43, who lives ten minutes from the course, rolled back the years with a 68 for the halfway lead before Uihlein powered three shots ahead by defying blustery conditions with a third round 67 that was an exercise in control and patience.

Uihlein, 24 years old on the opening day of the tournament, had Thomas Levet, who with six titles has more wins on The European Tour than any other Frenchman, and Bourdy as his closest pursuers. The American did little wrong, finding birdies at 15 and 17, but Bourdy sank putts totalling 85 feet at 16, 17 and 18 for a ticker tape finish that earned pole position in The Ryder Cup race to Gleneagles.

Graeme Storm

L-R: Espen Kofstad, Paul McGinley and John Parry

Golf Development Wales mascots

EUROPEAN TOUR
RACE TO DUBAI

OMEGA EUROPEAN MASTERS
Crans-sur-Sierre GC (Seve Ballesteros Course), Crans Montana, Switzerland September 5-8, 2013

1	**THOMAS BJÖRN**		66	66	67	65	264	-20
2	Craig Lee		71	65	61	67	264	-20
3	Victor Dubuisson		68	65	66	66	265	-19
4	Alejandro Cañizares		69	65	65	67	266	-18
5	Ross Fisher		71	69	63	66	269	-15
	Miguel Angel Jiménez		65	68	69	67	269	-15
7	Grégory Havret		68	69	70	63	270	-14
	Brooks Koepka		68	66	69	67	270	-14
9	Tommy Fleetwood		65	68	69	70	272	-12
	Stephen Gallacher		67	65	72	68	272	-12
	Thongchai Jaidee		68	69	70	65	272	-12

Total Prize Fund €2,200,000   **First Prize** €366,660

L-R: Stephen Urquhart, President of Omega, Gaston Barras, President of the Organising Committee and Thomas Björn

"I made a promise to myself to stay focused and determined and I did that this week so it was very sweet for me to get it over the line in a play-off"

Thomas Björn

The spectacular 13th Hole

Alejandro Cañizares

Ross Fisher

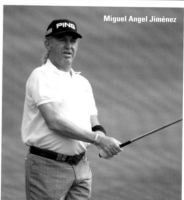
Miguel Angel Jiménez

Mountain High

There was a new look to Crans-sur-Sierre - innovative water features protecting a number of greens notably the now spectacular short 13th with its individual gallery accommodating 3,000 spectators - which provided the ultimate "River Deep, Mountain High" setting 5,000 feet above the Rhone Valley.

Nevertheless, it was a familiar face which emerged as champion with Thomas Björn, following his win in 2011, becoming the fifth player, after Seve Ballesteros, Hugh Baiocchi, Manuel Pinero and Eduardo Romero, to record multiple victories since the tournament became part of The European Tour in 1972.

Three-time Asian Tour winner Anirban Lahari fired an opening 64, two ahead of Paul Casey, Tommy Fleetwood and Miguel Angel Jiménez, making his 25th successive appearance in the tournament, before Björn followed his opening 65 with a 66 to share the halfway lead with Stephen Gallacher.

Then Craig Lee changed the whole complexion with in his own words comfortably the finest round of his career as he notched six successive birdies then two more at the eighth and ninth for an outward 28 and with another at the tenth sparked thoughts of a 59. His momentum was not halted by a bogey at 12 as he birdied 13 and 14 and although

that dream score did not materialise a 61 propelled him into the driving seat on 16 under – two in front of Björn, Alejandro Cañizares and Victor Dubuisson.

Björn showed all his experience with five birdies in an outward 31, after Cañizares had begun the final day eagle-birdie-birdie, but Lee, out in 35, fought his way back with three birdies in four holes from the 12th then lipped out at the last for what would have been a maiden victory. The play-off lasted one hole with Björn, who recorded only two bogeys all week, making his 23rd birdie of the tournament by holing from 12 feet, fist pumping the air and saluting his 14th European Tour triumph.

Victor Dubuisson

Craig Lee

EUROPEAN TOUR RACE TO DUBAI

KLM OPEN
Kennemer G&CC, Zandvoort, The Netherlands September 12-15, 2013

1	**JOOST LUITEN**		69	65	66	68	**268**	**-12**
2	Miguel Angel Jiménez		64	67	70	67	268	-12
3	Simon Dyson		69	63	71	68	271	-9
	Ross Fisher		69	68	68	66	271	-9
	Grégory Havret		67	70	68	66	271	-9
	Damien McGrane		65	70	67	69	271	-9
7	Julien Quesne		67	65	70	70	272	-8
8	Søren Kjeldsen		68	67	72	66	273	-7
9	David Horsey		71	66	70	67	274	-6
	Pablo Larrazábal		65	66	77	66	274	-6

Total Prize Fund €1,800,000   **First Prize** €300,000

Camiel Eurlings, President & CEO of KLM and Joost Luiten

"I'll never forget this day. To win your national Open is an unbelievable feeling. I'm so proud. And I'll never forget the support I received – I'm so pleased I was able to give the fans this win"

Joost Luiten

Damien McGrane

Grégory Havret

Ross Fisher

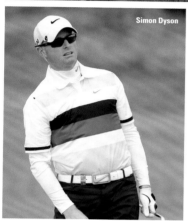
Simon Dyson

Double Dutch

Joost Luiten completed a weekend of "Double Dutch" delight as he notched a rare victory on home soil on The European Tour only minutes after compatriot Daan Huizing captured the Kharkov Superior Cup on the European Challenge Tour – the first time two players from The Netherlands had triumphed on the two Tours on the same day.

The record books were ripe to be plundered once Luiten completed his fourth successive sub-70 round to tie Miguel Angel Jiménez, who at 49 years and 253 days was bidding to extend his own record (48 years and 318 days) as the oldest winner in European Tour history.

Jiménez topped the leader-board on Day One with eight birdies in a 64 to continue his remarkable sequence of results since returning to the game following a broken leg sustained in a skiing accident at the back end of 2012. He was joined at the front at halfway by Spanish compatriot Pablo Larrazábal, who shot 66, before Luiten defied strong winds and torrential rain in the third round –

chipping in twice for birdies and holing a monster putt for another at the 17th for a superb 66, a ten under par total and a one shot advantage over Jiménez.

Four birdies in the first six holes enabled Jiménez to seize control again with a last round outward 32 but Luiten remained composed to shoot 68 to his rival's 67 then played the first extra hole in textbook fashion, much to the pleasure of the home audience, to gain his second success of the season and the third of his career.

Miguel Angel Jiménez

#	Player		R1	R2	R3	R4	Total	Score
1	**JULIEN QUESNE**		70	68	71	67	276	-12
2	David Higgins		67	69	73	68	277	-11
	Steve Webster		67	69	73	68	277	-11
4	Felipe Aguilar		69	66	72	71	278	-10
	Fredrik Andersson Hed		73	67	71	67	278	-10
	Nicolas Colsaerts		65	71	70	72	278	-10
	Emiliano Grillo		70	72	68	68	278	-10
8	Seve Benson		68	70	72	69	279	-9
	Robert-Jan Derksen		71	69	71	68	279	-9
	Marcus Fraser		66	71	68	74	279	-9
	Hennie Otto		71	67	70	71	279	-9
	Alvaro Quiros		71	67	73	68	279	-9
	Romain Wattel		71	72	66	70	279	-9

Total Prize Fund €1,500,000   **First Prize** €250,000

L-R: Franco Chimenti, President of the Italian Golf Federation, Julien Quesne and Antonio Bulgheroni, President of Lindt Italia

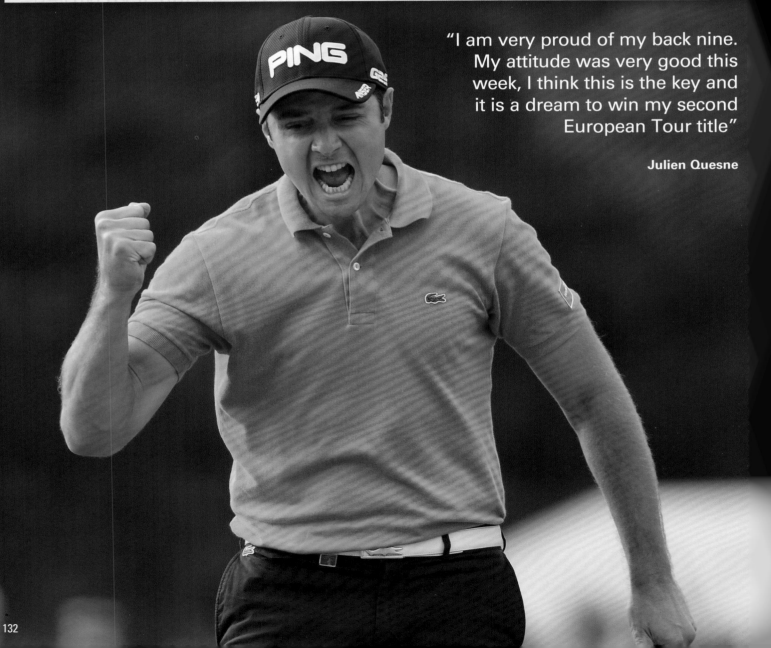

"I am very proud of my back nine. My attitude was very good this week, I think this is the key and it is a dream to win my second European Tour title"

Julien Quesne

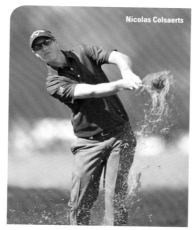
Nicolas Colsaerts

Emiliano Grillo

Gonzalo Fernández-Castaño and Fredrik Andersson Hed discover how Lindt chocolates are made

Steve Webster

Powers of Recovery

Just four tournaments into The Ryder Cup qualification race for places in Europe's team and two French players have recorded victories and, of course, we are talking about Gleneagles in 2014 and not Le Golf National, Paris, in 2018. Nevertheless with Raphaël Jacquelin (Open de España) winning earlier in the season and Julien Quesne following Grégory Bourdy (ISPS Handa Wales Open) onto the victor's podium it does appear that momentum is building with this being the 29th French victory on The European Tour International Schedule.

Coincidentally it was announced on the final day in Turin that the 2014 race would conclude at next year's Open d'Italia on August 31 when, of course, Quesne will be defending his title and, perhaps, seeking to secure a place in Paul McGinley's team.

Quesne demonstrated the powers of recovery so often required in the biennial contest being compelled to come from four behind starting the final round then digest the disappointment of a double bogey six on his second hole. Indeed he had mainly played a supporting role as Max Kieffer, who lost a nine hole play off to Jacquelin for the Open de España title in April, tied Nicolas Colsaerts and Ricardo Gonzalez on 65 before Francesco Molinari, encouraged by an impassioned crowd at the club where he became a member aged eight, surged into a share of the halfway lead with Felipe Aguilar and Simon Thornton.

Marcus Fraser posted a third round 68 for a one shot lead and for much of the final day, when at one time no fewer than ten players were separated by one shot, he looked to be in the driving seat. Then Quesne launched his charge by making birdies at four and six then two more at the 10th and 11th before three in the last four holes – he chipped in at 17 and holed from six feet at 18 – brought him home in 31 for a 67 and a one shot win ahead of David Higgins, gaining only his second top three finish in more than 200 European Tour events spanning 20 years, and Steve Webster.

Felipe Aquilar

David Higgins

1	**DAVID HOWELL**		67	68	63	67	265	-23
2	Peter Uihlein		71	60	65	69	265	-23
3	Tom Lewis		64	65	73	64	266	-22
	Shane Lowry		68	66	64	68	266	-22
5	Tommy Fleetwood		65	66	69	67	267	-21
6	Garth Mulroy		66	69	65	68	268	-20
7	Ricardo Gonzalez		67	69	63	70	269	-19
	Martin Kaymer		69	66	63	71	269	-19
	Thomas Levet		68	64	68	69	269	-19
	Charl Schwartzel		68	68	66	67	269	-19
	Chris Wood		66	69	69	65	269	-19

Total Prize Fund $5,000,000   **First Prize** €589,562

David Howell, Alfred Dunhill Links Champion

"It's been a long, long road from the depths of despair but it doesn't get much better than winning the Alfred Dunhill Links Championship at the Home of Golf"

David Howell

Peter Uihlein

Shane Lowry

Tom Lewis

Ricardo Gonzalez and Martin Kaymer

Thomas Levet and David Sayer

Ernie Els and Johann Rupert

Sir Bobby Charlton

Hugh Grant

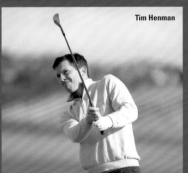
Tim Henman

James Nesbitt

David Horsey and Sir Ian Botham

Padraig Harrington and JP McManus

Charl Schwartzel

Tommy Fleetwood

Majesty of The Moment

It was the cool, composed manner with which he emerged from the intensity of the situation that immediately struck home as David Howell brought closure to seven years and 124 days and 200 events without a win on The European Tour International Schedule by calmly holing an eight foot birdie putt in sudden-death time on the 18th green at St Andrews.

Then Howell, who in September, 2010, was as low as 569th in the Official World Golf Ranking, thanked his coach Jonathan Wallet, caddie Steve Brotherhood and his wife Emily and digested the majesty of the moment on re-visiting his CV, which includes two Ryder Cup appearances, by adding this win at the Home of Golf to those, among others, in the flagship BMW PGA Championship and HSBC Champions.

Howell accelerated into contention on the Old Course in the third round when eight birdies and an eagle at the fifth for a 63 lifted him into a share of second place, alongside Ernie Els, Martin Kaymer, who

had nine birdies in a 63, Shane Lowry, Joost Luiten and Richard McEvoy, two shots behind Peter Uihlein, who holed his wedge shot for an eagle at the last.

Uihlein had come within a whisker of last hole glory the previous day at Kingsbarns where after eight birdies and two eagles his 25 foot putt to become the first player to shoot 59 on The European Tour stopped inches from the hole but nevertheless propelled him into the fray as Tom Lewis followed an opening 64 at Kingsbarns with a 65 at St Andrews for a one shot halfway lead ahead of Luiten.

Lewis would by sharing third place with Lowry, who momentarily led following six birdies in his first 11 holes, climb from 155th to 90th in The Race to Dubai but first Howell, out in 31, then Uihlein with scores of 67 and 69 respectively would set a new record score of 23 under par before the Englishman edged out the American with that birdie at the second extra hole.

Garth Mulroy

Chris Wood

A Veritable Golfing Treat

Continental Europe Team Captain, José María Olazábal, with the trophy

138

José María Olazábal watches intently, surrounded by members of the Continental Europe Team

Paul Lawrie and Stephen Gallacher

Joost Luiten and Grégory Bourdy

Severiano Ballesteros played golf like a matador with style and grace....but he was also a gladiator who relished the more personal head-to-head encounters provided by match play golf.

His record shows how much. He won five World Match Play titles when the event was played at Wentworth Club, its spiritual home, and we all know how passionate, inspirational and successful he was in The Ryder Cup.

He loved The Ryder Cup. He saved The Ryder Cup and it was no surprise when in 2000 he decided he wanted a Ryder Cup of his own – The Seve Trophy.

In non-Ryder Cup years, Seve's match pits the best professionals in Continental Europe against the best in Great Britain and Ireland.....and so it was for the third successive time we gathered at delightful Saint-Nom-La-Bretèche, former home of the elegant Trophée Lancôme, on the outskirts of Versailles, for the eighth edition of this enthralling team competition.

The tree-lined composite course just happens to be perfect for match play – a comfortable start, some tricky holes in mid-round and a 3-5-4-5-4 finish where, quite simply, anything can happen... and did.

The players served up a veritable golfing treat and, as captains José María Olazábal and Sam Torrance, both having led winning Ryder Cup teams, had predicted, the match, liberally sprinkled with awesome approach shots, holed chips and wonder bunker recoveries, was a desperately close affair.

Because it was an opportunity for the younger players on both sides to experience the unique pressures of team golf, the 2014 European Captain Paul McGinley spent the week watching, assessing form and wondering who might make his team.

At the 2013 Seve Trophy by Golf+, the Continentals were trying to end a run of six consecutive defeats and on a mellow autumn Thursday they started well taking the first series of five four balls.

Gonzalo Fernandez-Castaño and Nicolas Colsaerts

Gonzalo Fernandez Castaño, devastating on the fast greens, and big hitting Nicolas Colsaerts were ten under par as a team for their 5 and 3 defeat of Scots Marc Warren and Scott Jamieson but the other tartan duo of Paul Lawrie and Stephen Gallacher were 3 and 2 winners over Olazabal`s most experienced pairing Miguel Angel Jiménez, who has never missed a Trophy match, and Thomas Björn who has missed only one.

Dutchman Joost Luiten, revelling in the moment, shot to the turn in 29 although he and partner Grégory Bourdy were taken to the 17th by determined Jamie Donaldson and David Lynn.

Torrance's men responded on Friday by taking the second series of fourballs 3-2.   Luiten and Bourdy and Fernndez-Castaño and Colsaerts continued in winning form but Jamieson and Lynn snatched a vital point from Matteo Manassero and Francesco Molinari. After two days the Continentals were ahead 5½ - 4½.

For professionals used to playing their own ball foursomes are always more difficult and of the eight foursomes on Saturday four came to the last and

four went to the 17th. Jiménez, 49, and Manassero, 21, linked well to beat Paul Casey and Tommy Fleetwood and by lunch Europe led by two points. In the afternoon Luiten and Bourdy, dove-tailing well, remained unbeaten for the Continentals but that was their team's only point. When Lynn, partnering Casey, holed from six feet on the last to beat Jiménez and Manassero the overall score was 9-9 with ten singles remaining.

In early Sunday drama England's Simon Khan was forced to withdraw because of a back injury and Björn, was paired with him for a halved match. Making the scenario more intriguing was the fact that the Continentals had won more singles series but overall Great Britain and Ireland had won most singles points.

Captain Torrance, looking for three points from the first three games, only got 1½ - a point from lively newcomer Fleetwood, who beat Luiten by 3 and 2, and a half from Donaldson against stubborn Fernandez-Castaño. Casey, who had impressed during the week, lost his battle with Colsaerts on the last green. Now it was 11-11.

Then Bourdy, the only Frenchman involved, made history by beating Jamieson 4 and 3 to become the first man to win five points out of five in a Seve Trophy. Jiménez beat Lynn and Manassero was too good for Gallacher but with Warren's 4 and 3 defeat of Thorbjørn Olesen and Lawrie's 2 and 1 victory against Mikko Ilonen the overall result was dependent on the last match involving Chris Wood against Ryder Cup anchorman Molinari.

The Italian did not let his team mates down winning in style with a majestic tee shot and a birdie two at the short 16th to give Continental Europe victory.

It was their first win since 2000. It may not have been as intense a week as it will be at Gleneagles next September but both teams had played with great determination, enthusiasm and passion. Seve would have loved it.

Renton Laidlaw

Francesco Molinari

"I'm very proud that Continental Europe has won the trophy for the first time since the inaugural match in 2000 – everything was decided on the last day, the last match, which added to the drama"

José María Olazábal

Total Prize Fund €1,750,000
Per player winning team €100,000
Per player losing team €75,000

Sam Torrance, José María Olazábal and Jean Van de Velde, Tournament Host, present a cheque for €100,000 to Carmen Ballesteros, for the Seve Ballesteros Foundation

CONTINENTAL EUROPE

Captain: José María Olazábal

Day 1 - Fourballs

Continental Europe		GB & Ireland	
T Björn & M A Jiménez	0	Pa Lawrie & S Gallacher (3 & 2)	1
M Ilonen & T Olesen (1 hole)	1	T Fleetwood & C Wood	0
F Molinari & M Manassero (halved)	½	P Casey & S Khan (halved)	½
J Luiten & G Bourdy (2 & 1)	1	J Donaldson & D Lynn	0
N Colsaerts & G Fernandez-Castaño (5 & 3)	1	M Warren & S Jamieson	0
	3½		**1½**

Day 2 - Fourballs

Continental Europe		GB & Ireland	
M Ilonen & T Olesen	0	P Casey & S Khan (3 & 2)	1
F Molinari & M Manassero	0	D Lynn & S Jamieson (1 hole)	1
T Björn & M A Jiménez	0	J Donaldson & M Warren (4 & 2)	1
J Luiten & G Bourdy (1 hole)	1	T Fleetwood & C Wood	0
N Colsaerts & G Fernandez-Castaño (6 & 5)	1	Pa Lawrie & S Gallacher	0
	2		**3**

Day 3 - Foursomes

Continental Europe		GB & Ireland	
N Colsaerts & G Fernandez-Castaño (halved)	½	S Gallacher & Pa Lawrie (halved)	½
J Luiten & G Bourdy (2 & 1)	1	J Donaldson & M Warren	0
T Olesen & F Molinari	0	C Wood & S Jamieson (2 & 1)	1
M A Jiménez & M Manassero (1 hole)	1	P Casey & T Fleetwood	0
	2½		**1½**

Day 3 - Foursomes

Continental Europe		GB & Ireland	
N Colsaerts & G Fernandez-Castaño	0	Pa Lawrie & S Gallacher (2 & 1)	1
T Björn & M Ilonen	0	J Donaldson & M Warren (2 & 1)	1
J Luiten & G Bourdy (2 holes)	1	C Wood & S Jamieson	0
M A Jiménez & M Manassero	0	P Casey & D Lynn (1 hole)	1
	1		**3**

Day 4 - Singles

Continental Europe		GB & Ireland	
G Fernandez-Castaño (halved)	½	J Donaldson (halved)	½
N Colsaerts (1 hole)	1	P Casey	0
J Luiten	0	T Fleetwood (3 & 2)	1
T Björn (halved)	½	S Khan (halved) (withdrew due to injury)	½
G Bourdy (4 & 3)	1	S Jamieson	0
T Olesen	0	M Warren (4 & 3)	1
M Manassero (3 & 2)	1	S Gallacher	0
M Ilonen	0	Pa Lawrie (2 & 1)	1
M A Jiménez (6 & 4)	1	D Lynn	0
F Molinari (3 & 2)	1	C Wood	0
	6		**4**

GREAT BRITAIN & IRELAND

Captain: Sam Torrance

CONTINENTAL EUROPE	15	GREAT BRITAIN & IRELAND	13

PORTUGAL MASTERS
Oceânico Victoria Golf Course, Algarve, Portugal October 10-13, 2013

1	**DAVID LYNN**		65	65	73	63	**266**	**-18**
2	Justin Walters		69	63	69	66	267	-17
3	Stephen Gallacher		70	67	65	66	268	-16
	Paul Waring		67	63	67	71	268	-16
	Bernd Wiesberger		66	65	70	67	268	-16
6	Jamie Donaldson		65	68	66	70	269	-15
	Hennie Otto		66	64	69	70	269	-15
8	Robert-Jan Derksen		69	68	67	66	270	-14
	Chris Doak		67	64	69	70	270	-14
	Ross Fisher		67	66	71	66	270	-14
	Pablo Larrazábal		69	67	64	70	270	-14
	Simon Thornton		65	69	65	71	270	-14

Total Prize Fund €2,000,000 **First Prize** €333,330

David Lynn and Adolfo Mesquita Nunes, Secretary of State for Tourism, Portugal

"It was a cracking day's golf. I went out to set a target and make it tough for the guys in the wind. I caught fire on the front nine and it's a delight to win again"

David Lynn

Justin Walters

Paul Waring

Many Happy Returns

David Lynn celebrated his 40th birthday one week early, reeling in the field from six behind with an inspired closing round of 63, to land his first title for nine years and 66 days, although in terms of scoring the talk before that was of the one that got away.

For third rounds do not come much better than that compiled by Scott Jamieson who, after 11 birdies, had the magical figure of 59 in his sights, played a lovely approach to the 18th then watched in dismay as first the ball bounced through the green and then his superbly executed chip grazed the hole.

That 60 – the 18th such official score in Tour history - elevated Jamieson from 52nd to tied second entering the final round of an intriguing contest that began with Lynn sharing the first round lead with Felipe Aguilar, Jamie Donaldson, Max Kieffer, Alvaro Quiros, Graeme Storm and Simon Thornton before Hennie Otto and Paul Waring, who

recorded 14 birdies and one eagle between them in the second round, led at halfway with Lynn.

Jamieson would earn the plaudits on Day Three, moving alongside Donaldson, Otto and Thornton in second place as Lynn retreated and Waring, back following wrist surgery, swept two ahead with a 67. Lynn, however, returned to the leaderboard with five birdies in an outward 30 in a testing breeze then shrugged aside a "crazy" three putt bogey at the tenth with birdies at 11, 14, 15 and 17 to set an 18 under par clubhouse target that proved decisive.

Justin Walters, who arrived in 126th place in The Race to Dubai, provided the enthusiastic crowd with more to cheer in the sunshine as he followed four successive birdies from the 14th with a 50-foot par save at 18 to finish runner-up and keep his playing privileges only two weeks after his mother sadly passed away.

Bernd Wiesberger

Stephen Gallacher

EUROPEAN TOUR
RACE TO DUBAI

1	**JIN JEONG**		68	72	69	69	278	-10
2	Ross Fisher		72	67	71	68	278	-10
3	Brody Ninyette		72	69	67	72	280	-8
	Dimitrios Papadatos		69	71	72	68	280	-8
	Danny Willett		72	71	68	69	280	-8
6	Brett Rumford		71	73	65	72	281	-7
7	Richard Finch		72	69	69	72	282	-6
	JB Hansen		70	73	66	73	282	-6
	Joel Sjöholm		71	73	67	71	282	-6
10	Fredrik Andersson Hed		69	73	68	73	283	-5
	Peter Hedblom		68	69	75	71	283	-5

Total Prize Fund $2,000,000   **First Prize** €245,438

Jin Jeong and Midori Miyasaki, ISPS Executive Director of International Affairs

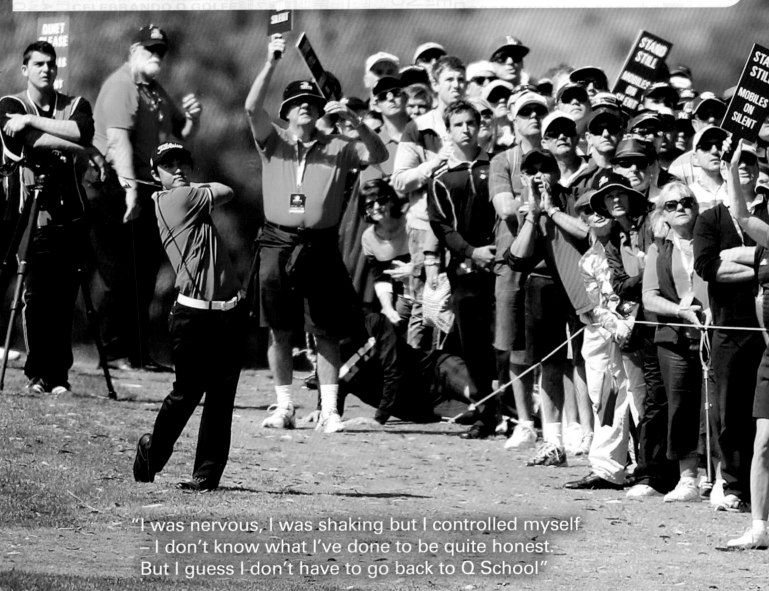

"I was nervous, I was shaking but I controlled myself
– I don't know what I've done to be quite honest.
But I guess I don't have to go back to Q School"

Jin Jeong

Danny Willett

Brett Rumford

Heart to Heart

Joy in golf does not always simply belong to the victor as Peter Lawrie would heartily agree after finishing joint 18th behind Jin Jeong whose play-off success over Ross Fisher earned him a maiden European Tour triumph.

For as Jeong celebrated a life-changing two year exemption to The European Tour so Lawrie retained his playing privileges for a 12th successive season despite a near heart-stopping finish.

Lawrie started the week 115th in The Race to Dubai – "I haven't slept or eaten properly for eight weeks" – needing to climb into the elite top 110. The tournament within a tournament, ultimately deciding Qualifying School attendance for a number of players, saw Lawrie, boosted by five birdies in the first 12 holes of his final round, climb to 109th despite dropping three late shots.

Meanwhile Jeong, who shared the first round lead, stayed in touch as Peter Hedblom led at halfway. Tied second behind Western Australian Brody Ninyette entering the last day, he recovered from a four-putt first hole to notch five birdies in a 69 and tie Fisher, who came home in 33 for a 68, before winning at the first extra hole. It was the first Korean win since Y E Yang in the Volvo China Open in 2010 – the year Jeong won the British Amateur Championship before finishing 14th in The Open Championship prior to turning professional.

Peter Lawrie

Ross Fisher

EUROPEAN TOUR
RACE TO DUBAI

BMW MASTERS PRESENTED BY SRE GROUP

Lake Malaren Golf Club (Masters Course), Shanghai, China October 24-27, 2013

1	GONZALO FERNANDEZ-CASTAÑO		71	71	67	68	277	-11
2	Thongchai Jaidee		70	70	72	66	278	-10
	Francesco Molinari		72	71	71	64	278	-10
4	Luke Guthrie		65	71	72	71	279	-9
5	Thomas Björn		73	72	69	66	280	-8
	Pablo Larrazábal		70	73	69	68	280	-8
	Peter Uihlein		69	75	69	67	280	-8
8	Rafa Cabrera-Bello		73	68	67	73	281	-7
	Paul Casey		70	70	71	70	281	-7
	Peter Hanson		79	68	71	63	281	-7
	Scott Jamieson		72	68	71	70	281	-7

Total Prize Fund $7,000,000   **First Prize** €851,346

L-R: George O'Grady, Chief Executive of The European Tour, Gonzalo Fernandez-Castaño and Ian Robertson, Member of the Board of Management, BMW AG

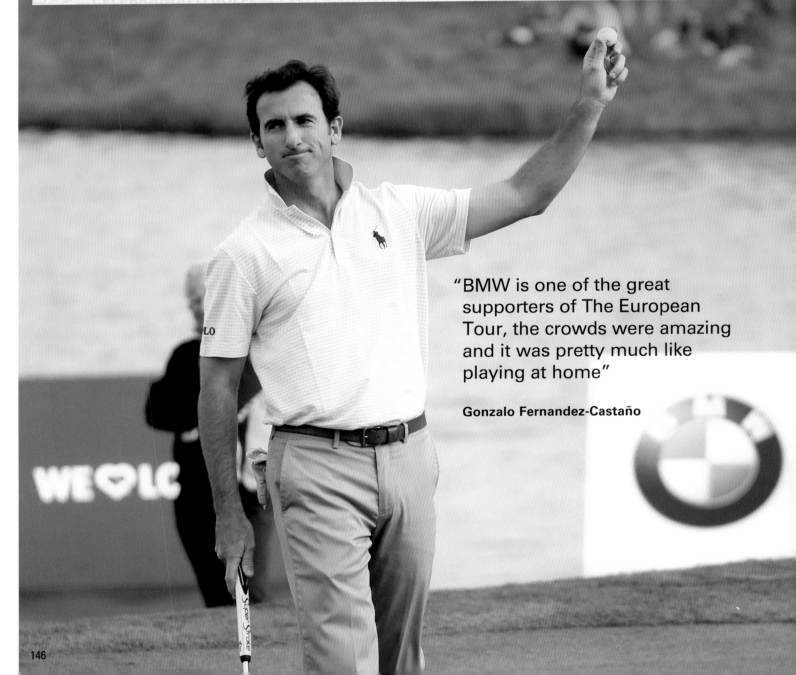

"BMW is one of the great supporters of The European Tour, the crowds were amazing and it was pretty much like playing at home"

Gonzalo Fernandez-Castaño

Home from Home

There might be more than 10,000 kilometres between Madrid and Shanghai but as Gonzalo Fernandez-Castaño celebrated making history by winning the first tournament on The European Tour's inaugural Final Series in The Race to Dubai so he reflected on feeling as at home in the largest city by population in China as he would in the Spanish capital where he was born and lives.

Fernandez-Castaño admitted to being inspired not only by the atmosphere, paying tribute to the amazing support of the spectators, but also the sponsorship of BMW as this was his third success in an European Tour event sponsored by the German automobile company following wins in last year's Italian Open and the 2006 Asian Open.

Players from no fewer than 11 countries were represented in the top 14 on Day One albeit that the $30.5 million Final Series began with

Luke Guthrie, after only 19 putts in an opening 65 in blustery conditions, leading an American 1-2-3 before surging four shots ahead at halfway.

Then the Spanish 'Armada' challenged the American with Rafa Cabrera-Bello's third round 67 taking him alongside Guthrie — one ahead of Fernandez-Castaño, who closed his 67 with a rare birdie at the 18th, and Pablo Larrazábal also among the contenders.

Two of Europe's 'Miracle Men' of Medinah, Peter Hanson, who notched 11 birdies, and Francesco Molinari, who followed an eagle at the 13th with four straight birdies, showed with closing rounds of 63 and 64 respectively their intention to retain their Ryder Cup places. However, Fernadez-Castaño, who eventually beat Thongchai Jaidee, who closed with a 66, and Molinari by one shot, put Gleneagles and a Ryder Cup debut firmly in his sights.

Thongchai Jaidee

Pablo Larrazábal

Thomas Björn

Rafa Cabrera-Bello

Francesco Molinari

WGC - HSBC CHAMPIONS
Sheshan International GC, Shanghai, China October 31–November 3, 2013

L-R: Giles Morgan, HSBC Global Head of Sponsorship and Events, Dustin Johnson and Gordon French, HSBC Head of Global Banking and Markets, Asia-Pacific

1	**DUSTIN JOHNSON**		69	63	66	66	264	-24
2	Ian Poulter		71	67	63	66	267	-21
3	Graeme McDowell		69	69	64	66	268	-20
4	Sergio Garcia		70	68	69	63	270	-18
5	Justin Rose		68	71	65	68	272	-16
6	Graham Delaet		71	68	65	69	273	-15
	Rory McIlroy		65	72	67	69	273	-15
8	Jamie Donaldson		67	74	66	67	274	-14
	Martin Kaymer		70	74	62	68	274	-14
	Bubba Watson		68	69	69	68	274	-14

Total Prize Fund $8,500,000   **First Prize** €1,012,146

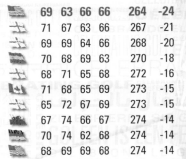

"It's the biggest win of my career and it feels really good"

Dustin Johnson

Graeme McDowell

Sergio Garcia

Justin Rose

Ian Poulter

EUROPEAN TOUR
RACE TO
DUBAI

In the future, talent will emerge from anywhere.

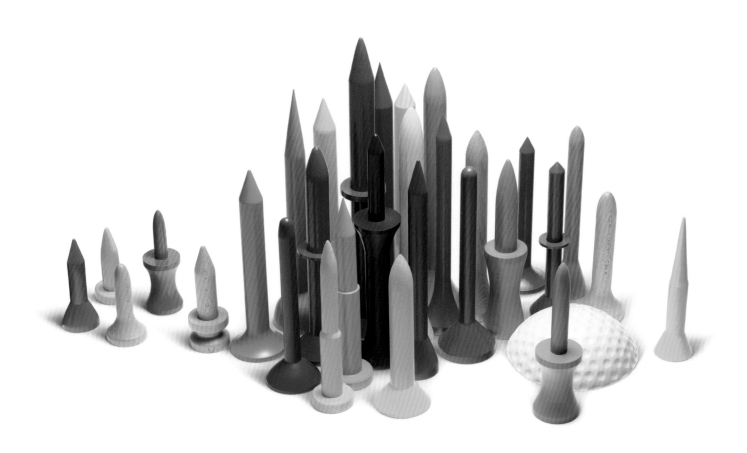

Golf is one of the fastest growing sports in Asia and across emerging markets, where disposable income is helping to bring new talent into the game. HSBC is proud to be investing in golf in these territories. From major tournaments and European Tour events to grassroots initiatives, we're opening up opportunities for both emerging talent and our customers.

www.hsbcgolf.com

HSBC

Issued by HSBC Holdings plc.

Rory McIlroy

Martin Kaymer

A golf fan in traditional dress

Game On! Game Over!

The second leg of the Final Series evolved into a battle royal between the 'Miracle Men' and the 'Maximum Man' of Medinah. Dustin Johnson, who claimed three points from three matches for the United States in The 2012 Ryder Cup, produced a final flourish to deny a chasing pack breathtakingly led by defending champion Ian Poulter and Graeme McDowell in which no fewer than six of José María Olazábal's winning European team eventually finished in the top ten.

Johnson had observed "this course suits my eye" and playing partner McDowell noted, as the American swept five shots ahead at halfway following Rory McIlroy's pacesetting 65, that "You could probably build a four or five bedroom house with garden in the space between our drives. My drives fly through the air between 270 and 275 yards but every one of his was over 320."

The prodigious driving Johnson, out in 30 in the third round for the second day in succession, did hold out a hand of friendship by taking seven at the 18th so enabling Poulter, who notched five successive birdies from the third and added an eagle at the 14th, to close to within three with a superbly constructed 63 with McDowell only one further back after six birdies and a chip-in eagle at the 16th for a flawless 64.

Game on! Most certainly as Poulter led Johnson and McDowell by one standing on the 13th. Game over! Most certainly as Johnson played the last six birdie-birdie-par-eagle-birdie-par to match the 66s of his playing partners and win by three. Consolation for Poulter, who had 15 birdies and an eagle in his last 36 holes, and McDowell as they boosted their prospects of Race to Dubai glory and satisfaction, too, for Sergio Garcia, who closed with a 63 for fourth, Justin Rose, McIlroy and Martin Kaymer, who shot 62-68 on the weekend.

Jamie Donaldson

EUROPEAN TOUR
RACE TO DUBAI

TURKISH AIRLINES OPEN BY THE MINISTRY OF CULTURE AND TOURISM
The Montgomerie Maxx Royal, Antalya, Turkey November 7-10, 2013

Hamdi Topçu, Chairman of the Board of Turkish Airlines and Victor Dubuisson

1	**VICTOR DUBUISSON**		67	65	63	69	264	-24
2	Jamie Donaldson		68	67	68	63	266	-22
3	Justin Rose		70	66	67	65	268	-20
	Tiger Woods		70	63	68	67	268	-20
5	Raphaël Jacquelin		67	72	62	68	269	-19
	Ian Poulter		66	66	68	69	269	-19
7	Henrik Stenson		64	68	69	69	270	-18
	Marc Warren		69	70	66	65	270	-18
	Bernd Wiesberger		68	72	66	64	270	-18
10	Ross Fisher		68	68	70	65	271	-17
	Justin Walters		66	66	70	69	271	-17

Total Prize Fund $7,000,000   **First Prize** €848,930

"I wanted to cry on the 18th. I had been watching the leaderboard, seeing all these great players coming at me – it was the longest day I have ever had on a golf course"

Henrik Stenson

Tiger Woods

Raphaël Jacquelin

To Victor the Spoils

Victor Dubuisson set off in the final round of the third leg of The Final Series holding a five shot lead, courtesy of synchronised scoring in the sun as he followed an opening 67 with a 65 then nine birdies in a flawless 63, with a maiden European Tour win in his sights and a chasing pack intent on inflicting serious pressure on him.

In-form Ian Poulter led the pursuers and followed an outward 32 with a birdie at the tenth. World Number One Tiger Woods stalked the field; US Open champion Justin Rose roared to the turn in 29 with four birdies and an eagle; and Race to Dubai leader Henrik Stenson, Raphaël Jacquelin and Jamie Donaldson waited in the wings.

Nevertheless Dubuisson stayed composed, following nine straight pars with a birdie at the tenth. Then after a bogey at the 14th so Rose with a third birdie in four holes from the 14th tied him for the lead. Donaldson, quite dramatically, gathered seven birdies

then holed in one at the 16th en route to completing a fabulous 63 with a birdie at the last. Meanwhile Stenson and Woods both launched birdie barrages on the back nine to further raise the tempo.

Dubuisson's response? A birdie at the 15th, a treacherous 30 foot putt holed for another at the 17th and then the coup de grâce – a thundering drive at 18, a smart second, a glance at the leaderboard, a perfectly judged pitch to six feet from where he had two for the title but required only one so finishing two ahead of Donaldson.

Almost speechless, Dubuisson had climbed from 108th to 39th in the Official World Ranking. He had become the highest placed Frenchman in the history of the Ranking, beating the 41st achieved by Thomas Levet in January 2005. Dubuisson also went to Number One in the European Ryder Cup Points Table and to ninth in The 2013 Race to Dubai still led by Stenson with Rose, Graeme McDowell and Poulter all within 350,000 points.

Ian Poulter

Justin Rose

Jamie Donaldson

EUROPEAN TOUR RACE TO DUBAI

Emperor of Europe

THE RACE ENDS HERE

ROLEX

EUROPEAN TOUR

DP WOR

"This has been a dream season. Everyone who has won The Race to Dubai before me has been World Number One - it would not be fair if I didn't try to follow them"

Henrik Stenson

1	**HENRIK STENSON**		68	64	67	64	263	-25
2	Ian Poulter		69	68	66	66	269	-19
3	Victor Dubuisson		70	66	64	71	271	-17
4	Joost Luiten		73	68	65	66	272	-16
5	Luke Donald		73	66	67	67	273	-15
	Rory McIlroy		71	67	68	67	273	-15
	Lee Westwood		70	70	65	68	273	-15
8	Jamie Donaldson		68	72	67	67	274	-14
	Miguel Angel Jiménez		72	66	66	70	274	-14
10	Peter Hanson		70	68	70	67	275	-13
	Justin Rose		70	67	68	70	275	-13

Total Prize Fund $8,000,000   **First Prize** €985,476

L-R: Mohammed Sharaf, Group CEO DP World, Henrik Stenson, H.E. Sultan Ahmed bin Sulayem and George O'Grady, Chief Executive The European Tour

Henrik Stenson took care of one statistic that threatened to irritate his record-breaking celebrations when with an imperious performance he won the DP World Tour Championship, Dubai on the Earth Course at Jumeirah Golf Estates.

For as he targeted becoming the 42nd European Tour Number One he was well aware that not one of the players before him had failed to win a tournament during The European Tour season in which they earned that coveted honour.

Stenson, however, ensured that his name would make no such annoying invasion into the record books as he completed a remarkable victory march in the season-ending DP World Tour Championship, Dubai by drilling a phenomenal 260 yards three wood to within eight inches at the 18th where the spectators in the packed grandstand provided a vociferous, heart-felt reception for the amicable Swede.

What the victory also cemented was a very special slice of golfing history as by winning the DP World Tour Championship, Dubai and

The Race to Dubai, Stenson completed an astonishing 'double-double' having won the Tour Championship and FedExCup on American soil exactly 56 days earlier.

Stenson's success, following a well-documented tumble outside of the world's leading 200, enabled him to follow in the footsteps of the first four winners of The Race to Dubai – Lee Westwood, Martin Kaymer, Luke Donald and Rory McIlroy – and his peers graciously acknowledged that, quite simply, he was on another planet in the second half of 2013 when his rise to Number One was ignited by finishing tied third in the Aberdeen Asset Management Scottish Open then runner-up in The 142nd Open Championship.

"Everyone goes through ups and downs," said Stenson. "I had a

Joost Luiten

Victor Dubuisson

Ian Poulter

couple of slumps, a bit deeper than you would like to see, but if you keep fighting and keep your belief then anything is possible."

The man from Gothenburg, who now lives in Florida, had relocated at the start of the new Millennium to Dubai – "I've got my family here this week and great support from a lot of friends from living here for ten years" - so there could hardly have been a more appropriate place for him to celebrate the closure of such a stellar season than in the United Arab Emirates. Stenson recognised, of course, that this was no foregone conclusion with Justin Rose, Graeme McDowell and the ebullient Ian Poulter all snapping at his heels in The Race to Dubai. Not that he actually saw much of them in the lead-up to the action unfolding.

Electing, wisely, to rest his injured wrist, Stenson stayed away from the course. What he missed was the potential distraction of McDowell, Poulter and Rose naturally talking up their own prospects, all excited by the possibility of finishing Number One, although

such was his focus when he eventually teed off that one sensed that not even the Red Arrows could divert his attention from the task at hand.

The British Royal Air Force Aerobatic Team – the official name of the Red Arrows led by Squadron Leader Jim Turner – provided a unique salute to the 56 strong field with a spectacular fly-past timed to emblazon the skies in red, white and blue – maybe it should have been blue and yellow - with Rose and Stenson minutes away from starting their first rounds.

This further enhanced a truly enterprising entertainment programme for the fans with the DP World Tour Championship becoming a sporting and social spectacular and Jumeirah Golf Estates the centre of the global golfing spotlight with something to interest everyone in the Championship Village, including popular bands The Maplejacks and Suburban Voodoo playing live each night.

The special relationship between The European Tour and Dubai was underlined at the

start of the week when David Howell, Brett Rumford, Peter Uihlein and Rose simultaneously struck shots from the impressive teaching bays to officially open the new state-of-the-art European Tour Performance Institute (ETPI) at Jumeirah Golf Estates which recently became part of European Tour Property's expanding network of world class Destination Venues. Yousuf Kazim, General Manager, Jumeirah Golf Estates, performed the Opening Ceremony jointly with George O'Grady, Chief Executive of The European Tour, and commented: "This marks another important milestone for the on-going development at Jumeirah Golf Estates and in addition to recently gaining European Tour Destination status we are delighted to be further enhancing our relationship with The European Tour."

Then The European Tour announced that The Race to Dubai had been extended through to the 2017 season with the next edition once again concluding with the season-ending finale at Jumeirah Golf

Estates. O'Grady said: "Thanks to the leadership and vision of DP World, the tremendous contribution of everyone at Jumeirah Golf Estates, and the continued commitment of our partners, the future of The Race to Dubai is exceptionally positive. This is the perfect venue to finish our year. The climate is excellent, the facilities superb and the welcome from everyone in Dubai is simply outstanding."

Nearly 55,000 spectators over the four days were rewarded with golf of the highest calibre from Day One which ended not with any one of the Race to Dubai protagonists leading – that honour went to Spaniard Alejandro Cañizares with an excellent 66 – although they all made their presence felt. Stenson's 68, despite a three putt at the 18th, was a statement of intent. Poulter, oozing confidence, aggressively seeking birdies at every hole, viewed his 69 as a good rather than a great score and Rose and McDowell, courtesy of three successive birdies from the 14th, shot 70 and 72 respectively.

L-R: Justin Rose; Majid al Ghurair, Board Member, Jumeirah Golf Estates; George O'Grady, Chief Executive, The European Tour; Yousuf Kazim, General Manager, JGE; David Howell

Serge Zaalof, President and Managing Director of Atlantis, The Palm presents the players with their trophies after the DP World Tour Championship Atlantis Golf Challenge

The Championship Village

Luke Donald

Rory McIlroy

If Stenson did require an antidote for that injured wrist then he found it with an outstanding, flawless second round of 64 with which he moved one ahead of Canizares. Victor Dubuisson, buoyed by his winning performance the previous Sunday, charged into contention with a 66 although Stenson, naturally enough, had his eyes on Rose and Poulter, who shot 67 and 68 respectively, when he said: "They are chasing me as hard as they can so I better keep by head down, my foot down and maintain the momentum."

In fact Poulter caught Stenson at one stage during a hugely impressive third round of 66 but the Swede responded with four birdies in the last five holes for a 67. Poulter was confident he was still firmly in the hunt and if that was not enough then Stenson also had that other matter of winning the tournament on his mind as Dubuisson remained in the form of his life. The Frenchman notched 11 birdies in a 64 to close to within one of the leader.

Stenson knew that to become the Emperor of Europe he could show no mercy on the final day. Splendid nine iron approaches brought birdies at the first and third, a wedge to within inches another at the fifth and with a two putt birdie at the seventh he was out in 32. Dubuisson gallantly birdied three of his first seven holes then dropped a shot at the eighth. The Frenchman was still a threat as was Poulter

who, despite a three putt at the first, predictably attacked the course. Seven birdies brought a second successive 66 on the weekend but he was still compelled to accept second place as Dubuisson bravely birdied the last to take third place on his own. Joost Luiten sealed his own personal best season with fourth place and the quality of the field was emphasised with Donald, McIlroy and Westwood sharing fifth place.

That left Stenson standing over that eight inch putt on the 18th green following birdies at the 12th, where in the blustery conditions he hit an absolutely fabulous 'baby' five iron from 173 yards to 18 inches, and 14th. So to a season-ending tap-in eagle, a closing 64 a record 25 under par winning score of 263 and a comprehensive six shot victory. He had missed only four greens and five fairways in 72 holes on the immaculate 7,675 yards Earth Course. Many great names have won the Harry Vardon Trophy – now awarded annually to the winner of The Race to Dubai – but probably no player has brought the curtain down on a season with such a commanding performance than the 71st recipient of this famous trophy.

For Henrik Stenson had taken care of business and written his name in the record books for all the right reasons.

Mitchell Platts

Lee Westwood

The Red Arrows

THE RACE TO DUBAI ON THE 2013 EUROPEAN TOUR INTERNATIONAL SCHEDULE

Pos	Name	Country	Played	Points
1	Henrik STENSON	(SWE)	(17)	4103796.34
2	Ian POULTER	(ENG)	(14)	3172728.95
3	Justin ROSE	(ENG)	(13)	2665375.77
4	Graeme MCDOWELL	(NIR)	(14)	2420305.62
5	Jamie DONALDSON	(WAL)	(23)	2181113.44
6	Victor DUBUISSON	(FRA)	(21)	2031674.58
7	Gonzalo FDEZ-CASTAÑO	(ESP)	(22)	1767155.95
8	Richard STERNE	(RSA)	(22)	1687014.11
9	Thongchai JAIDEE	(THA)	(25)	1585520.55
10	Thomas BJÖRN	(DEN)	(26)	1546735.56
11	Matteo MANASSERO	(ITA)	(26)	1414471.28
12	Joost LUITEN	(NED)	(26)	1411909.63
13	Francesco MOLINARI	(ITA)	(27)	1367565.59
14	Peter UIHLEIN	(USA)	(24)	1360267.81
15	Lee WESTWOOD	(ENG)	(13)	1299694.37
16	Sergio GARCIA	(ESP)	(13)	1280581.11
17	Brett RUMFORD	(AUS)	(26)	1277022.04
18	Branden GRACE	(RSA)	(25)	1224191.58
19	Stephen GALLACHER	(SCO)	(27)	1173314.96
20	Ernie ELS	(RSA)	(16)	1166711.91
21	David HOWELL	(ENG)	(30)	1158048.97
22	Miguel Angel JIMÉNEZ	(ESP)	(19)	1157142.01
23	Mikko ILONEN	(FIN)	(25)	1065066.36
24	Martin KAYMER	(GER)	(18)	1042036.52
25	Grégory BOURDY	(FRA)	(29)	1011374.88
26	Tommy FLEETWOOD	(ENG)	(32)	1007872.32
27	Charl SCHWARTZEL	(RSA)	(13)	1006691.60
28	Bernd WIESBERGER	(AUT)	(25)	998332.13
29	Chris WOOD	(ENG)	(22)	998281.26
30	Paul CASEY	(ENG)	(25)	969421.63
31	Scott JAMIESON	(SCO)	(31)	966320.55
32	Thorbjørn OLESEN	(DEN)	(24)	963876.06
33	Marc WARREN	(SCO)	(30)	925853.69
34	Pablo LARRAZÁBAL	(ESP)	(31)	908223.68
35	Rory MCILROY	(NIR)	(13)	862176.63
36	Shane LOWRY	(IRL)	(21)	834042.83
37	Raphaël JACQUELIN	(FRA)	(27)	801530.73
38	Nicolas COLSAERTS	(BEL)	(18)	799098.43
39	Kiradech APHIBARNRAT	(THA)	(17)	797868.11
40	Ross FISHER	(ENG)	(18)	767933.48
41	Rafa CABRERA-BELLO	(ESP)	(29)	767904.31
42	Julien QUESNE	(FRA)	(26)	749927.86
43	Luke DONALD	(ENG)	(13)	745154.12
44	Thomas AIKEN	(RSA)	(26)	739772.74
45	Marcus FRASER	(AUS)	(22)	738937.79
46	Jonas BLIXT	(SWE)	(7)	728760.36
47	Louis OOSTHUIZEN	(RSA)	(15)	727151.74
48	Darren FICHARDT	(RSA)	(25)	722287.49
49	Peter HANSON	(SWE)	(14)	704835.23
50	Felipe AGUILAR	(CHI)	(27)	703070.10
51	Alejandro CAÑIZARES	(ESP)	(28)	694466.83
52	David LYNN	(ENG)	(16)	685808.09
53	Marcel SIEM	(GER)	(18)	674890.42
54	George COETZEE	(RSA)	(17)	667214.76
55	Simon KHAN	(ENG)	(21)	647807.31
56	Alex NOREN	(SWE)	(20)	612104.33
57	David HORSEY	(ENG)	(27)	594033.83
58	Eduardo DE LA RIVA	(ESP)	(27)	593360.74
59	Craig LEE	(SCO)	(30)	581828.04
60	Garth MULROY	(RSA)	(23)	579076.13
61	Søren KJELDSEN	(DEN)	(33)	532750.39
62	Danny WILLETT	(ENG)	(22)	531446.87
63	Paul LAWRIE	(SCO)	(23)	513307.25
64	Justin WALTERS	(RSA)	(31)	512157.98
65	Ricardo SANTOS	(POR)	(29)	499756.14
66	Ricardo GONZALEZ	(ARG)	(25)	499650.75
67	Steve WEBSTER	(ENG)	(26)	498979.28
68	Padraig HARRINGTON	(IRL)	(16)	464326.11
69	Paul WARING	(ENG)	(25)	459862.22
70	Richie RAMSAY	(SCO)	(22)	459252.43
71	Grégory HAVRET	(FRA)	(31)	425240.01
72	Simon DYSON	(ENG)	(28)	417331.76
73	Maximilian KIEFFER	(GER)	(29)	416910.37
74	Robert-Jan DERKSEN	(NED)	(23)	411958.70
75	Graeme STORM	(ENG)	(29)	401263.55
76	Eddie PEPPERELL	(ENG)	(25)	389766.24
77	John PARRY	(ENG)	(24)	388415.21
78	Wen-chong LIANG	(CHN)	(15)	382265.08
79	JB HANSEN	(DEN)	(28)	375036.62
80	David DRYSDALE	(SCO)	(31)	364720.97
81	Morten Ørum MADSEN	(DEN)	(23)	357416.63
82	Damien MCGRANE	(IRL)	(28)	342164.57
83	Anders HANSEN	(DEN)	(17)	339943.89
84	Romain WATTEL	(FRA)	(26)	332032.30
85	Robert ROCK	(ENG)	(25)	330344.61
86	Jaco VAN ZYL	(RSA)	(21)	325974.10
87	Matthew BALDWIN	(ENG)	(31)	324140.78
88	Peter WHITEFORD	(SCO)	(29)	324128.27
89	Emiliano GRILLO	(ARG)	(28)	324123.88
90	Hennie OTTO	(RSA)	(20)	323562.73
91	Edoardo MOLINARI	(ITA)	(14)	319759.66
92	Michael HOEY	(NIR)	(22)	318959.72
93	Jin JEONG	(KOR)	(2)	308336.11
94	Tom LEWIS	(ENG)	(25)	303354.30
95	Gareth MAYBIN	(NIR)	(26)	300961.91
96	Jorge CAMPILLO	(ESP)	(32)	299671.80
97	Seve BENSON	(ENG)	(22)	297958.66
98	Andy SULLIVAN	(ENG)	(26)	279998.60
99	Lee SLATTERY	(ENG)	(27)	277013.07
100	Mark FOSTER	(ENG)	(24)	275872.02
101	Chris DOAK	(SCO)	(27)	261506.55
102	Gaganjeet BHULLAR	(IND)	(13)	259803.97
103	Kristoffer BROBERG	(SWE)	(27)	258105.03
104	Alvaro QUIROS	(ESP)	(20)	256761.31
105	Matthew NIXON	(ENG)	(26)	252179.04
106	Magnus A CARLSSON	(SWE)	(26)	251434.33
107	Dawie VAN DER WALT	(RSA)	(10)	249550.00
108	Richard BLAND	(ENG)	(26)	247732.69
109	Alexander LEVY	(FRA)	(24)	240540.09
110	Peter LAWRIE	(IRL)	(28)	233630.35
111	James KINGSTON	(RSA)	(15)	225150.30
112	Richard GREEN	(AUS)	(21)	218462.72
113	Brooks KOEPKA	(USA)	(12)	217761.62
114	Mark TULLO	(CHI)	(25)	216164.60
115	David HIGGINS	(IRL)	(22)	215355.85
116	Alexandre KALEKA	(FRA)	(29)	209865.66
117	Lorenzo GAGLI	(ITA)	(29)	209227.00
118	Oliver FISHER	(ENG)	(28)	207537.99
119	Andreas HARTØ	(DEN)	(30)	199447.41
120	Scott HENRY	(SCO)	(31)	197601.30
121	Darren CLARKE	(NIR)	(13)	195129.65
122	Chris PAISLEY	(ENG)	(31)	194369.24
123	Fredrik ANDERSSON HED	(SWE)	(25)	192381.54
124	Mikko KORHONEN	(FIN)	(16)	187399.14
125	Richard FINCH	(ENG)	(29)	186533.64
126	José María OLAZÁBAL	(ESP)	(23)	182049.91
127	Paul MCGINLEY	(IRL)	(17)	177096.44
128	Simon THORNTON	(IRL)	(11)	176688.53
129	Tjaart VAN DER WALT	(RSA)	(20)	175130.99
130	Rikard KARLBERG	(SWE)	(17)	171371.22
131	Soren HANSEN	(DEN)	(22)	161721.99
132	Jbe KRUGER	(RSA)	(23)	157403.29
133	Jeev Milkha SINGH	(IND)	(23)	156643.41
134	Simon WAKEFIELD	(ENG)	(30)	155490.28
135	Espen KOFSTAD	(NOR)	(30)	155439.52
136	Thomas LEVET	(FRA)	(25)	153231.41
137	Keith HORNE	(RSA)	(25)	152933.11
138	Joel SJÖHOLM	(SWE)	(31)	143899.43
139	James MORRISON	(ENG)	(29)	141098.62
140	Fabrizio ZANOTTI	(PAR)	(27)	139304.41
141	Gary LOCKERBIE	(ENG)	(27)	131615.29
142	Björn ÅKESSON	(SWE)	(25)	125117.23
143	Matteo DELPODIO	(ITA)	(26)	118252.89
144	Joakim LAGERGREN	(SWE)	(20)	117521.78
145	S.S.P CHOWRASIA	(IND)	(22)	117446.67
146	Gareth SHAW	(NIR)	(5)	116654.29
147	Scott HEND	(AUS)	(12)	114044.50
148	Alessandro TADINI	(ITA)	(27)	113905.42
149	Andrew DODT	(AUS)	(24)	110837.61
150	Richard MCEVOY	(ENG)	(22)	108223.41

Pos	Name	Country	Played	Points
151	Oscar FLOREN	(SWE)	(22)	104473.68
152	Niclas FASTH	(SWE)	(27)	104031.11
153	Chris LLOYD	(ENG)	(23)	103395.78
154	José Manuel LARA	(ESP)	(29)	103014.69
155	Johan EDFORS	(SWE)	(25)	102908.26
156	Shiv KAPUR	(IND)	(12)	99512.98
157	Phillip PRICE	(WAL)	(23)	98485.66
158	Robert COLES	(ENG)	(28)	96528.07
159	Ignacio GARRIDO	(ESP)	(26)	90590.07
160	Prom MEESAWAT	(THA)	(15)	89821.22
161	Seuk-hyun BAEK	(KOR)	(4)	88304.13
162	Adilson DA SILVA	(BRA)	(9)	86355.13
163	Anthony SNOBECK	(FRA)	(21)	86141.19
164	Peter HEDBLOM	(SWE)	(21)	84778.81
165	Sam LITTLE	(ENG)	(22)	77804.27
166	Berry HENSON	(USA)	(5)	74761.46
167	Ashun WU	(CHN)	(7)	70954.78
168	Mikael LUNDBERG	(SWE)	(23)	69389.47
169	Andrew MARSHALL	(ENG)	(15)	68731.25
170	Wen-yi HUANG	(CHN)	(5)	67633.35
171	Lasse JENSEN	(DEN)	(20)	64128.19
172	Jean-Baptiste GONNET	(FRA)	(25)	63268.83
173	Michael CAMPBELL	(NZL)	(17)	63164.74
174	Estanislao GOYA	(ARG)	(22)	63149.19
175	Matthew SOUTHGATE	(ENG)	(20)	62367.06
176	Thaworn WIRATCHANT	(THA)	(6)	60996.98
177	Alvaro VELASCO	(ESP)	(5)	58635.00
178	Trevor FISHER JNR	(RSA)	(10)	57735.15
179	Michael JONZON	(SWE)	(16)	55693.24
180	Maarten LAFEBER	(NED)	(25)	53637.43
181	Daniel POPOVIC	(AUS)	(9)	52204.97
182	Rhys DAVIES	(WAL)	(14)	51715.00
183	Steven TILEY	(ENG)	(3)	51582.31
184	Moritz LAMPERT	(GER)	(22)	45251.28
185	Alastair FORSYTH	(SCO)	(12)	40992.80
186	Jake ROOS	(RSA)	(9)	40383.69
187	George MURRAY	(SCO)	(9)	40371.03
188	Alan DUNBAR	(NIR)	(6)	39960.00
189	Oliver BEKKER	(RSA)	(11)	39845.00
190	Thomas PIETERS	(BEL)	(3)	39463.64
191	Callum MACAULAY	(SCO)	(20)	39125.00
192	Roope KAKKO	(FIN)	(4)	36224.29
193	Martin WIEGELE	(AUT)	(29)	35114.98
194	Himmat RAI	(IND)	(5)	35100.00
195	Jason KNUTZON	(USA)	(3)	34644.75
196	Chinnarat PHADUNGSIL	(THA)	(4)	34533.96
197	Jamie ELSON	(ENG)	(8)	33910.00
198	Stephen DODD	(WAL)	(10)	33860.00
199	Chapchai NIRAT	(THA)	(5)	33770.00
200	Daniel GAUNT	(AUS)	(15)	32698.00

FLAGS OF THE WORLD

	Abu Dhabi		Kenya
	Argentina		Malaysia
	Australia		Mauritius
	Austria		Morocco
	Bahrain		The Netherlands
	Barbados		New Zealand
	Belgium		Northern Ireland
	Brunei		Norway
	Bulgaria		Oman
	Chile		Paraguay
	China		Phillipines
	Chinese Taipei		Poland
	Colombia		Portugal
	Czech Republic		Qatar
	Denmark		Russia
	Dubai		Scotland
	England		Singapore
	Estonia		South Africa
	Fiji		South Korea
	Finland		Spain
	France		Sweden
	Germany		Switzerland
	Hong Kong		Taiwan
	Iceland		Thailand
	India		Trinidad & Tobago
	Indonesia		Turkey
	Ireland		Ukraine
	Italy		USA
	Jamaica		Venezuela
	Japan		Wales
	Kazakhstan		Zimbabwe

THE 2013 EUROPEAN TOUR INTERNATIONAL SCHEDULE

Stroke Average

Pos	Name	Stroke Average	Total Strokes	Total Rounds	Pos	Name	Stroke Average	Total Strokes	Total Rounds	Pos	Name	Stroke Average	Total Strokes	Total Rounds
1	Charl SCHWARTZEL	69.63	2855	41	51	David DRYSDALE	71.01	7243	102	76	Padraig HARRINGTON	71.22	3490	49
2	Henrik STENSON	69.72	4183	60	52	Marcel SIEM	71.03	4404	62		Paul LAWRIE	71.22	5484	77
3	Ross FISHER	69.83	4539	65	53	Wen-chong LIANG	71.04	3552	50	78	Andy SULLIVAN	71.23	5342	75
4	Joost LUITEN	69.92	5803	83	54	Mikko KORHONEN	71.05	4405	62	79	Matthew BALDWIN	71.25	7125	100
5	Justin ROSE	70.00	3220	46		Rafa CABRERA-BELLO	71.05	6963	98	80	Ricardo SANTOS	71.26	6271	88
6	Richard STERNE	70.04	4903	70	56	Emiliano GRILLO	71.06	5543	78	81	David LYNN	71.28	3350	47
7	Victor DUBUISSON	70.13	4418	63		Nicolas COLSAERTS	71.06	3624	51	82	Gonzalo FDEZ-CASTAÑO	71.31	5277	74
8	Adilson DA SILVA	70.16	1754	25	58	Grégory HAVRET	71.07	6538	92		Tom LEWIS	71.31	4992	70
9	Bernd WIESBERGER	70.24	6532	93		John PARRY	71.07	5046	71	84	Richard BLAND	71.32	5420	76
10	Jonas BLIXT	70.25	1967	28	60	Alejandro CAÑIZARES	71.08	6326	89	85	Magnus A CARLSSON	71.33	5564	78
11	Martin KAYMER	70.40	4787	68	61	Maximilian KIEFFER	71.10	6186	87		Rory MCILROY	71.33	2853	40
	Sergio GARCIA	70.40	3379	48		Richie RAMSAY	71.10	5119	72	87	Alvaro QUIROS	71.34	4209	59
13	Peter UIHLEIN	70.42	5493	78	63	Thomas AIKEN	71.11	5262	74	88	Jaco VAN ZYL	71.35	4638	65
14	Jamie DONALDSON	70.45	5143	73	64	Graeme MCDOWELL	71.13	2845	40	89	Eddie PEPPERELL	71.37	5567	78
15	Lee WESTWOOD	70.54	3386	48	65	James KINGSTON	71.14	2988	42	90	Raphaël JACQUELIN	71.38	6281	88
16	Garth MULROY	70.55	5291	75	66	Lee SLATTERY	71.15	6048	85		Rikard KARLBERG	71.38	3783	53
17	Peter HANSON	70.57	2964	42		Morten Ørum MADSEN	71.15	5123	72	92	Eduardo DE LA RIVA	71.39	5925	83
18	Tommy FLEETWOOD	70.58	7482	106	68	Jorge CAMPILLO	71.16	6974	98		Justin WALTERS	71.39	6282	88
19	Ian POULTER	70.61	3107	44	69	Kiradech APHIBARNRAT	71.18	3915	55		Marc WARREN	71.39	6211	87
20	David HORSEY	70.63	6215	88		Romain WATTEL	71.18	5623	79	95	Branden GRACE	71.41	5427	76
	Paul WARING	70.63	5297	75		Scott HEND	71.18	2349	33		Soren HANSEN	71.41	4856	68
	Simon THORNTON	70.63	2472	35		Søren KJELDSEN	71.18	7047	99		Thorbjørn OLESEN	71.41	4927	69
23	Paul CASEY	70.64	6216	88	73	Chris WOOD	71.19	4556	64	98	Alexander LEVY	71.48	4646	65
24	Ricardo GONZALEZ	70.65	5581	79		Steve WEBSTER	71.19	5126	72		George COETZEE	71.48	3717	52
25	Darren FICHARDT	70.69	5302	75	75	Craig LEE	71.20	6622	93	100	Mark TULLO	71.49	5290	74
	Thomas BJÖRN	70.69	6009	85										
	Thongchai JAIDEE	70.69	5938	84										
28	Matteo MANASSERO	70.71	6152	87										
29	Alex NOREN	70.74	4386	62										
	Brooks KOEPKA	70.74	2971	42										
	Hennie OTTO	70.74	4103	58										
	Miguel Angel JIMÉNEZ	70.74	4669	66										
33	Ernie ELS	70.77	3680	52										
34	Danny WILLETT	70.78	5238	74										
	Seve BENSON	70.78	4884	69										
36	Pablo LARRAZÁBAL	70.82	6303	89										
	Shane LOWRY	70.82	4745	67										
38	David HOWELL	70.83	7366	104										
39	Robert-Jan DERKSEN	70.85	5668	80										
40	Grégory BOURDY	70.87	6874	97										
41	Stephen GALLACHER	70.91	6027	85										
42	Felipe AGUILAR	70.93	6029	85										
43	Anders HANSEN	70.96	3761	53										
	Francesco MOLINARI	70.96	5961	84										
	Mikko ILONEN	70.96	5748	81										
46	Simon DYSON	70.98	5962	84										
47	Mark FOSTER	70.99	5182	73										
48	Julien QUESNE	71.00	5538	78										
	Louis OOSTHUIZEN	71.00	2911	41										
	Marcus FRASER	71.00	5254	74										

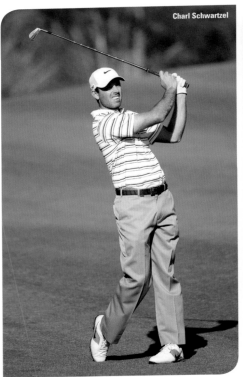

Charl Schwartzel

Brett Rumford

Driving Distance (yds)

Pos	Name	Average Yards	Stats Rounds
1	Brooks KOEPKA	318.2	35
2	Scott HEND	316.5	33
3	Alvaro QUIROS	309.5	58
4	Nicolas COLSAERTS	308.7	51
5	Charl SCHWARTZEL	307.8	39
6	Scott HENRY	306.4	82
7	Peter UIHLEIN	305.5	71
8	Gaganjeet BHULLAR	303.2	30
9	Andy SULLIVAN	302.3	73
10	Seve BENSON	301.9	67
11	Joakim LAGERGREN	301.3	57
12	Henrik STENSON	301.2	60
13	Björn ÅKESSON	300.4	62
14	Rory MCILROY	300.3	40
15	Alexander LEVY	299.3	63
16	Bernd WIESBERGER	299.2	91
17	Justin WALTERS	299.2	85
18	Paul WARING	299.2	74
19	Kiradech APHIBARNRAT	299.1	55
20	Victor DUBUISSON	298.8	60
21	Espen KOFSTAD	298.1	76
22	Alexandre KALEKA	297.9	72
23	Carlos DEL MORAL	297.2	31
24	Louis OOSTHUIZEN	297.1	41
25	George COETZEE	297.0	52

Driving Accuracy (%)

Pos	Name	%	Stats Rounds
1	Adilson DA SILVA	81.4	24
2	Simon WAKEFIELD	80.9	83
3	Richie RAMSAY	71.9	72
4	Grégory BOURDY	71.8	95
	Phillip PRICE	71.8	59
6	Felipe AGUILAR	71.5	84
7	Francesco MOLINARI	71.4	84
	Joost LUITEN	71.4	83
	Matthew SOUTHGATE	71.4	50
10	David DRYSDALE	71.0	99
	Thomas AIKEN	71.0	71
12	Edoardo MOLINARI	70.9	35
13	Mikko KORHONEN	70.8	62
14	Gaganjeet BHULLAR	70.6	30
15	David HIGGINS	69.9	64
16	Eduardo DE LA RIVA	69.8	82
17	Tjaart VAN DER WALT	69.6	57
18	Graeme MCDOWELL	69.5	40
19	Miguel Angel JIMÉNEZ	68.8	66
	Simon THORNTON	68.8	32
21	James KINGSTON	68.5	39
22	Andy SULLIVAN	68.4	73
	Chris DOAK	68.4	79
	Grégory HAVRET	68.4	88
25	David HORSEY	67.7	84

Average Putts Per Round

Pos	Name	Putts per Round	Stats Rounds
1	Brett RUMFORD	27.9	83
2	Darren FICHARDT	28.1	72
3	Fredrik ANDERSSON HED	28.5	65
4	Christian CÉVAËR	28.6	59
	Marcus FRASER	28.6	72
6	Alex NOREN	28.7	60
7	Jeev Milkha SINGH	28.8	53
8	Miguel Angel JIMÉNEZ	28.9	66
	Peter HANSON	28.9	42
	Wen-chong LIANG	28.9	49
11	David HOWELL	29.0	102
	Mikael LUNDBERG	29.0	60
	Rikard KARLBERG	29.0	48
14	Damien MCGRANE	29.1	83
	David HORSEY	29.1	84
	Garth MULROY	29.1	74
	George COETZEE	29.1	52
	James KINGSTON	29.1	39
	Jamie DONALDSON	29.1	72
	Jean-Baptiste GONNET	29.1	59
	Matteo MANASSERO	29.1	86
	Mikko ILONEN	29.1	78
23	David LYNN	29.2	47
	Jbe KRUGER	29.2	60
	José María OLAZÁBAL	29.2	67

Greens In Regulation (%)

Pos	Name	%	Stats Rounds
1	Soren HANSEN	76.8	66
2	Magnus A CARLSSON	76.6	76
3	Adilson DA SILVA	76.4	24
4	Emiliano GRILLO	76.3	77
5	Ross FISHER	75.8	62
6	Paul CASEY	75.6	86
7	Henrik STENSON	75.3	60
	Steve WEBSTER	75.3	69
9	Eduardo DE LA RIVA	75.1	82
10	Ricardo GONZALEZ	74.9	78
11	Felipe AGUILAR	74.2	84
12	Victor DUBUISSON	74.1	60
	Joost LUITEN	74.1	83
14	Louis OOSTHUIZEN	73.7	41
15	Thomas AIKEN	73.6	71
16	Seve BENSON	73.5	67
17	Rafa CABRERA-BELLO	73.3	96
18	David DRYSDALE	73.1	99
	Justin ROSE	73.1	46
20	Simon DYSON	73.0	82
	Bernd WIESBERGER	73.0	91
22	Grégory BOURDY	72.8	95
	Stephen GALLACHER	72.8	85
24	Maximilian KIEFFER	72.7	84
25	Thongchai JAIDEE	72.6	84

Sand Saves (%)

Pos	Name	%	Stats Rounds
1	Gaganjeet BHULLAR	85.7	30
2	José Manuel LARA	83.7	62
3	Adilson DA SILVA	75.0	24
4	Peter HANSON	70.7	42
5	Mark TULLO	67.9	72
6	Matteo MANASSERO	67.4	86
7	Ricardo SANTOS	67.3	86
8	James KINGSTON	66.7	39
9	Jonas BLIXT	65.4	24
10	Alex NOREN	64.9	60
11	John PARRY	64.8	67
12	Seve BENSON	64.7	67
13	David HOWELL	64.5	102
14	S.S.P CHOWRASIA	64.0	61
15	Christian CÉVAËR	63.6	59
16	Gonzalo FDEZ-CASTAÑO	63.3	74
17	Andrew MARSHALL	62.1	39
18	Maximilian KIEFFER	61.7	84
19	Grégory HAVRET	61.5	88
20	Jeev Milkha SINGH	61.2	53
21	Ignacio GARRIDO	61.1	63
22	Miguel Angel JIMÉNEZ	60.9	66
23	George COETZEE	60.8	52
24	Jbe KRUGER	60.2	60
25	Justin ROSE	60.0	46

Putts Per Green In Regulation

Pos	Name	Putts per GIR	Stats Rounds
1	Darren FICHARDT	1.710	72
2	Garth MULROY	1.719	74
3	Mikko ILONEN	1.729	78
4	Brett RUMFORD	1.730	83
5	Alex NOREN	1.736	60
6	Fredrik ANDERSSON HED	1.741	65
7	Matteo MANASSERO	1.742	86
8	Pablo LARRAZÁBAL	1.744	84
9	Victor DUBUISSON	1.745	60
10	David HOWELL	1.746	102
	James KINGSTON	1.746	39
12	Thomas BJÖRN	1.747	85
	Wen-chong LIANG	1.747	49
14	Marcus FRASER	1.749	72
	Shane LOWRY	1.749	64
16	Jonas BLIXT	1.750	24
	Oliver BEKKER	1.750	16
18	Peter HANSON	1.754	42
	Peter LAWRIE	1.754	74
	Sergio GARCIA	1.754	48
21	Alejandro CAÑIZARES	1.755	87
	Charl SCHWARTZEL	1.755	39
23	Kiradech APHIBARNRAT	1.757	55
24	Peter UIHLEIN	1.758	71
25	Jeev Milkha SINGH	1.759	53

Scrambles

Pos	Name	%	AVE SPR	AVE Missed GPR	Total Missed GIR	Total Scrambles	Stats Rounds
1	Robert-Jan DERKSEN	63.5	3.5	6	438	278	79
2	Jamie DONALDSON	63.3	3.5	6	398	252	72
3	David HORSEY	62.4	3.4	5	458	286	84
4	Marcus FRASER	61.6	3.9	6	456	281	72
5	Peter HANSON	61.3	3.5	6	243	149	42
6	Joost LUITEN	61.0	2.8	5	387	236	83
7	Brett RUMFORD	60.9	4.3	7	585	356	83
8	Miguel Angel JIMÉNEZ	60.8	3.7	6	401	244	66
9	Wen-chong LIANG	60.4	3.6	6	288	174	49
10	Bernd WIESBERGER	60.0	2.9	5	443	266	91
	Søren KJELDSEN	60.0	3.3	5	505	303	93
12	S.S.P CHOWRASIA	59.4	3.9	7	397	236	61
13	Anders HANSEN	59.2	3.3	6	294	174	53
14	Alex NOREN	59.1	3.5	6	352	208	60
15	Rikard KARLBERG	59.0	3.7	6	300	177	48
16	Damien MCGRANE	58.9	3.6	6	511	301	83
	Stephen DODD	58.9	4.0	7	190	112	28
18	Adilson DA SILVA	58.8	2.5	4	102	60	24
	Darren FICHARDT	58.8	3.7	6	454	267	72
	Jbe KRUGER	58.8	3.7	6	376	221	60
21	Gonzalo FDEZ-CASTAÑO	58.7	3.4	6	429	252	74
	Jeev Milkha SINGH	58.7	3.9	7	356	209	53
	Tjaart VAN DER WALT	58.7	3.4	6	332	195	57
24	David HOWELL	58.6	3.3	6	570	334	102
	Mikael LUNDBERG	58.6	4.0	7	415	243	60

Average One Putts Per Round

Pos	Name	One Putts Average
1	Jean-Baptiste GONNET	6.93
2	Pablo LARRAZÁBAL	6.61
3	Peter EROFEJEFF	6.43
4	Fredrik ANDERSSON HED	6.38
5	Peter HANSON	6.36
	Garth MULROY	6.36
7	Alastair FORSYTH	6.33
8	Mikael LUNDBERG	6.32
9	Darren FICHARDT	6.24
	Marcus FRASER	6.24
11	Brett RUMFORD	6.23
12	Marc WARREN	6.12
13	Rory MCILROY	6.10
14	Edoardo MOLINARI	6.09
15	Grégory HAVRET	6.08
16	Phillip PRICE	6.07
17	James KINGSTON	6.05
	Jbe KRUGER	6.05
19	Peter LAWRIE	6.00
	Chris PAISLEY	6.00
	Simon THORNTON	6.00
22	Christian CÉVAËR	5.98
	Raphaël JACQUELIN	5.98
24	Sergio GARCIA	5.96
25	Joel SJÖHOLM	5.94

THE 2013 EUROPEAN TOUR INTERNATIONAL SCHEDULE

Date		Event	Venue
Dec	6 - 9	Nelson Mandela Championship presented by ISPS Handa	Royal Durban GC, Durban, South Africa
	13 - 16	Alfred Dunhill Championship	Leopard Creek CC, Malelane, South Africa
Jan	10 - 13	Volvo Golf Champions	Durban CC, Durban, South Africa
	17 - 20	Abu Dhabi HSBC Golf Championship	Abu Dhabi GC, Abu Dhabi, UAE
	23 - 26	Commercial Bank Qatar Masters	Doha GC, Doha, Qatar
	31 - 3	Omega Dubai Desert Classic	Emirates GC, Dubai, UAE
Feb	7 - 10	Joburg Open	Royal Johannesburg & Kensington GC, South Africa
	14 - 17	Africa Open	East London GC, East London, Eastern Cape, South Africa
	20 - 24	WGC - Accenture Match Play Championship	Golf Club at Dove Mountain, Marana, Arizona, USA
	28 - 3	Tshwane Open	Copperleaf Golf & Country Estate, Centurion, South Africa
Mar	7 - 10	WGC - Cadillac Championship	Doral Golf Resort & Spa, Doral, Florida, USA
	14 - 17	Avantha Masters	Jaypee Greens Golf & Spa Resort, Greater Noida, Delhi/NCR, India
	21 - 24	Maybank Malaysian Open	Kuala Lumpur G&CC, Kuala Lumpur, Malaysia
Apr	11 - 14	MASTERS TOURNAMENT	Augusta National GC, Augusta, Georgia, USA
	28 - 31	Trophée Hassan II	Golf du Palais Royal, Agadir, Morocco
	18 - 21	Open de España	Parador de El Saler, Valencia, Spain
	25 - 28	Ballantine's Championship	Blackstone GC, Icheon, Seoul, South Korea
May	2 - 5	Volvo China Open	Binhai Lake GC, Tianjin, China
	16 - 19	Volvo World Match Play Championship	Thracian Cliffs Golf & Beach Resort, Kavarna, Bulgaria
	23 - 26	BMW PGA CHAMPIONSHIP	Wentworth Club, Surrey, England
	16 - 19	Madeira Islands Open - Portugal - BPI	Clube de Golf do Santo da Serra, Madeira, Portugal
	30 - 2	Nordea Masters	Bro Hof Slott GC, Stockholm, Sweden
Jun	6 - 9	Lyoness Open powered by Greenfinity	Diamond CC, Atzenbrugg, Vienna, Austria
	13 - 16	Najeti Hotels et Golfs Open presented by Neuflize OBC	Aa Saint Omer GC, Lumbres, France
	13 - 16	U.S. OPEN CHAMPIONSHIP	Merion GC, Ardmore, Pennsylvania, USA
	27 - 30	Irish Open	Carton House GC, Maynooth, Co. Kildare, Ireland
	20 - 23	BMW International Open	Golfclub München Eichenried, Munich, Germany
Jul	4 - 7	Alstom Open de France	Le Golf National, Paris, France
	11 - 14	Aberdeen Asset Management Scottish Open	Castle Stuart Golf Links, Inverness, Scotland
	18 - 21	THE 142nd OPEN CHAMPIONSHIP	Muirfield, Gullane, East Lothian, Scotland
	25 - 28	M2M Russian Open	Tseleevo Golf & Polo Club, Moscow Region, Russia
Aug	1 - 4	WGC – Bridgestone Invitational	Firestone CC, Akron, Ohio, USA
	8 - 11	US PGA CHAMPIONSHIP	Oak Hill CC, Rochester, New York, USA
	22 - 25	Johnnie Walker Championship at Gleneagles	The Gleneagles Hotel, Perthshire, Scotland
	29 - 1	ISPS Handa Wales Open	Celtic Manor Resort, City of Newport, Wales
Sep	5 - 8	Omega European Masters	Crans-sur-Sierre, Crans Montana, Switzerland
	12 - 15	KLM Open	Kennemer G&CC, Zandvoort, The Netherlands
	19 - 22	70° OPEN D'ITALIA LINDT	Golf Club Torino, Turin, Italy
	26 - 29	Alfred Dunhill Links Championship	Old Course, St Andrews, Carnoustie & Kingsbarns, Scotland
Oct	3 - 6	Seve Trophy by Golf+*	Saint-Nom-La-Bretèche, Paris, France
	10 - 13	Portugal Masters	Oceânico Victoria Golf Course, Algarve, Portugal
	17 - 20	ISPS HANDA Perth International	Lake Karrinyup CC, Perth, Western Australia, Australia
		THE FINAL SERIES	
	24 - 27	BMW Masters presented by SRE Group	Lake Malaren GC, Shanghai, China
	31 - 3	WGC - HSBC Champions	Sheshan International GC, Shanghai, China
Nov	7 - 10	Turkish Airlines Open by the Ministry of Culture and Tourism	Montgomerie Maxx Royal, Antalya, Turkey
	14 - 17	DP WORLD TOUR CHAMPIONSHIP, DUBAI	Jumeirah Golf Estates, Dubai, UAE
	21 - 24	ISPS HANDA World Cup of Golf*	Royal Melbourne GC, Melbourne, Victoria, Australia

* Denotes Approved Special Event **play-off
^ Reduced to 36 holes due to inclement weather   ^^ Reduced to 54 holes due to inclement weather

Winner	Score	First Prize/Prize Fund
Scott Jamieson, SCO^**	66-57=123 (-7)	€118,875/ €1,000,000
Charl Schwartzel, RSA	67-64-64-69=264 (-24)	€237,750 / €1,500,000
Louis Oosthuizen, RSA	68-64-74-66=272 (-16)	€350,000 / €2,000,000
Jamie Donaldson, WAL	67-70-69-68=274 (-14)	€336,725 / $2,700,000
Chris Wood, ENG	67-70-64-69=270 (-18)	€310,917 / $2,500,000
Stephen Gallacher, SCO	63-70-62-71=266 (-22)	€309,233 / $2,500,000
Richard Sterne, RSA	63-65-68-64=260 (-27)	€206,050 / €1,300,000
Darren Fichardt, RSA	69-67-65-71=272 (-16)	€158,500 / €1,000,000
Matt Kuchar, USA	2 and 1	€1,114,636 / $8,750,000
Dawie Van Der Walt, RSA	68-65-67-67=267 (-21)	€237,750 / €1,500,000
Tiger Woods, USA	66-65-67-71=269 (-19)	€1,139,523 / $8,750,000
Thomas Aiken, RSA	67-69-62-67=265 (-23)	€300,000 / €1,800,000
Kiradech Aphibarnrat, THA^^	65-68-70=203(-13)	€350,411 / $2,750,000
Adam Scott, AUS**	69-72-69-69=279 (-9)	€1,104,379 / $8,000,000
Marcel Siem, GER	64-68-69-70=271 (-17)	€250,000 / €1,500,000
Raphaël Jacquelin, FRA**	73-66-73-71=283 (-5)	€250,000 / €1,500,000
Brett Rumford, AUS**	73-67-69-68=277 (-11)	€367,500 / €2,205,000
Brett Rumford, AUS	68-67-69-68=272 (-16)	€407,906 / RMB20,000,000
Graeme McDowell, NIR	2 and 1	€800,000 / €3,000,000
Matteo Manassero, ITA**	69-71-69-69=278 (-10)	€791,660 / €4,750,000
Peter Uihlein, USA	72-64-69-68=273 (-15)	€100,000 / €600,000
Mikko Ilonen, FIN	70-63-65-69=267 (-21)	€250,000 / €1,500,000
Joost Luiten, NED	65-68-67-71=271 (-17)	€166,660 / €1,000,000
Simon Thornton, IRL**	74-70-65-70=279 (-5)	€83,330 / €500,000
Justin Rose, ENG	71-69-71-70=281 (+1)	€1,101,397 / $8,000,000
Paul Casey, ENG	68-72-67-67=274 (-14)	€333,330 / €2,000,000
Ernie Els, RSA	63-69-69-69=270 (-18)	€333,330 / €2,000,000
Graeme McDowell, NIR	69-69-70-67=275 (-9)	€500,000 / €3,000,000
Phil Mickelson, USA**	66-70-66-69=271 (-17)	€579,079 / €3,000,000
Phil Mickelson, USA	69-74-72-66=281 (-3)	€1,097,570 / £5,250,000
Michael Hoey, NIR	70-67-65-70=272 (-16)	€166,660 / €1,000,000
Tiger Woods, USA	66-61-68-70=265 (-15)	€1,139,341 / $8,750,000
Jason Dufner, USA	68-63-71-68=270 (-10)	€1,095,693 / $8,000,000
Tommy Fleetwood, ENG	68-65-67-70=270 (-18)	€272,272 / £1,400,000
Grégory Bourdy, FRA	67-72-70-67=276 (-8)	€348,660 / £1,800,000
Thomas Björn, DEN**	66-66-67-65=264 (-20)	€366,660 / €2,200,000
Joost Luiten, NED**	69-65-66-68=268 (-12)	€300,000 / €1,800,000
Julien Quesne, FRA	70-68-71-67=276 (-12)	€250,000 / €1,500,000
David Howell ENG**	67-68-63-67=265 (-23)	€589,562 / $5,000,000
Continental Europe	15 - 13	€100,000 / €1,750,000
David Lynn ENG	65-65-73-63=266 (-18)	€333,330 / €2,000,000
Jin Jeong, KOR**	68-72-69-69=278 (-10)	€245,438 / $2,000,000
Gonzalo Fernandez-Castaño, ESP	71-71-67-68=277 (-11)	€851,346 / $7,000,000
Dustin Johnson, USA	69-63-66-66=264 (-24)	€1,012,146 / $8,500,000
Victor Dubuisson, FRA	67-65-63-69=264 (-24)	€848,930 / $7,000,000
Henrik Stenson, SWE	68-64-67-64=263 (-25)	€985,476 / $8,000,000
		$8,000,000

THE EUROPEAN TOUR QUALIFYING SCHOOL
PGA Catalunya Resort (Stadium and Tour Courses) Girona, Spain November 10-15, 2013

Carlos Del Moral and Angel Gallardo, Vice Chairman of The European Tour Board of Directors

Moral's Marathon Masterclass

Pos		Country	R1	R2	R3	R4	R5	R6	AGG	PAR	€
1	**Carlos DEL MORAL**	ESP	67	71	69	63	65	67	402	-26	16,000.00
2	Fabrizio ZANOTTI	PAR	66	70	67	68	68	68	407	-21	11,500.00
3	Marco CRESPI	ITA	71	70	67	68	67	70	413	-15	9,000.00
4	Gary STAL	FRA	71	68	69	68	68	70	414	-14	7,200.00
5	Mikael LUNDBERG	SWE	69	68	70	71	66	71	415	-13	5,240.00
6	Adrien SADDIER	FRA	71	66	69	71	67	71	415	-13	5,240.00
7	John HAHN	USA	66	66	73	68	71	71	415	-13	5,240.00
8	Connor ARENDELL	USA	72	70	71	65	70	68	416	-12	4,085.00
9	Wade ORMSBY	AUS	69	67	70	69	70	71	416	-12	4,085.00
10	Stuart MANLEY	WAL	68	71	67	69	69	72	416	-12	4,085.00
11	James MORRISON	ENG	72	67	63	70	71	73	416	-12	4,085.00
12	James HEATH	ENG	69	71	70	69	69	69	417	-11	3,190.00
13	Simon WAKEFIELD	ENG	69	68	67	69	75	69	417	-11	3,190.00
14	Jens DANTORP	SWE	66	68	68	72	73	70	417	-11	3,190.00
15	Brinson PAOLINI	USA	70	71	68	64	72	72	417	-11	3,190.00
16	Patrik SJÖLAND	SWE	66	72	67	67	73	72	417	-11	3,190.00
17	Kevin PHELAN	IRL	73	67	68	71	70	69	418	-10	2,440.00
18	Andreas HARTØ	DEN	67	70	69	72	69	71	418	-10	2,440.00
19	Daniel BROOKS	ENG	65	71	69	66	76	71	418	-10	2,440.00
20	Thomas PIETERS	BEL	64	73	72	68	68	73	418	-10	2,440.00
21	Lucas BJERREGAARD	DEN	65	70	69	69	72	73	419	-9	1,936.67
22	Jason KNUTZON	USA	70	69	71	69	69	71	419	-9	1,936.67
23	Mikko KORHONEN	FIN	69	71	68	70	70	71	419	-9	1,936.67
24	Estanislao GOYA	ARG	66	70	67	73	72	71	419	-9	1,936.67
25	Jack DOHERTY	SCO	68	70	66	71	73	71	419	-9	1,936.67
26	Adam GEE	ENG	66	70	71	69	69	74	419	-9	1,936.67
27	Alastair FORSYTH	SCO	65	70	70	69	71	74	419	-9	1,936.67

Fabrizio Zanotti

Marco Crespi

Gary Stal

Carlos Del Moral secured his return to The European Tour with a hugely impressive five shot win in the Qualifying School Final Stage at PGA Catalunya Resort where 27 players from 15 countries earned their place on The 2014 Race to Dubai.

Del Moral, twice a winner on the European Challenge Tour, had good reason to feel delighted with his six days work north of Barcelona as he became the first Spaniard since Carlos Rodiles in 2006 to win the Qualifying School.

Indeed Del Moral produced a marathon masterclass with in all five sub-70 rounds, including a stunning 63 on the fourth day, with three of those scores concluding his victory march on the Neil Coles and Angel Gallardo-designed Stadium Course.

Del Moral, who has now qualified from the Final Stage four times in the past six years, said: "It feels very special to be the winner of the event. It's such a long week and after the year I have gone through it is a pay-off for all the hard work."

The 28-year-old former English, European and Spanish Boys champion from Valencia finished with a 26 under par total of 402 and ahead of Paraguay's Fabrizio Zanotti, Italy's Marco Crespi and Frenchman Gary Stal.

Zanotti, also a winner on the Challenge Tour with several runners-up finishes on The European Tour, ensured a fifth successive campaign on The Race to Dubai with a powerful performance from an opening 66 to four successive closing sub-70 rounds.

Among those who graduated there were five European Tour winners - Scotsman Alastair

Forsyth, who endured a roller-coaster two over par final round of 74 which included three double-bogeys and five birdies before making it on the mark, Swedes Mikael Lundberg and Patrik Sjöland, as well as England's James Morrison and Estanislao Goya of Argentina.

Ten of those who qualified earned a rookie season on The Race to Dubai, including a number of former amateur prodigies such as 2013 Walker Cup player Kevin Phelan of Ireland and Belgium's Thomas Pieters, who impressed on the American collegiate circuit.

Following the recent success stories on The European Tour of Americans Peter Uihlein, named 2013 Sir Henry Cotton Rookie of the Year and Brooks Koepka, a record four USA natives also qualified, three of whom were under the age of 25.

Neil Ahern

John Hahn

Adrien Saddier

Mikael Lundberg

The 2014 Ryder Cup

The Gleneagles Hotel, Perthshire, Scotland: September 26-28, 2014

The Endless Charm of Gleneagles

That Gleneagles would one day host The Ryder Cup, which will be the case when Europe seeks a successful defence against the United States on September 26-28, 2014, seems to have been written in the stars.

For not only did the illustrious resort survive the threat of the First World War, but it emerged in the "Roaring Twenties" to become recognised by the rich and famous as "The Riviera of the Highlands." Now, little more than a century after Donald Matheson had the vision for a Grand Hotel, Gleneagles will celebrate its 90th Anniversary year by welcoming the 40th edition of arguably the most enthralling show in golf on a course designed by a man recognised by most observers as the greatest golfer to ever replace a divot.

 Jack Nicklaus, whose record of winning 18 professional Major Championships from the 1962 US Open to the 1986 Masters Tournament represents 25 years of unparalleled sporting supremacy, states, unequivocally, that "Scotland has always been considered the 'home of golf' and, in some ways, it has felt like a second home to me." All of which is hardly surprising since he made his Walker Cup debut in 1959 at Muirfield, where in 1966 he won the first of his three Open Championships. The other two were secured in 1970 and 1978 on the Old Course at St

Andrews, where in 2005 he said farewell to Major Championship competition.

Nicklaus has always believed that a course should both challenge and inspire. When his layout opened in 1993 at Gleneagles as The Monarch's Course, it achieved all that and more for the Hotel guests. Subsequently, the demand for quality golf shots and decision-making has been enhanced through a collective effort by Nicklaus Design and Gleneagles to ensure that the re-named PGA Centenary Course is a true modern-day challenge to confront the players captained by Paul McGinley and Tom Watson.

Matheson was taking time out in 1910, from his role of general manager of the Caledonian Railway Company, in the picturesque surroundings of the Scottish Highlands, when, in his mind, he conceived the idea that would become Gleneagles. He submitted his proposal in October, 1912, for a "Grand Hotel" and three golf courses, and the rest, as they say, is history.

Vision is in the eye of the beholder and, with hindsight, sometimes too easy to see. So while there can be no question that

James Braid

Jack Nicklaus, Dirk Bouts, Senior Design Associate, Nicklaus Design, and Scott Fenwick, Golf Courses and Estate Manager, The Gleneagles Hotel, walking the PGA Centenary Course in June, 2011

Ian Marchbank

the Perthshire hills provided the perfect setting for such a Grand Hotel and golf to come together, it nevertheless required commitment, energy and foresight on the part of Matheson to keep his dream alive as the First World War interrupted construction.

The King's Course, officially opened on May 1, 1919, then followed by The Queen's Course—initially nine holes—were both creations of James Braid, winner of five Open Championships and the leading golf course designer in the 1920s and 1930s. Still, work on the hotel did not resume until 1922. The Grand Opening Gala in June, 1924, was a lavish affair, and came a full 14 years after Matheson, by profession a civil engineer and architect, had his dream, while holidaying in Strathearn, that a hotel possessing the cultured razzamataz of the grand establishments on the Continent could be built in the valley through which his company's railway line ran, so providing the perfect mode of transportation at that time for discerning guests.

Those guests, enjoying the luxury of The Gleneagles Hotel and the relaxing challenge of the golf, could not help be smitten by the majesty of the scenery as Ed Hodge in his excellent book "Jewel in the Glen – Gleneagles, Golf and The Ryder Cup" so eloquently writes: "With the sun emerging above the verdant Ochil Hills in the foreground and the uplifting magnificence of the rugged Grampian Mountains and the Trossachs beyond there are few settings that inspire such breathlessness."

Braid, on being engaged by Matheson, instantly recognised—just as Nicklaus would

more than 60 years later—that the land of sand and gravel, deposited when the last ice sheet finally melted some 15,000 years earlier, was perfect for golf courses. In appointing Braid, Matheson also knew that the quality of the courses would provide the opportunity for professional competition, which started with a tangible link to The Ryder Cup when an historic, first-ever "International Challenge Match" was played on The King's Course between British and American professionals on June 6, 1921, as a prelude to the Glasgow Herald 1,000 Guineas tournament taking place.

Nevertheless, while the match and the tournament won the plaudits of the players and the spectators, the Americans were not entirely impressed by their accommodation,

since construction had only just re-started on the hotel. They were compelled to fetch and carry their own water to the five waterless railway carriages in which they were housed in a siding at the station near Auchtermuchty in Fife.

By the time that Nicklaus first visited Gleneagles—for a famous "Big Three" match with Arnold Palmer and Gary Player on The King's Course in 1966—there was no talk of the resort hosting The Ryder Cup. Yet Ian Marchbank, the Gleneagles head professional from 1962 to 1992, admits to in 1971 "trying very hard to promote Gleneagles as a potential venue" despite being aware at the time that the next edition would be taking place at Muirfield.

Scottish Ryder Cup Captains Sam Torrance, Bernard Gallacher and Colin Montgomerie with Alex Salmond, First Minister of Scotland

EY

Building a better
working world

**TEAMS GET RESULTS
WHEN THE TOP TALENT
WORKS TOGETHER.**

Discover more about building
high-performing teams.

Visit ey.com/rydercup.

OFFICIAL PARTNER OF THE 2014 RYDER CUP

RYDER CUP
2014

OFFICIAL
PARTNER

built on a site occupied at that time by the courses named Glendevon, opened in 1980, and Prince's, which began life as the Wee Course in 1928 and was extended to 18 holes in 1974.

Nicklaus was an obvious choice and not simply because of his reputation as a player. He had developed, unquestionably, a design company which for many astute observers was the best in the world. Moreover, he believed wholeheartedly in creating courses that were aesthetically pleasing and had not lost sight of the fact that everything he was able to pursue in design and business followed because of his ability to play golf.

Even so Nicklaus' determination to put back into golf something that would further enhance its values had much to do with his desire to design courses and, indeed, gave birth to the dream to build Muirfield Village Golf Club just outside his hometown of Columbus, Ohio, and conceive the concept of the Memorial Tournament.

Making a contribution to the future success of the game whetted Nicklaus' appetite and in Muirfield Village and the Memorial Tournament he has a legacy of which he is justifiably proud.

Now The Gleneagles Hotel and The PGA Centenary Course are about to take their place in the history books. Nicklaus, following a first planning meeting with then Managing Director Peter Lederer and Golf Courses and Estate Director Jimmy Kidd,

Nicklaus was, of course, by that time the master of the fairways in full flow towards building a career record which included a remarkable 18 professional Major Championships—six Masters, five US PGA Championships, four US Opens and three Open Championships—and, although in no way diluting his quest for titles (he would eventually win in total 120 worldwide), he was already embarking in golf course design. That would evolve into the family-run, globally acclaimed Nicklaus Design, now with a résumé built over more than 40 years.

 When The 2014 Ryder Cup is played on The PGA Centenary Course, his company will have in 36 countries and 39 US states approaching 400 golf courses open for play, including a fourth of the courses having played host to a professional tournament.

It was in March, 1988, that Nicklaus signed a contract with Gleneagles to build his first course in Scotland with the aim being to create a 21st century challenge that would complement the existing King's and Queen's courses. The new course would be

Harold Macmillan, then Prime Minister, and Sir Alec Douglas-Home at The Gleneagles Hotel in 1957

described the land on which he would go to work in Scotland as "the finest in the world I have ever been given to work with. Great terrain; nice rolling turf; a lot of terrific places; beautiful views—when you see the views." You could almost hear Braid saying much the same as the challenge began on the then Monarch's Course, which was officially opened on May 15, 1993, and re-named The PGA Centenary Course on January 1, 2001, to commemorate the PGA's Centenary Year.

 Time stands still for no man and golf, similarly, requires constant review. Gleneagles had made some minor changes but then Nicklaus was invited to return to modernise and re-invigorate the layout because as Patrick Elsmie, the Managing Director of Gleneagles, points out: "When we started looking at what we thought we might need to do to The PGA Centenary Course some years ago we had a very simple motto: We wanted to have memorable holes for the fantastic match-play event that is The Ryder Cup, but we wanted it to be known as a fantastic course, for everyday play, not just because it's going to have three days of The Ryder Cup. It was a great opportunity for us to hook those changes onto The Ryder Cup. To re-engage with Jack was exciting."

Nicklaus explains: "When we built the course it was a pretty challenging layout. With the equipment and the golf ball—in 1993 we were still using wound balls—and everything going much farther, it needed alterations. So we set out to make it more relevant in today's game, from some of the bunkering to the strategy."

The PGA Centenary Course has successfully hosted a European Tour event since 1999,

in its present form known as the Johnnie Walker Championship at Gleneagles, but the work undertaken during the winter of 2011-12 transformed the course with changes being made to no fewer than 12 holes, in addition to the bunkers on all holes being remodelled. The most significant alterations were to the ninth, which is like beauty and the beast as it is both aesthetically striking and artfully challenging, and the 18th holes.

Nicklaus Design supplied Gleneagles with a very detailed and extensive plan on how to develop the 18th and then left it with them to make a decision based on time and available resources. Nicklaus explained: "Among the adjustments we collectively decided to move forward with was to place a bunker off the right side of the first landing area. Obviously the more you challenge the bunker, the better the opportunity to reach the green in two. We also added a group of diagonal bunkers short and right of the new green which gives the golfer three options on how to play the hole—hit short and right and leave a pitch; play left to open the green for a pitch; or take it all the way home."

 In a nutshell, the ninth and 18th are now par fives that provide a risk-and-reward element that transcends the course, offering the opportunity for the players, especially in the match-play environment afforded by The Ryder Cup, to raise the excitement level. The lowering of the 18th green to create an amphitheatre effect has installed the space for more spectators to enjoy those matches which go to the wire.

The flow of The PGA Centenary Course has, however, not changed. You start out playing southeast towards the famed Glen of Eagles,

sweeping up the Ochil Hills to the summit of the pass below Ben Shee, which joins it to Glen Devon. As you move westwards, the course, which now sits so naturally in the Perthshire countryside that it might have been there since the 1920s, the rugged Grampians provide a breath-taking backdrop with the majesty of Ben Vorlich and the mountains above the Trossachs.

 There is a bewitching kaleidoscope of colours every step of the way, with the lush panorama of the rich Perthshire straths framed by tall pines, beech and firs, silver birch and golden gorse, purple heather and dominant-brown ferns in a spectacular moorland setting dotted by burns and lochs. The charm of Gleneagles is endless, with the call of wild geese, duck, grouse, partridge, pheasant, snipe and woodcock. Perhaps there has never been a more appropriate setting, given that Samuel Ryder, the seed merchant who provided The Ryder Cup for competition, named his business the Heath and Heather Company.

Coincidentally, The Gleneagles Hotel and The Ryder Cup began life in the "Roaring Twenties," recognised as the breakout decade for sports across the modern world, and when the hotel opened on June 7, 1924, the music was broadcast all over Britain by the BBC. Such is the appeal of The Ryder Cup there is no question that the attention of the whole world will in late September, 2014, focus on the teams of Europe and the United States and on The Gleneagles Hotel with The PGA Centenary Course that Jack Nicklaus built.

Mitchell Platts

Results: 1979-2012

1979 The Greenbrier, White Sulphur Springs, West Virginia, USA
Europe: 11 - USA 17

1981 Walton Heath, Surrey, England
Europe 9½ - USA 18½

1983 PGA National Golf Club, Palm Beach Gardens, Florida, USA
Europe 13½ - USA 14½

1985 The Belfry, Sutton Coldfield, West Midlands, England
Europe 16½ - USA 11½

1987 Muirfield Village, Columbus, Ohio, USA
Europe 15 - USA 13

1989 The Belfry, Sutton Coldfield, West Midlands, England
Europe 14 - USA 14 (Europe retained Cup)

1991 Ocean Course, Kiawah Island, South Carolina, USA
Europe 13½ - USA 14½

1993 The Belfry, Sutton Coldfield, West Midlands, England
Europe 13 - USA 15

1995 Oak Hill Country Club, Rochester, New York, USA
Europe 14½ - USA 13½

1997 Club de Golf Valderrama, Sotogrande, Spain
Europe 14½ - USA 13½

1999 The Country Club, Brookline, Massachusetts, USA
Europe 13½ - USA 14½

2002 The Belfry, Sutton Coldfield, West Midlands, England
Europe 15½ - USA 12½

2004 Oakland Hills Country Club, Bloomfield Township, Michigan, USA
Europe 18½ - USA 9½

2006 The K Club, Straffan, Co. Kildare, Ireland
Europe 18½ - USA 9½

2008 Valhalla Golf Club, Louisville, Kentucky, USA
Europe 11½ - USA 16½

2010 The Celtic Manor Resort, City of Newport, Wales
Europe 14½ - USA 13½

2012 Medinah Country Club, Illinois, Chicago, USA
Europe 14½ - USA 13½

Future Venues

2016 Hazeltine National Golf Club, Chaska, Minnesota, USA
2018 Le Golf National, Paris, France
2020 Whistling Straits, Kohler, Wisconsin, USA
2024 Bethpage State Park, Black Course, New York, USA

France will host The Ryder Cup for the first time in 2018. The historic announcement, which will see golf's greatest team event return to the Continent of Europe for the first time in 21 years, was made by Ryder Cup Europe on May 17, 2011, at Wentworth Club, Surrey, England.

Le Golf National (pictured above) on the outskirts of Versailles near Paris, the well-established home of the Alstom Open de France, will become only the second Continental venue – following Club de Golf Valderrama, in Spain in 1997 - when the 42nd edition of The Ryder Cup between Europe and the United States is contested in the autumn of 2018.

The PGA Centenary Course
by Jack Nicklaus

Card of the Course

Hole	Yards	Metres	Par	Hole	Yards	Metres	Par
1	426	390	4	10	208	190	3
2	516	472	5	11	350	320	4
3	431	394	4	12	445	407	4
4	239	219	3	13	481	440	4
5	461	422	4	14	320	293	4
6	201	184	3	15	463	423	4
7	468	428	4	16	543	497	5
8	419	383	4	17	194	177	3
9	618	565	5	18	513	469	5
OUT	3779	3457	36	IN	3517	3216	36
				TOTAL	7296	6673	72

GLENEAGLES   GLENEAGLES

BRACKEN BRAE/FERN HILL
Par 4 – 426 Yards; 390 Metres:

The first hole at Gleneagles is slightly downhill and a slight dogleg to the right. There's a bunker on the right side of the fairway which should not present a great problem for most of the players in The Ryder Cup. However, if you hit the ball in the rough, the green is a relatively narrow one protected by a bunker in the front and a grass hollow behind it.

WESTER GREENWELLS/NAME OF THE RUINED CROFT
Par 5 – 516 Yards; 472 Metres:

This has an elevated tee shot, and doglegs left around a bunker on the left side of the fairway. It is protected on the left side of the green with bunkers and a pond. Over the green is a deep grass hollow. Most of the competitors will reach the green in two. So this hole presents a very good birdie chance for most of the players, and there will be a fair number of eagle possibilities here.

SCHIEHALLION/HILL OF SCOTS
Par 4 – 431 Yards; 394 Metres:

A dogleg right, with an elevated tee shot. Bunkers protect the right side of the fairway. The second shot is slightly uphill. The green is protected in the front by two bunkers. This is a good, solid par four. The loch on the left was filled during construction and was incorporated into the design.

GOWDEN BEASTIE/GOLDEN BEAR
Par 3 – 239 Yards; 219 Metres:

The longest of all the par threes. It can play up to 239 yards. I'm sure that both tee options will be used here, depending on how much excitement they want to create in the matches. It is protected by a little pot bunker short right and a bunker to the left of the green. The ball feeds in a bit from the right. It's a good, long par three that requires an accurate tee shot.

5

CROOKIT CRATUR/ TWISTED AND UNDULATING
Par 4 – 461 Yards; 422 Metres:

A very narrow tee shot, protected on both sides by trees and hills, this hole has a bog mire—a Site of Scientific Interest—short of the green and a bunker left of the green. This is one of the more difficult holes on the golf course, and probably the number one handicap hole. It's a beautiful golf hole, just relatively difficult especially with the prevailing wind against you.

6

7

MICKLE SKELP/SMALL HIT, Par 3 – 201 Yards; 184 Metres:

This par three can play to just over 200 yards. There is a bunker on the left side of the green, and a wetland—sort of an existing pond— short of the green. This hole requires a very accurate tee shot. There is a little bit of bailout out to the right, which will actually help feed the ball a little bit into the green. Back left will be a difficult hole location to get to on this green.

LARCH GAIT/LARCH WALK, Par 4 – 468 Yards; 428 Metres:

This hole doglegs right. The tee shot is slightly elevated and plays into a nice valley. The approach is into a green tucked in against the hillside on the right and drops off on the left. This hole simply requires two good, solid shots. Nothing tricky about the hole; it just requires good golf.

8

SIDLIN' BROWS/SUCCESSION OF UNDULATIONS ALONG THE SIDE OF THE HILL
Par 4 – 419 Yards; 383 Metres:

This hole presents players options. A great majority of the players will play the ball out to the right, trying to get a good view into the green. The green is protected by bunkers on both sides. However, there will be certain conditions that might lead players to try to drive it over the four bunkers on the left side, attempting to shorten the hole down to a short sand wedge into the green. So there is an option for players. I'm sure that some will take the option to take the bunkers out of play; however, I think the great majority will probably play the ball out into the fairway and hit a middle to short iron into the green.

We're on course to make the turn after a great front nine.

What great club selection.

Ryder Cup Travel Services have been the Official Travel Services Operator for The Ryder Cup since 1997. Over the years we have ensured over 55,000 people have been in the thick of the action as the drama and spectacle of this unique golf event unfolds.

Now, after Team Europe's stunning victory at Medinah, we have put together some great travel programmes for the next Ryder Cup back on European soil at Gleneagles, Scotland in 2014.

All details of these value travel opportunities can be found on our website. So, why not book yourself a greenside seat to cheer on the very best golfers in the world as they battle head to head for that precious Team victory.

www.rcts.co.uk

VALDERRAMA 1997
THE COUNTRY CLUB 1999
THE BELFRY 2002
OAKLAND HILLS 2004
THE K CLUB 2006
VALHALLA 2008
CELTIC MANOR 2010
MEDINAH 2012
GLENEAGLES 2014

RYDER CUP 2014

GLENEAGLES
SCOTLAND 2014

CROOK O'MOSS/NAME OF THE SOURCE OF THE WATER SUPPLY
Par 5 – 618 Yards; 565 Metres:

A very pretty hole which begins with a demanding tee shot—an elevated tee shot with two ponds to play between, hillsides, bunker on the right, and bunkers long on the left. The second shot presents a choice of what you want to do: Do you want to take the ball and play it conservatively out to the left of the pond, or do you want to try to take it at the green? Even though the hole plays over 600 yards, I'm sure that under certain conditions a number of players will take it at the green. Many of them will play it out left to get the proper angle to play down the length of the green. A good hole, and a very, very pretty hole.

10

SLEEKIT HOWE/TRICKY HOLLOW
Par 3 – 208 Yards; 190 Metres:

An exciting short hole with an elevated tee shot that plays down the hill. There is a little pot bunker on the left and a bunker to the right. This hole requires just a good, solid tee shot. Nothing fancy. I'm sure that the elements, when the wind is blowing, will affect the tee shot as the ball falls a great distance from a tee that is very exposed.

11

LAICH BURN/NAME OF THE STREAM YOU PLAY OVER
Par 4 – 350 Yards; 320 Metres:

A short par four where you drive the ball out to the left with probably an iron or a metal wood. It plays across a ravine, with water that flows through it, to a green sitting on the side of a hill. There will be a lot of birdies here.

12

CARN MAIRG/HILL OF SORROW OR DIFFICULTY
Par 4 – 445 Yards; 407 Metres:

You have to make up your mind on the tee shot how much you want to bite off on the left side, as it plays over dunes. There are bunkers on the right side that frame the hole. A long tee shot here will provide a fairly simple but demanding second shot, with a little pot bunker that protects the left front of the green and a small bunker at the back right. I think this is one of the nicest holes on the golf course.

13

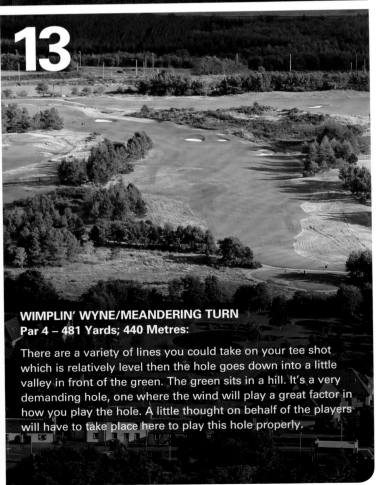

WIMPLIN' WYNE/MEANDERING TURN
Par 4 – 481 Yards; 440 Metres:

There are a variety of lines you could take on your tee shot which is relatively level then the hole goes down into a little valley in front of the green. The green sits in a hill. It's a very demanding hole, one where the wind will play a great factor in how you play the hole. A little thought on behalf of the players will have to take place here to play this hole properly.

NEBIT KNOWE/POINTED HILLOCK
Par 4 – 320 Yards; 293 Metres:

Quite possibly a drivable par four. It is set up to be so. There are some key bunkers on the right side that you have to carry, if you want to get it to the green which is the smallest on the course. They sit about 280 yards off the tee. There are two bunkers on the left side of the fairway, which you must play inside. I'm not sure whether everybody will try to drive this green or try to play it just short and hit sand wedge in. There are certainly a lot of options here.

15

OCHIL SICHT/VIEW OF THE OCHIL HILLS
Par 4 – 463 Yards; 423 Metres:

There is a nice bunker on the right side of the fairway, and the hole drops off on the left side of the fairway. Very pretty tee shot, as is the second shot. The second shot plays downhill into a long, narrow green that is bunkered well on the right side. It's a good, strong hole, and it sits at a place in the match where a lot of times this hole will be won with a par. It should be one of the pivotal holes.

16

LOCHAN LOUP/
LEAP OVER THE SMALL LOCH
Par 5 – 543 Yards; 497 Metres:

There is a bunker in the centre of the fairway, which should not be an issue. But there are also bunkers on the right side, which will be an issue. A good drive here will put a player in position to play over the pond that sits well short of the green into a landing area or into the green. It's a par five that a lot of the players will reach in two. Matter of fact, most all of the players will. A lot of birdies and eagle possibilities.

1st Worldwide Partner of The Ryder Cup.

Standard Life Investments is proud to be the first Worldwide Partner in the history of The Ryder Cup. This ground-breaking agreement with one of sport's most iconic global brands reflects our shared values, a distinctive team ethos and a commitment to excellence.

Look forward to history in the making at www.standardlifeinvestments.com/rydercup

Potential.   Delivered.

Equities • Fixed Income • Real Estate • Multi-asset • Private Equity

WORLDWIDE
PARTNER

17

CA' CANNY/BE CAREFUL
Par 3 – 194 Yards; 177 Metres:

The final par three is slightly downhill. It is very well bunkered - left, right and back. Here is a hole where I think coming as it will towards the end of a match, a very accurate tee shot will be required and could be very well rewarded.

18

DUN ROAMIN'/RETURNING HOME
Par 5 – 513 Yards; 469 Metres:

This can be played as a par five or a par four. I think it's a really nice, shortish par five, or a strong par four that plays up the hill, into the wind. Great amphitheatre around the green, with a great gallery situation here. I think the players will take a run at this one. Nevertheless, if they are too aggressive and go through the green to the left, they will leave themselves a very awkward chip shot from a deep valley. The hole is well bunkered short of the green. It's a great viewing hole and hopefully many of the matches will reach this far.

Paul McGinley –
The 2014 European Ryder Cup Captain

The intriguing background to Paul McGinley making history by becoming the first Irishman to captain a Ryder Cup team is that somewhere between the playing fields of Gaelic football and the European Commission he might have been lost to the world of golf.

For many observers of the Gaelic game were absolutely convinced that the young McGinley possessed the speed and skill, the tenacity and the talent, to one-day graduate to playing for Dublin in the All-Ireland Final at the iconic Croke Park before an appalling injury that broke his knee-cap terminated a promising career.

Instead he followed an educational path by finishing school then gaining a diploma in marketing and management in his native Dublin before accepting a role on the Year of the Environment project in the European Commission in Brussels where he also studied French.

 Then came that "Robert Frost – The Road Not Taken" moment when Eamon Gallagher, then Ireland's senior E.U. Diplomat, with support from Padraig O'Huiginn, then Secretary to the Department of the Taoiseach and like McGinley a member at The Grange Golf Club in Dublin, and Frank Fahey, the Minister for Sport, opened the door to a scholarship at the United States International University, San Diego, and McGinley chose the route that would make all the difference to his life.

In truth, McGinley was swayed quite easily because as someone who aspired to making something of himself in sport, as his enthusiasm for playing and watching hurling and the more orthodox form of football emphasised, he was also blessed with the innate ability to hit a golf ball even if he initially courted little desire to make the game a career.

McGinley said: "The idea of me being a pro golfer was like me going to the moon. There was no way. As far as I was concerned Gaelic football was everything that golf was not. It's a fast, tough, hard-running game whereas golf is much more sedate. I enjoyed the odd game of golf but there was no doubt about which sport I wanted to play. I was going to be a Gaelic footballer because that is what I was best at and loved the most. I wanted to play for Dublin, I also enjoyed my hurling and for work the business world beckoned. The injury to my left knee and then to move on from the European Commission to go study and play golf in San Diego were both blessings in disguise that changed my life."

His initial contact with golf was as a caddie for his father, Michael, who not only played Gaelic football himself for Donegal but also struck the golf ball with such authority that he was always considered better than the one handicap he held for several years. The young McGinley, despite being distracted by his addiction to Gaelic football, played to an acceptable five handicap. Such was his application to succeed that once he focused on golf he was able to swiftly reduce his handicap at The Grange Golf Club in the heart of Rathfarnham, a south side suburb of Dublin where he grew up, so that by the time he turned professional he played off plus four.

Desire, dedication and determination decreed that McGinley, born in Dublin on December 16, 1966, would significantly develop his golf game. In San Diego, he successfully studied for his degree in International Business and his strong work ethic on the practice range under the studious eye of coach Gordon Severson, who sadly passed away in 2006, transformed his game.

McGinley said: "I learned more from Gordon than anyone else. He took me from a shabby amateur to a golf professional. Later I worked with Bob Torrance and he took me from shabby professional to a good professional. But it was with Gordon that I really started to learn how to play the game properly."

 McGinley revelled in the opportunity to practice under the hot Californian sun and in the competitive world of American inter-collegiate golf his self-belief prospered as he became mentally and physically stronger. He took time out to come home and in the 1989 Irish Close – the Blue Riband of the Irish amateur game - at Rosses Point, his perseverance and patience were key as he overcame five opponents to win the match-play title.

On graduating from San Diego he concentrated on the amateur circuit – losing in the 1990 final of the North of Ireland to Darren Clarke while in 1991 beating Padraig Harrington on the way to winning the South of Ireland match play – before being selected for Great Britain and Ireland for the 1991 Walker Cup which by a lovely coincidence was that year being played at Portmarnock in Dublin. The United States would win but McGinley brought the curtain down on his amateur career with a brilliant second shot to eight feet at the last which set up a famous foursomes win with Liam White against Phil Mickelson and Bob May.

By now McGinley knew that his future would be on The European Tour, to which he has been committed from Day One, and he immediately grasped the nettle by winning the Under-25s European Open in the autumn of 1991 then started 1992 by making his European Tour debut in the Johnnie Walker Asian Classic a few weeks after earning his playing privileges by finishing tied second at the Qualifying School.

 McGinley's first significant European Tour performance arrived at the Mont Agel course later that summer when four successive rounds in the 60s enabled him to finish tied sixth behind Ian Woosnam in the European Monte Carlo Golf Open. There can be few more spectacular courses than the Monte Carlo Golf Club at Mont Agel, perched high above the principality of Monaco, to kick-start a career but the quintessential Dubliner remained grounded.

McGinley had at 25 arrived relatively late to the professional ranks but he did so with a mature sense of balance and outlook on life. He said: "I don't want to make myself achieve what I want to achieve in a given amount of time. I've got an awful lot to learn about myself and my golf. Steady improvement, even if it's slow, will mean that my time will come."

Not that he was anything other than ambitious. So he correctly celebrated as he ticked all the boxes with his first European Tour win in the Hohe Brücke Open in Austria in 1996, storming from out of the pack from eight behind with 11 birdies in a superb 62, and the champagne flowed again later that year when he married Allison Shapcott, then a professional on the ladies tour.

A family would follow – Niamh, born in 1999, Killian (2000) and Maia (2002) – and further individual success highlighted by his win in the 2005 Volvo Masters at Club de Golf Valderrama. It had been McGinley's finest season but also his most frustrating. He had lost a play-off to Paul Casey in the TCL Classic in China then finished runner-up to Angel Cabrera in the flagship BMW PGA Championship where both had closed with 67s at Wentworth Club and narrowly lost 2 and 1 to Michael Campbell in the HSBC Match Play Championship back at Wentworth Club.

Now at the season-ending tournament in the south of Spain, McGinley would post a third round 65 – by two shots the best round of the day – to be four behind joint leaders Sergio Garcia and Colin Montgomerie and with a closing 67 he climbed to the top of the pack with which he would finish third in the then Order of Merit. They say that when McGinley took a stranglehold on the title with a wonderful wedge over water to the treacherous 17th green and a ten foot birdie putt that the cheers in The Grange clubhouse could be heard all the way across Rathfarnham to the Yellow House pub where McGinley enjoyed his first glass of Guinness.

By then, of course, McGinley had also established his international career – representing Ireland 13 times in the World Cup, famously winning the prestigious title with Padraig Harrington at Kiawah Island in 1997 and so emulating the triumph of Christy O'Connor and Harry Bradshaw 39 years previously, and seven times in the Alfred Dunhill Cup; playing in the Royal Trophy three times and playing a significant role in helping Great Britain and Ireland win The Seve Trophy in 2002 and 2005 – winning his singles on both occasions and losing only twice in eight matches alongside Harrington.

McGinley's almost uncanny knack of

claiming team success continued when he captained Great Britain and Ireland to further victories in The Seve Trophy against Continental Europe in 2009 and 2011 although what remains the pièce de résistance in his international playing career is The Ryder Cup.

That began with that time-stopping moment on the 18th green at The Belfry in 2002 when McGinley gloriously holed the ten foot putt that secured Europe's success and he was bear-hugged by captain Sam Torrance. It continued at Oakland Hills in Michigan in 2004 when he went unbeaten as Europe won 18 ½ - 9 ½ on American soil and he kept his unbeaten singles record intact two years later at The K Club little more than 20 miles from where he grew-up as Europe again won 18 ½ - 9 ½. Moreover, his unbeaten run has continued as a Vice Captain to Colin Montgomerie in 2010 and José María Olazábal in 2012.

 McGinley's love affair with The Ryder Cup is driven by passion. He says: "I love the whole atmosphere of The Ryder Cup. I love everything that goes with it, the pomp and the pageantry. I get a real buzz out of being in the same room where everyone is pulling for the team. It's inspirational, you can touch the camaraderie, and I do reach for another level when involved in team golf. My heart ticks a bit faster, my adrenalin flows more."

So Gaelic football's loss has been golf's gain and the land that bred the likes of Bradshaw and Daly, O'Connor and O'Connor jnr, Clarke and Harrington, McDowell and McIlroy, to play Ryder Cup golf now has in Paul McGinley the most consummate of professionals as their first European Ryder Cup Captain.

Mitchell Platts

The winning 2012 European Ryder Cup Team

Tom Watson –
The 2014 United States Ryder Cup Captain

The young American was met early in the morning at the Ballybunion Golf Club by Ted Higgins, the professional, and Sean Walsh, the secretary/manager, not to mention 2,000 local enthusiasts eager to witness with their own eyes the Number One Golfer in the World.

Tom Watson had chosen to hone his game ahead of his 1981 defence of The Open Championship on the revered links set by the Shannon estuary in Co. Kerry on the west coast of Ireland. He teed-up with his good friends Sandy Tatum and Harry Easterly, both former Presidents of the United States Golf Association, and they played a convivial round with Walsh before enjoying what Watson, on his first visit, described as a "cheerful lunch" before retiring to the Marine Links Hotel.

 That should have been that except that Watson and Tatum could not resist returning to the course - "After playing Ballybunion for the first time a man would think that the game of golf originated here," Watson later said - but their attempt to enjoy a quiet 18 holes was foiled as word quickly spread that they were back on the course and the crowd which Watson warmly embraced swiftly grew again in numbers.

All of which goes some of the way to explaining why Thomas Sturges Watson is held in the highest respect in the world of sport. Quite simply, he has always understood the importance of entertaining the public even if he never courted the fame which inevitably disrupts private life.

Watson said: "Fame's not important to me. Doing what I do for a living well is important to me. I am there to play golf, to entertain, to compete, to play my absolute best. That was always the dream from the age of 14."

Ray Watson, his late father, an insurance broker, and at one time a scratch golfer, introduced Tom, born the second of three sons in Kansas City, Missouri, on September 4, 1949, to golf at the country club where he was a member and his influence extended beyond teaching the fundamentals to passing on a love for the game. Meanwhile his mother, Sally, chauffeured her son to compete in junior events on a variety of courses as he developed the swing initially shaped by first teacher Stan Thirsk.

Watson, naturally talented and massively determined, sensibly did not allow golf to become an obsession. He put down the clubs to play quarterback on the High School football team, winning the conference championship, and was an outstanding shooting guard when the basketball season began. He won trophies for sportsmanship but also did not escape punishment when once suspended for smoking at a dance.

Watson moved to Stanford University - the Harvard of the West - to prepare for a career in the insurance business, graduated with a degree in psychology and confessed: "Four years at Stanford didn't prepare me for the business world. I made the decision that my only talent was golf!"

Watson had won four Missouri State Amateur Championships in five years. He had the game, the skill, the heart and the desire. Blessed with powerful arms and hands, strong legs and wide shoulders, he developed a brisk, business-like swing and earned in High School from his football coach Leon Flappan the nickname Huckleberry Dillinger.

The Dillinger evolved from his gangster-like nerve - his putting touch was lethal - and Jim Murray, the legendary Los Angeles Times sportswriter, later wrote: "Once upon a time there was this young golfer who looked as if he had just arrived by raft from the Mississippi River.

 "He had this red hair and freckled face and a gap-toothed smile that made him look as if he had just slipped off the pages of Mark Twain. He looked out of place with shoes on. You wanted to sift his pockets for live lizards or balls of string, and ask him where he put his fishing pole. You wanted to ask him if his name was 'Huckleberry.'"

Pretty soon Murray and the world's leading sports writers were capturing Watson's deeds in words. He turned professional, very nearly won in his rookie season in 1972, losing the Quad Cities event by one stroke to Deane Beman, who eventually became US PGA Tour Commissioner. Then, after some frustrating results, two men entered his life and helped transform his career.

First, he took on Bruce Edwards as his caddie in 1973. They formed arguably the most formidable of fairway partnerships, winning titles with a smile and with grace. Sadly, Edwards passed away in 2004 after a courageous battle with Lou Gehrig's disease (ALS).

Then after being the 54-hole leader in the 1974 US Open, faltering only in the final round, Watson was approached by Byron Nelson, who was commentating having retired following an outstanding career, and welcomed the words of encouragement so much so that Nelson would become teacher, mentor and friend.

Watson made the 1974 Western Open his first PGA Tour win and his second, perhaps predictably, came in the Byron Nelson Golf Classic in May, 1975.

 Two months later he captured his first Major Championship, holing a 20-foot putt on the last green to tie Australian Jack Newton then winning the 18-hole play-off with a 71 to a 72 in The Open Championship at Carnoustie.

Four of his five Open Championships were won in Scotland and the next in 1977 took him centre stage as for the second time in three months - he had won his first Masters in April - Watson pushed Jack Nicklaus into second place. The "Duel in the Sun" at Turnberry in which Watson and Nicklaus went head for head, Watson prevailing by closing 65-65 to Nicklaus's 65-66, was an epic encounter that

captured the imagination of the world and, unquestionably, confirmed his emergence as the game's dominant player of the time. Watson would win eight Majors - another Masters in 1981 when Nicklaus was second again, The Opens of 1980, 1982 and 1983, and the US Open in 1982 - and in all 39 US PGA Tour titles in addition to six PGA Players of the Year Awards.

Watson, regarded as the finest striker of the golf ball since Nicklaus, also possessed the ability to improvise shots and in that 1982 US Open at Pebble Beach one shot was quite breath-taking - a 'touchy' chip from knotted rough for a sensational two and for good measure he birdied the last to once more deny Nicklaus.

Nicklaus showed his respect as they walked off the 18th - "You little son of a gun; you're something else. That was nice going. I'm really proud of you, and I'm pleased for you." Watson says: "Playing head to head with Jack was what I dreamed it would be. Was Turnberry in 1977 the most exciting career moment of my life? Yes, with the exception maybe of Pebble Beach."

Arguably there has not been two better losers in golf. Watson's reverence for the game blended to his intelligence and imagination are distinctive qualities that set him apart as does his loyalty and his charity work. He has been a long-time supporter of the Children's Mercy Hospital in Kansas City, Missouri. He co-founded the Bruce Edwards Foundation for ALS to raise funds to find a cure for the debilitating disease that claimed the life of his caddie and friend. He has played an enormous role in Clubs for Kids, the precursor to the First Tee in Kansas City for which Watson is the Chairman of the Advisory Board, and he participated in trips to Iraq to "deliver a little bit of home to the troops."

Then in the sunset of his career Watson arrived at a potential curtain call. He had told his wife Hilary on the eve of The 2009 Open Championship at Turnberry that he had a good chance

of winning. Four days of brilliant play brought him to within one hole of creating a unique piece of history as at the age of 59 he was set to rip-up the record books and in the process equal Harry Vardon's record of six Opens. The golfing gods, however, decreed otherwise.

 Victory would have given Watson the opportunity to ride off into that sunset and retire to his farm on the outskirts of Kansas City. Instead he continued with the day job and in May, 2011, he became at the age of 61 the oldest player to win a Major Championship since the Senior Tour began by winning the Senior PGA Championship for his sixth Senior Major including the three Senior Open Championships (2003, 2005, 2007) he has won in Britain.

Now at the age of 65 years and 22 days on September 26, 2014, he will make history again by becoming the oldest Ryder Cup captain. This is because he is the right man for the job, the last winning American captain (1993) on British soil, an Ambassador to the game he cherishes, a man who commands the respect of all. His most memorable Ryder Cup moment remains the Opening Ceremony at Royal Lytham & St Annes in 1977 which he says was "spine-tingling to listen to Captain Dow Finsterwald's speech introducing the players and to see the flags go up - I had never done that before and it affected me greatly."

What transpired to take Watson back to Scotland, scene of four of the Open Championship triumphs, to lead the United States on, coincidently, a Jack Nicklaus designed course, can be attributed to the foresight of Ted Bishop, the PGA of America President, and the genius essayist Jim Huber who, sadly, is no longer with us. Bishop had read "Four Days in July," Huber's emotive account of Watson's enthralling challenge for Open glory two months short of his 60th birthday, and decided that this was the man he wanted to lead them in 2014. So "Four Days in July" becomes "Three Days in September" and another special milestone in the life of Tom Watson.

Mitchell Platts

Tom Watson (right) and the winning 1981 United States Ryder Cup Team

Wins Around the World

From America to Asia, South America to South Africa, European Tour Members further enhanced their global reputations as no fewer than 24 captured a total of 32 titles. Henrik Stenson led the way as with two wins he claimed the FedExCup on the US PGA Tour on which Jonas Blixt and Graeme McDowell were also successful while also on American soil winning 2004 European Ryder Cup Captain Bernhard Langer, Number One on the Champions Tour Money List for a fifth time, and David Frost both won twice on the Champions Tour. Meanwhile 2005 BMW Championship winner Angel Cabrera was within a whisker of winning a third Major title, losing a play-off for the Masters Tournament to Adam Scott, but one week later in his native Argentina he won the 82nd Abierto OSDE del Centro in Cordoba where at the age of ten as a caddy he started to play the game.

Graeme McDowell - RBC Heritage

Henrik Stenson - Deutsche Bank Championship (below), Tour Championship by Coca-Cola and FedExCup

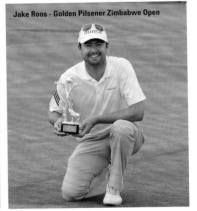
David Frost - Toshiba Classic (below) and Regions Tradition

Jake Roos - Golden Pilsener Zimbabwe Open

Anton Haig - Sunshine Big Easy Tour-Irene Country Club

Wade Ormsby - Panasonic Open India

Mohd Siddikur - Hero Indian Open

Anirban Lahiri - SAIL-SBI Open presented by Incredible India, Ministry of Tourism

Thaworn Wiratchant - Yeangder Tournament Players Championship (TPC)

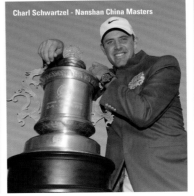
Charl Schwartzel - Nanshan China Masters

Liang Wen-chong - Resorts World Manila Masters

192

Jaco Van Zyl - Dimension Data-Pro Am (below), Telkom PGA Championship Final Wrap and Investec Cup

Adilson da Silva - Zambia Sugar Open (above) and Sun City Challenge

Jonas Blixt - The Greenbrier Classic

Michael McGeady - Irish PGA Championship

Jean Hugo - Vodacom Origins of Golf Langebaan

Wu Ashun - Heiwa PGM Dream Cup in Kasumigaura

James Kingston - Investec Royal Swazi Open

Scott Hend - Chiangmai Golf Classic presented by PTT (below), Mercuries Taiwan Masters and Venetian Macau Open

Tjaart Van der Walt - Lion of Africa Cape Town Open

Oliver Bekker - Telkom PGA Pro-Am

Bernhard Langer - ACE Group Classic (below) and Greater Gwinnett Championship

Bernd Wiesberger - CIMB Niaga Indonesian Masters

Angel Cabrera - 82nd Abierto OSDE del Centro
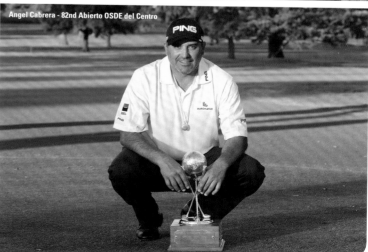

Changing of the Guard

Paul Wesselingh

From the record breaking achievements of Carl Mason to the historic double Major triumph of Roger Chapman, the history of the European Senior Tour is decorated with the stories of players for whom life began at 50.

The 2013 campaign provided yet more plotlines to this narrative as a new generation of players came to the fore, led by two long-term club professionals and a Dane who would become known as the Senior Tour's 'Ironman'.

It was an Englishman, Paul Wesselingh, who was at the forefront of a new generation of Senior Tour players, showing a remarkable consistency and win conversion rate that even his compatriot Mason, the Tour's most prolific winner, would have been proud of.

Wesselingh had sealed the 2012 Rookie of the Year accolade at Constance Belle Mare Plage in Mauritius, 11 months after securing his card at Qualifying School and his second season was one in which he sensationally built on those solid foundations, winning three times to return to the season-ending MCB Tour Championship leading the challenge to seal another trophy on the sunshine island, this time the John Jacobs

Trophy awarded to the Number One player on the European Senior Tour.

The six-time PGA Cup player, who shunned Tour life in the 1990s in favour of a career as a club professional so he could be around his young family, successfully defended his title in the ISPS HANDA PGA Seniors Championship in England in August, adding a second victory a month later in the Bad Ragaz PGA Seniors Open in Switzerland.

Both were achieved with closing rounds of 64, the first to finish ahead of nine-time runner up Angel Franco, of Paraguay, and former World Number One Ian Woosnam, and the latter to force a play-off with compatriot Kevin Spurgeon - winner of the 2009 Mauritius Commercial Bank Open - which Wesselingh won with a 25ft birdie putt on the third extra hole.

As Mauritius then appeared on the horizon, and the race for the John Jacobs Trophy began to heat up, Wesselingh swept from

behind to masterfully seize control of the Order of Merit from Steen Tinning by claiming his third victory of 2013, finishing one shot clear of home favourite Wen-teh Lu to win the Fubon Senior Open in Taipei.

Kohki Idoki

Steen Tinning

For the former Kedleston Park professional, who had spent five years preparing meticulously for life alongside some of the game's great names, to be regularly competing alongside them, and to be battling for the John Jacobs Trophy which Woosnam won in 2008, was as touching a personal fairy tale as Mason winning a record 25 times on the Senior Tour, or Chapman's historic double of the US Senior PGA Championship and US Senior Open in the same season in 2012.

"It was always a dream to play at the top level but for various reasons I never quite got there," he told his fellow professionals in a touching speech at the Senior Tour's Annual Awards Dinner. "Maybe I didn't think I was quite good enough and then the family came along and I wanted to spend time with them.

"But having watched these players for so many years, they inspire you. We have legends everywhere on this Tour.

"I remember, like most people, Sam Torrance holing that massive putt on the 18th at The Belfry in The 1985 Ryder Cup, arms aloft and tears streaming down his face. That was a defining moment in golf, an iconic one.

"And then you go to 1991, when Ian Woosnam holed that six-footer on the 18th at Augusta to win the Masters Tournament and went ballistic, his caddie chucking him around the green.

"And who am I, playing with them? Sam Torrance and Ian Woosnam! That's a dream – and I'm living the dream."

It was Tinning, another player determined to take full advantage of his second career-break on the Senior Tour, who ensured the battle for the John Jacobs Trophy went right to the wire in Mauritius.

A two-time winner in 18 seasons on The European Tour, the Dane returned to competitive golf at the 2012 MCB Tour Championship in Mauritius after an absence of nearly a decade, joining an established order of European Tour champions and Ryder Cup Captains and players already continuing their careers on the Senior Tour.

During his hiatus, Tinning took up the gruelling sport of ironman to help him prepare for life on the over 50s circuit, and his endurance became very much his asset in 2013 in a year-long quest to return to Mauritius for the 2013 season-finale as Senior Tour Number One.

Tinning made his winning breakthrough in his rookie campaign in the Berenberg Masters in Germany, where he withstood the challenge of home favourite and two-time Masters Champion Bernhard Langer, before fending off fellow newcomer Santiago Luna, of Spain, to claim the English Senior Open at Rockliffe Hall in October.

"I could not have predicted doing so well coming into my first Senior Tour season," said Tinning. "My ironman training and competition has a lot to do with how my mind works on a course. I try to challenge myself in all areas of the game. It was an awesome feeling to win and then to win again."

Ian Woosnam

Jamie Spence

Philip Golding

Paul Eales

Miguel Angel Martin

Andrew Oldcorn

Kenny Perry

Colin Montgomerie

Tinning's latter victory meant he joined Wesselingh as a multiple winner in 2013, with the two consequently going head-to-head for the John Jacobs Trophy.

The only other man to triumph on more than one occasion in 2013 was Englishman Simon P Brown, whose route to the Senior Tour resembled a remarkably similar tale to Wesselingh's.

Brown, like his compatriot Wesselingh a year previously, finished runner up at Qualifying School in Portugal having spent three decades as head professional at Golf Club Rhein-Sieg in Germany, a period of service that was punctuated with a brief flirtation with Tour life in the mid-nineties.

He also took to life on the Senior Tour effortlessly, claiming his maiden title with a superb wire-to-wire victory in the lucrative Russian Open Golf Championship (Senior) ahead of Mason and 2009 Rookie of the Year Mike Harwood of Australia.

Brown then doubled his haul of silverware courtesy of his triumph in the Dutch Senior Open, after the final round was washed out in Amsterdam with the Englishman two shots clear of Scotland's Ross Drummond on completion of 36 holes.

Despite owing a nod to the golfing rain gods, Brown could also rightly take pride in his considerable achievements during a maiden season where he found himself joining Tinning and Wesselingh at the business end of the Order of Merit.

"It's amazing that I have two victories," he said. "I never thought anything like this would happen in my first year on the Senior Tour."

Brown and Tinning were among an impressive line-up of first time winners in 2013, with the pair joined by Japan's Kohki Idoki (US Senior PGA Championship presented by KitchenAid), England's Philip Golding (Speedy Services Wales Senior Open), Americans Mark Wiebe (The Senior Open Championship Presented by Rolex) and Kenny Perry (US Senior Open Championship), Luna (SSE Scottish Senior Open) and Colin Montgomerie (Travis Perkins plc Senior Masters).

Mark Wiebe

David J Russell and Des Smyth

Mark James and Barry Lane

Whilst there were also titles for more recognised Senior Tour players in Scotland's Gordon Brand Jnr (WINSTONgolf Senior Open) and Australia's Peter Fowler (French Riviera Masters), the success of this group of maiden winners in 2013 undoubtedly heralded a 'changing of the guard' year like no other.

Notable among the 'new breed' was the name of Montgomerie, who became the latest in a line of Ryder Cup Captains to join the Senior Tour, following in the spike marks of Sir Nick Faldo, Mark James, Torrance, Woosnam, and Langer, the German who missed out on a second Senior Open Championship when he lost to Wiebe in a play-off at Royal Birkdale.

It took 2010 European winning Ryder Cup Captain Montgomerie just three events to find his feet and join some of his predecessors in the Senior Tour winners' club, the Scot dominating the Travis Perkins plc Senior Masters at Woburn Golf Club as August turned to September.

Carl Mason

Having eased himself into life on the Senior Tour with top 30 finishes in the US Senior Open and The Senior Open Championship Presented by Rolex, Montgomerie carded consecutive rounds of 68 followed by a closing 70 to finish six shots clear of Spaniard Miguel Angel Martin and Wesselingh, claiming his first tournament victory for more than six years.

"Joining the Senior Tour has been a new chapter in my life," said Montgomerie. "I feel very lucky. When I turned 50 I became a member of three tours: the Senior Tour, the Champions Tour in America, and The European Tour. How often does that happen in life? How often is it that when you get older, you have more opportunities available? It's a fabulous time.

"It is like a new lease of life turning 50 in golf. I can't think of any other sports where you take a fresh step on in your career at such an age and to have such a fine Tour, such an excellent brand, as the Senior Tour as part of that is brilliant."

In addition to offering another chance to win the Major Championship that has so far

Gordon Brand Jnr

eluded him, Montgomerie's new beginnings presents an opportunity for the 31-time European Tour winner to challenge for another Order of Merit crown.

The World Golf Hall of Fame member claimed the Harry Vardon Trophy a record eight times, finishing as European Tour

Number One for seven straight seasons between 1993 and 1999, and again in 2005.

So far, Woosnam is the only man to lift both the Harry Vardon Trophy and the John Jacobs Trophy, receiving the former in both 1987 and 1990 and the latter in his debut Senior Tour season in 2008.

Santiago Luna

Greg Turner

RUSSIAN OPEN GOLF CHAMPIONSHIP (Se
13-15 сентября 2013 года | 13-15 September 2013

Simon P Brown

To emulate Woosnam's achievement, Montgomerie will face stern competition from the Senior Tour's new guard, led by Brown, Golding, Luna, Tinning and Wesselingh, supported by the likes of Englishmen Paul Eales and Jamie Spence and New Zealander Greg Turner, as well as enduring Senior Tour contenders such as England's Nick Job, Barry Lane, Mason, David J Russell and Gary Wolstenholme, Fowler, Scotland's Brand Jnr, Andrew Oldcorn and Torrance, Irishman Des Smyth and indeed Welshman Woosnam himself,

who showed he remains a force with three top five finishes in 2013.

The future is likely also to bring a potent new threat in the form of Spaniard Miguel Angel Jiménez, the oldest winner in the history of The European Tour at 49 years old, who 'comes of age' in January 2014.

With more victories beyond the age of 40 than any other player on The European Tour, logic would suggest that Jiménez might not take too long to add his name to the

growing roll call of honour on the Senior Tour when he decides to turn his attention to the over 50s circuit.

Further on the horizon is the arrival of Ryder Cup Captains José María Olazábal and Paul McGinley, who both turn 50 in 2016, swelling a Tour already rich in talent and with a growing strength in depth year-on-year.

Steve Todd

Peter Fowler

Nick Job

Constance Belle Mare Plage, Poste de Flacq, Mauritius

Gary Wolstenholme

Angel Franco

THE 2013 EUROPEAN SENIOR TOUR

	Date	Event	Venue	Winner	Score	First prize / Prize fund
May	23 - 26	US Senior PGA Championship presented by KitchenAid	Bellerive CC, St Louis, Missouri, USA	Kohki Idoki, JPN	71-69-68-65=273 (-11)	€295,428 / $2,100,000
Jun	6 - 9	ISPS HANDA PGA Seniors Championship	De Vere Mottram Hall, Cheshire, England	Paul Wesselingh, ENG	68-70-70-64=272 (-20)	€48,687 / £260,000
	14 - 16	Speedy Services Wales Senior Open	Royal Porthcawl GC, Bridgend, Wales	Philip Golding, ENG	66-79-66=211 (-2)	€44,004 / £250,000
Jul	5 - 7	Bad Ragaz PGA Seniors Open	Golf Club Bad Ragaz, Bad Ragaz, Switzerland	Paul Wesselingh, ENG**	71-66-64=201 (-9)	€42,000 / €280,000
	11 - 14	US Senior Open Championship*	Omaha CC, Omaha, Nebraska, USA	Kenny Perry, USA	67-73-64-63=267 (-13)	$500,000 / $2,600,000
	25 - 28	The Senior Open Championship Presented by Rolex	Royal Birkdale GC, Merseyside, England	Mark Wiebe, USA**	70-65-70-66=271 (-9)	$315,600 / $2,000,000
Aug	2 - 4	Berenberg Masters	Golf-und Land-Club Köln, Refrath, Germany	Steen Tinning, DEN	68-70-69=207 (-9)	€60,000 / €400,000
	16 - 18	SSE Scottish Senior Open	Torrance Championship Course, Fairmont St Andrews, Fife, Scotland	Santiago Luna, ESP	69-71-71=211 (-5)	€43,485 / £250,000
	30 - 1	Travis Perkins plc Senior Masters	Duke's Course, Woburn GC, Woburn, England	Colin Montgomerie, SCO	68-68-70=206 (-10)	€52,299 / £300,000
Sep	6 - 8	WINSTONgolf Senior Open	WINSTONopen Course, WINSTONgolf, Vorbeck, Germany	Gordon Brand Jnr, SCO	68-68-68=204 (-12)	€60,000 / €400,000
	13 - 15	Russian Open Golf Championship (Senior)	Moscow CC, Moscow Region, Russia	Simon P Brown, ENG	66-68-70=204 (-12)	€97,306 / $850,000
	20 - 22	French Riviera Masters	Terre Blanche Hotel, Spa & Golf Resort, Provence, France	Peter Fowler, AUS	68-71-66=205 (-11)	€60,000 / €400,000
Oct	4 - 6	English Senior Open	Rockliffe Hall, Hurworth-on-Tees, Darlington, England	Steen Tinning, DEN	69-63-67=199 (-17)	€35,898 / £200,000
	11 - 13	Dutch Senior Open	The International, Amsterdam, The Netherlands	Simon P Brown, ENG	72-71=143 (-3)	€30,475 / €200,000
Nov	15 - 17	Fubon Senior Open	Miramar G&CC, Taipei, Taiwan	Paul Wesselingh, ENG	69-68-70=207 (-9)	€59,869 / $450,000
Dec	13 - 15	MCB Tour Championship	Constance Belle Mare Plage, Poste de Flacq, Mauritius			€400,000

* Money won does not count towards the European Senior Tour Order of Merit

** denotes play-off

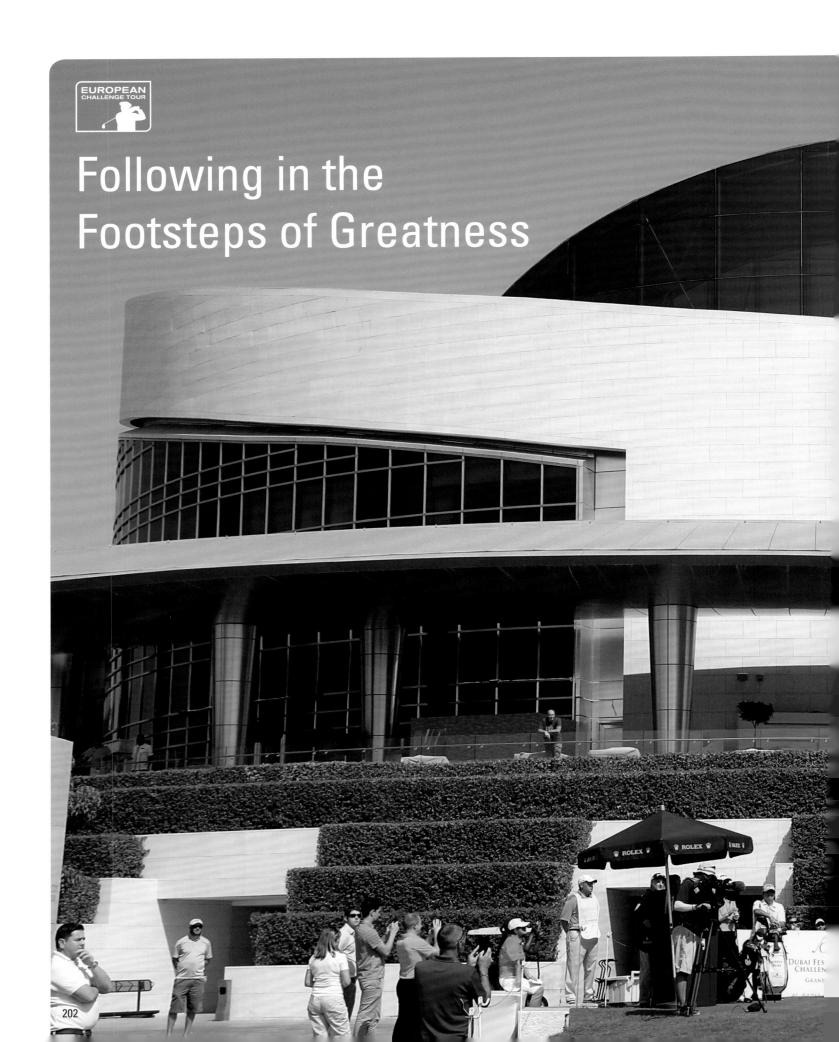

Following in the Footsteps of Greatness

Andrea Pavan

Andrea Pavan and Alain de Soultrait, Director of Challenge Tour

In the year that the European Challenge Tour celebrated its 25th Anniversary, there could not have been a more fitting figurehead for the success of the tour in the past quarter of a century than the 2013 Number One Andrea Pavan.

On the one hand, the 24 year old possesses the confidence, youthful exuberance and supreme talent which epitomises so many of the young stars who have passed through the gates of the developmental tour en route to stardom.

But there is another side to the Italian's story, which exemplifies one of the Challenge Tour's less celebrated, but equally important, facets.

Not only does it provide a constant conveyor belt of rising young stars, but it also acts as a crucial platform for players to re-focus and re-build after the disappointment of losing their playing rights on The European Tour.

In 2013, Pavan followed the path of many of the Tour's greatest alumni as he bounced back from European Tour disappointment in courageous fashion.

Pavan's pedigree was beyond reasonable doubt having burst on to the Challenge Tour scene in 2011 with two victories,

including one at the prestigious season finale, to finish second in the Rankings behind Englishman Tommy Fleetwood.

After struggling through a frustrating European Tour campaign in 2012, with so much expectation on his shoulders, Pavan's temperament and ability to deal with perceived failure were under the microscope.

Undeterred, the Roman proved unequivocally that he is made of world-beating stuff with a 2013 campaign in which he added an unerring consistency, missing just two cuts in 23 appearances, to his already indefatigable desire to win, doubling his victory count on the Challenge Tour to four with wins at the Bad Griesbach Challenge Tour by Hartl Resort in July and the Open Blue Green Côtes d'Armor Bretagne in September.

So many of the Challenge Tour's success stories down the years have played out as tales of recovering from adversity before rising to the highest echelons of the game.

Roope Kakko

Marco Crespi

Brooks Koepka

Pavan's friend and compatriot Edoardo Molinari is one of the most famous examples, returning from European Tour disappointment in 2008 to enjoy a record-breaking season on the Challenge Tour in 2009 before going on to claim two top-tier victories in 2010.

The Turin native's meteoric rise reached levels of Challenge Tour "folklore" when he earned an appearance in Colin Montgomerie's victorious European Ryder Cup Team at The Celtic Manor Resort in Wales in 2010

Pavan, a former amateur star both in Europe and the American collegiate system, believes the 2013 season could be a similarly life-changing one for him.

"It's a great accomplishment," said Pavan. "I'm so happy with how things turned out this year and I'm really looking forward to next year.

"I was proud to make such a good comeback. It's not easy to get back up and I showed that I can do it. Towards the end of 2012 I was struggling with my confidence. It was very disappointing but I learned from it and got back, worked hard in winter and got hungry again to get good results and get consistent again.

"This year has felt better than two years ago. In the first season, you come out and there is less pressure, but when you gain your card and fall back it can get harder for you. Edoardo took it to the next level. He really dominated the Challenge Tour in 2009. I know he is a tough competitor so he is an inspiration for me. I could not even think about The Ryder Cup right now. I just need to take it step by step. I know I have

Jens Dantorp

Adrian Otaegui

José-Filipe Lima

STAY AND PLAY AT A
WORLD-CLASS GOLF COURSE.

Al Badia Golf Club by InterContinental Dubai Festival City is a premium, lifestyle destination offering the ultimate golf and dining experience in Dubai and the Middle East. The iconic clubhouse provides a breathtaking retreat set within the grounds of an extraordinary, oasis-themed golf course, designed by Robert Trent Jones II. The facilities encompass a fully equipped pro shop, a world-class golf academy boasting the region's only TaylorMade Performance Lab, themed dining outlets and extensive meeting and outdoor event venues. Just a few minutes away, InterContinental Dubai Festival City ends a good day of play with an exceptional stay.

For more information or to make a booking,
Please call the golf club on +971 (4) 601 0101
email albadiagolf@ichdfc.ae
visit www.albadiagolfclub.ae

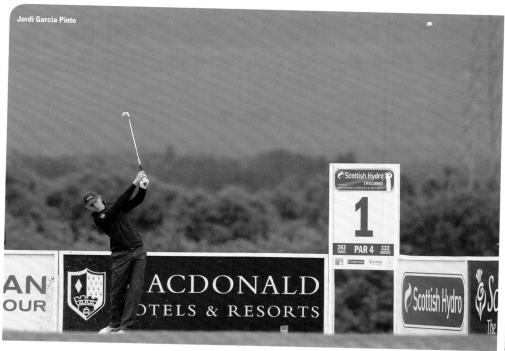

Jordi Garcia Pinto

Jens Fahrbring

Robert Dinwiddie

Peter Uihlein

François Calmels

the potential but it's about showing it with results."

The 2013 Challenge Tour season was another ground-breaking one for the tour, visiting Ukraine, Oman and the United Arab Emirates for the first time in its history, and it was a year bookended by two landmark victories for another player who is sure to return to The European Tour a different beast following a morale-boosting campaign.

Shiv Kapur had spent six seasons in the top tier before arriving on the Challenge Tour. He could not have made a finer start to 2013 as he won the season-opening Gujarat Kensville Challenge on home soil on February 3 – nine days before celebrating his 31st birthday.

His biggest one was yet to come, however, as he closed the season as he began it by celebrating a famous triumph with his win in the Dubai Festival City Challenge Tour Grand Final hosted by Al Badia Golf Club – becoming not only the first player from India to capture the showpiece finale but also to graduate from the Challenge Tour to The European Tour.

While Kapur was the central character in the opening and closing chapters of the 2013 season, the many plots and sub-plots which unfolded in between were just as gripping and none more so than the story of American rising star Brooks Koepka.

The confident young Floridian had already claimed a victory on the tour in 2012 before returning rejuvenated and even more determined and his win at the Montecchia Golf Open presented by POLAROID in May, followed by a June double at the Fred Olsen Challenge de España and Scottish Hydro Challenge hosted by Macdonald Hotels and Resorts meant he broke the record for the fastest graduation from the Challenge Tour in a calendar year.

In a period stretching less than 50 days, the 23 year old earned the right to be spoken of as a future superstar and he proved his credentials by finishing tied 12th in his first appearance as a full European Tour member at the Aberdeen Asset Management Scottish Open before a top ten at the Omega European Masters.

Simon Thornton

Dylan Frittelli

His season almost reached a stunning crescendo when he came close to winning on the US PGA Tour and it is surely only a matter of time before Koepka, who finished the season third in the Rankings, is being heralded as one of the Challenge Tour's great alumni.

His friend and compatriot Peter Uihlein is another who began the season as a Challenge Tour member but finished it being ear-marked as one of the next major players in world golf, after he claimed the Madeira Islands Open – Portugal – BPI title in May to make the step up before finishing 14th in The 2013 Race to Dubai and earning the Sir Henry Cotton Rookie of the Year Award.

While these two outstanding Americans dominated the headlines in the early part of the Challenge Tour season, there was one European who emerged from the pack in similarly spectacular fashion in the second half of the year in the shape of Dutchman Daan Huizing.

The 23 year old arrived on the Challenge Tour with a rather eye-catching CV in the amateur scene and he hit the ground running in June with a tied runner-up finish in his maiden professional appearance on the tour at the Kärnten Golf Open presented by Mazda.

That kicked off a run of eight events in which he never finished outside the top 20, securing two victories in consecutive

appearances in September – at the Northern Ireland Open Challenge Presented By Clannah and XJET and Kharkov Superior Cup in the Ukraine – on the way to a sixth place finish in the Rankings.

François Calmels was the fourth multiple winner to graduate from the 2013 Challenge Tour, finishing 13th in the Rankings after early victories at the Challenge de Madrid in April and the D+D Real Czech Challenge Open in June, and he was joined by French compatriot Victor Riu, whose maiden win at the Swiss Challenge helped him to an 11th place finish in the Rankings.

The Challenge Tour, of course, is no different to any of the major world golf

Tyrrell Hatton

Jamie McLeary

Victor Riu

Sihwan Kim

Stuart Manley

Nacho Elvira

Daan Huizing

tours in rewarding players with big performances at the big events and the most striking beneficiary in 2013 was Johan Carlsson, whose imperious victory at the lucrative Kazakhstan Open along with an extraordinarily consistent second half of the season yielded a fifth place in the Rankings.

Fellow Scandinavian Roope Kakko earned a second Challenge Tour title, his first as a professional, at the penultimate National Bank of Oman Golf Classic in late October, on the way to an eighth place finish in the Rankings.

A week before the Finn's crowning glory, Spaniard Nacho Elvira made his mark in the first of the final run of three thrilling

season-ending tournaments, The Foshan Open in China, before claiming the 14th European Tour card on offer with a top ten at the Grand Final in Dubai.

While big prize money at big events can prove the catalyst for success, the Challenge Tour is also built on the virtue of consistency and that has never been more evident than in the 2013 season, given that six of the 15 graduates had not recorded a win en route to European Tour promotion.

The most notable example was Portugal's José-Filipe Lima, winner of the 2004 Aa St Omer Open, whose three runners-up finishes, including the share of second place at the Dubai Festival City Challenge

Tour Grand Final hosted by Al Badia Golf Club, and five further top tens deservedly lifted him to second in the Rankings.

Promising 21 year old Spaniard Adrian Otaegui also racked up three runners-up finishes, including a tied second finish at the Kazakhstan Open, to finish seventh in the Rankings while Korean Sihwan Kim came close to victory on a number of occasions but was rewarded for eight top ten finishes, finishing ninth in the Rankings.

Englishman Tyrrell Hatton's incredible late surge in the season, which included back-to-back tied runnersup finishes at the Kazakhstan Open and The Foshan Open as well as a top ten at the season finale, was

Brinson Paolini

Johan Carlsson

Shiv Kapur

Daniel Gaunt

fairytale stories of the Grand Final when he charged to a tied runner-up finish in Dubai, initially thinking it may not have been enough before celebrating emotionally when confirmation eventually came through that, after seven long seasons on the Challenge Tour, his European Tour dreams had finally come true.

Those who could not revel in such end-of-season festivities despite experiencing the joy of victory on the Challenge Tour in 2013 were Spain's Jordi Garcia Pinto (Barclays Kenya Open), Australia's DanielGaunt (Telenet Trophy), South Africa's Dylan Frittelli (Kärnten Golf Open presented by Mazda), Italy's Marco Crespi (Mugello Tuscany Open), American Brinson Paolini (Le Vaudreuil Golf Challenge),Welshman Stuart Manley (Finnish Challenge) and Swedes Jens Fahrbring (Norwegian Challenge) and Jens Dantorp (Rolex Trophy).

Proof, if ever it were needed, that the Challenge Tour can so often be a school of hard knocks. But as the 15 stars of this milestone 25th season of the Challenge Tour - representing 12 different nations - have proven, for those who bounce back and battle to the bitter end, the rewards are endless as they seek to follow in the footsteps of greatness.

enough to secure a rookie season on The European Tour courtesy of a tenth place finish in the Rankings.

He was joined by compatriot Robert Dinwiddie, who claimed the 12th European Tour card on offer thanks in part to a tied fourth finish in the dual-ranking Najeti Hotels et Golfs Open presented by Neuflize OBC, which was won by 2011 Challenge Tour graduate Simon Thornton.

The final man in the top 15, Jamie McLeary, provided one of the great

Neil Ahern

THE 2013 EUROPEAN CHALLENGE TOUR

	Date	Event	Venue	Winner	Score	First Prize / Prizefund
Jan	31 - 3	Gujurat Kensville Challenge	Kensville G&CC, Ahmedabad, India	Shiv Kapur, IND	67-71-65-71=274 (-14)	€32,000 / €20,000
Feb	14 - 17	Barclays Kenya Open	Karen CC, Nairobi, Kenya	Jordi Garcia Pinto, ESP	69-66-68-69=272 (-12)	€31,200 / €195,000
Apr	24 - 27+	Challenge de Madrid	El Encín Golf Hotel, Alcala de Henares, Madrid, Spain	François Calmels, FRA	63-69-72-67=271 (-17)	€25,600 / €160,000
May	2 - 5	Montecchia Golf Open presented by POLAROID	Golf Club della Montecchia, Padova, Italy	Brooks Koepka, USA	66-67-62-66=261 (-23)	€25,600 / €160,000
	16 - 19	Madeira Islands Open - Portugal - BPI***	Club de Golf do Santo da Serra, Madeira, Portugal	Peter Uihlein, USA	72-64-69-68=273 (-15)	€100,000 / €600,000
	23 - 26	Telenet Trophy	Royal Waterloo GC, Lasne, Belgium	Daniel Gaunt, AUS**	69-66-69-69=273 (-11)	€25,600 / €160,000
	30 - 2	Fred Olsen Challenge de España	Tecina Golf, La Gomera, Canary Islands, Spain	Brooks Koepka, USA	64-66-64-66=260 (-24)	€25,600 / €160,000
Jun	6 - 9	D+D Real Czech Challenge Open	Golf & Spa Kunêticá Hora, Drîtec, Czech Republic	François Calmels, FRA	67-69-65-65=266 (-22)	€25,600 / €160,000
	13 - 16	Najeti Hotels et Golfs Open presented by Neuflize OBC*	Aa St Omer GC, Lumbres, France	Simon Thornton, IRL**	74-70-65-70=279 (-5)	€83,330 / €500,000
	20 - 23	Scottish Hydro Challenge hosted by Macdonald Hotels & Resorts	Macdonald Spey Valley GC, Aviemore, Scotland	Brooks Koepka, USA	70-66-62-68=266 (-18)	€35,200 / €220,000
	27 - 30	Kärnten Golf Open presented by Mazda	Jacques Lemans GC, St Veit - Längsee, Austria	Dylan Frittelli, RSA	67-64-65-71=267 (-17)	€25,600 / €160,000
Jul	4 - 7	Bad Griesbach Challenge Tour by Hartl Resort	Hartl Resort, Bad Griesbach, Germany	Andrea Pavan, ITA	68-67-66-68=269 (-19)	€27,200 / €170,000
	11 - 14	Swiss Challenge	Golf Sempachersee, Lucerne, Switzerland	Victor Riu, FRA	69-64-62-70=265 (-19)	€25,600 / €160,000
	18 - 21	Mugello Tuscany Open	UNA Poggio dei Medici GC, Scarperia, Florence, Italy	Marco Crespi, ITA	72-64-66-65=267 (-17)	€25,600 / €160,000
	25 - 28	Le Vaudreuil Golf Challenge	Golf PGA France du Vaudreuil, Le Vaudreuil, France	Brinson Paolini, USA	69-66-66-68=269 (-19)	€28,800 / €180,000
Aug	1 - 4	Finnish Challenge	Kytäjä Golf, Hyvinkää, Finland	Stuart Manley, WAL	65-69-64-69=267 (-21)	€27,200 / €170,000
	8 - 11	Norwegian Challenge	Losby G&CC, Finstadjordet, Oslo Norway	Jens Fahrbring, SWE	69-72-62-66=269 (-19)	€28,000 / €175,000
	21 - 24+	Rolex Trophy	GC de Genève, Geneva, Switzerland	Jens Dantorp, SWE	67-67-66-70=270 (-18)	€26,000 / €228,000
	29 - 1	Northern Ireland Open Challenge presented by Clannah and XJET	Galgorm Castle GC & Estates, Ballymena, Co. Antrim, Northern Ireland	Daan Huizing, NED**	65-66-66-74=271 (-13)	€27,200 / €170,000
Sep	5 - 8	Open Blue Green Côtes d'Armor Bretagne	Golf Blue Green de Pléneuf Val André, Pléneuf, France	Andrea Pavan, ITA	64-65-68-72=269 (-19)	€28,800 / €180,000
	12 - 15	Kharkov Superior Cup	Superior Golf & Spa Resort, Kharkov, Ukraine	Daan Huizing, NED	70-69-67-67=273 (-15)	€32,000 / €200,000
	19 - 22	Kazakhstan Open	Nurtau GC, Almaty, Kazakhstan	Johan Carlsson, SWE	69-67-67-67=270 (-18)	€64,000 / €400,000
Oct	17 - 20	The Foshan Open	Foshan GC, Shishan Town, Nanhai District, Foshan City, China	Nacho Elvira, ESP	68-68-66-72=274 (-14)	€41,234 / $350,000
	24 - 27	National Bank of Oman Golf Classic	Almouj Golf, The Wave, Muscat, Oman	Roope Kakko, FIN	70-69-66-69=274 (-14)	€35,029 / $300,000
	31 - 3	Dubai Festival City Challenge Tour Grand Final hosted by Al Badia Golf Club	Al Badia GC by Intercontinental, Dubai, UAE	Shiv Kapur, IND	69-66-67-70=272 (-16)	€56,650 / €330,000

* Dual Ranking Event   ** denotes play-off   *** Prize fund capped at €500,000

THE 2013 EUROPEAN CHALLENGE TOUR RANKINGS

Pos	Name	Country	Played	€	Pos	Name	Country	Played	€
1	Andrea PAVAN	(ITA)	(23)	147811.05	51	Jason BARNES	(ENG)	(21)	31635.89
2	José-Filipe LIMA	(POR)	(20)	123697.22	52	Daniel VANCSIK	(ARG)	(21)	28657.64
3	Brooks KOEPKA	(USA)	(10)	119423.33	53	Damian ULRICH	(SUI)	(15)	28484.50
4	Shiv KAPUR	(IND)	(9)	118322.87	54	George MURRAY	(SCO)	(19)	28163.23
5	Johan CARLSSON	(SWE)	(17)	113065.78	55	Christophe BRAZILLIER	(FRA)	(22)	26102.12
6	Daan HUIZING	(NED)	(12)	104870.40	56	Scott ARNOLD	(AUS)	(12)	25742.69
7	Adrian OTAEGUI	(ESP)	(20)	104811.40	57	Alvaro VELASCO	(ESP)	(21)	25737.90
8	Roope KAKKO	(FIN)	(17)	100293.30	58	Andrea ROTA	(ITA)	(17)	25724.00
9	Sihwan KIM	(KOR)	(22)	95707.65	59	Sam HUTSBY	(ENG)	(21)	25017.83
10	Tyrrell HATTON	(ENG)	(17)	92113.63	60	Raymond RUSSELL	(SCO)	(19)	24108.04
11	Victor RIU	(FRA)	(24)	87296.78	61	Gary STAL	(FRA)	(16)	23676.44
12	Robert DINWIDDIE	(ENG)	(19)	86489.38	62	Mark F HAASTRUP	(DEN)	(16)	23631.54
13	François CALMELS	(FRA)	(22)	85533.61	63	Pedro ORIOL	(ESP)	(17)	22805.46
14	Nacho ELVIRA	(ESP)	(20)	82784.81	64	Filippo BERGAMASCHI	(ITA)	(17)	22663.33
15	Jamie MCLEARY	(SCO)	(23)	78675.75	65	Carlos AGUILAR	(ESP)	(20)	22159.28
16	Sam WALKER	(ENG)	(20)	76105.54	66	Jerome LANDO CASANOVA	(FRA)	(19)	21643.00
17	Daniel IM	(USA)	(23)	75870.07	67	Luke GODDARD	(ENG)	(21)	21181.31
18	Marco CRESPI	(ITA)	(20)	74921.07	68	Andrew JOHNSTON	(ENG)	(12)	20975.00
19	Stuart MANLEY	(WAL)	(21)	71996.38	69	Pontus WIDEGREN	(SWE)	(7)	20200.83
20	Duncan STEWART	(SCO)	(20)	70226.85	70	Paul MADDY	(ENG)	(18)	19966.35
21	Jens DANTORP	(SWE)	(20)	67342.13	71	Gareth SHAW	(NIR)	(16)	19831.57
22	Edouard DUBOIS	(FRA)	(22)	66491.45	72	Tapio PULKKANEN	(FIN)	(15)	19661.82
23	Rhys DAVIES	(WAL)	(16)	66229.19	73	Luis CLAVERIE	(ESP)	(12)	19533.00
24	Jordi GARCIA PINTO	(ESP)	(22)	65610.99	74	Nicolo RAVANO	(ITA)	(21)	19219.24
25	Byeong-hun AN	(KOR)	(22)	64395.82	75	Roland STEINER	(AUT)	(14)	18762.10
26	Andrew MCARTHUR	(SCO)	(22)	62628.15	76	James HEATH	(ENG)	(11)	18586.00
27	Jens FAHRBRING	(SWE)	(19)	59174.57	77	Chan KIM	(USA)	(12)	17556.75
28	Phillip ARCHER	(ENG)	(22)	58733.56	78	Charles-Edouard RUSSO	(FRA)	(17)	17079.06
29	Brinson PAOLINI	(USA)	(12)	58562.77	79	Benjamin HEBERT	(FRA)	(19)	17021.78
30	Agustin DOMINGO	(ESP)	(22)	58289.31	80	Guillaume CAMBIS	(FRA)	(19)	16680.46
31	Tim SLUITER	(NED)	(19)	56612.00	81	Brandon STONE	(RSA)	(4)	16601.16
32	Dylan FRITTELLI	(RSA)	(20)	52659.17	82	Dodge KEMMER	(USA)	(17)	15340.50
33	Daniel GAUNT	(AUS)	(14)	52322.99	83	Ross McGOWAN	(ENG)	(9)	14602.75
34	Lucas BJERREGAARD	(DEN)	(18)	51545.60	84	Max GLAUERT	(GER)	(14)	14483.50
35	Jamie ELSON	(ENG)	(14)	51167.22	85	Markus BRIER	(AUT)	(12)	14169.99
36	Steven TILEY	(ENG)	(19)	50691.74	86	Florian PRAEGANT	(AUT)	(18)	13889.65
37	Bernd RITTHAMMER	(GER)	(17)	49096.53	87	Chris HANSON	(ENG)	(11)	13755.73
38	Jeppe HULDAHL	(DEN)	(18)	47597.06	88	Eirik Tage JOHANSEN	(NOR)	(9)	12307.00
39	Lloyd KENNEDY	(ENG)	(17)	46262.79	89	Edouard ESPANA	(FRA)	(9)	11350.71
40	Wil BESSELING	(NED)	(20)	45507.59	90	Adrien BERNADET	(FRA)	(20)	11309.32
41	Adam GEE	(ENG)	(21)	45103.51	91	Sebastian GARCIA RODRIGUEZ	(ESP)	(13)	11235.25
42	Oliver WILSON	(ENG)	(18)	44824.49	92	Wallace BOOTH	(SCO)	(18)	11187.50
43	Niklas LEMKE	(SWE)	(15)	44679.32	93	Baptiste CHAPELLAN	(FRA)	(16)	10850.62
44	Julien GUERRIER	(FRA)	(20)	41747.20	94	Paul DWYER	(ENG)	(18)	10691.72
45	Thomas NØRRET	(DEN)	(20)	40889.79	95	Lloyd SALTMAN	(SCO)	(18)	10229.79
46	Terry PILKADARIS	(AUS)	(18)	35666.72	96	Adrien SADDIER	(FRA)	(4)	9910.75
47	Pelle EDBERG	(SWE)	(18)	35540.79	97	Niccolo QUINTARELLI	(ITA)	(18)	9737.00
48	Matt FORD	(ENG)	(13)	35093.27	98	Matt HAINES	(ENG)	(12)	9634.00
49	Knut BORSHEIM	(NOR)	(20)	34990.30	99	Domenico GEMINIANI	(ITA)	(16)	9575.83
50	Daniel BROOKS	(ENG)	(15)	34088.73	100	Tom MURRAY	(ENG)	(19)	9523.83

The Graduates of the 2013 European Challenge Tour

THE 2013 RACE TO DUBAI EUROPEAN TOUR GOLFER OF THE MONTH AWARDS

The Race to Dubai European Tour Golfer of the Month Awards are presented throughout the year followed by an Annual Award. The winners receive an engraved alms dish and a jeroboam of Moët & Chandon champagne

GOLFER OF THE YEAR WINNERS

2012	Rory McIlory		1998	Lee Westwood	
2011	Luke Donald		1997	Colin Montgomerie	
2010	Martin Kaymer and Graeme McDowell		1996	Colin Montgomerie	
			1995	Colin Montgomerie	
2009	Lee Westwood		1994	Ernie Els	
2008	Padraig Harrington		1993	Bernhard Langer	
2007	Padraig Harrington		1992	Sir Nick Faldo	
2006	Paul Casey		1991	Severiano Ballesteros	
2005	Michael Campbell		1990	Sir Nick Faldo	
2004	Vijay Singh		1989	Sir Nick Faldo	
2003	Ernie Els		1988	Severiano Ballesteros	
2002	Ernie Els		1987	Ian Woosnam	
2001	Retief Goosen		1986	Severiano Ballesteros	
2000	Lee Westwood		1985	Bernhard Langer	
1999	Colin Montgomerie				

George O'Grady and Henrik Stenson

August
For his performances in the WGC-Bridgestone Invitational and US PGA Championship followed by victory in the Deutsche Bank Championship

September
For his victory in the Tour Championship by Coca-Cola and Number One finish in the FedEx Cup

Chris Wood - January
For his victory in the Commercial Bank Qatar Masters

Darren Fichardt - February
For his victory in the Africa Open

Marcel Siem - March
For his victory in the Trophée Hassan II

Raphaël Jacquelin - April
For his victory in the Open de España

Matteo Manassero - May
For his victory in the BMW PGA Championship

Justin Rose - June
For his victory in the US Open Championship

Graeme McDowell - July
For his victory in the Alstom Open de France

Gonzalo Fernandez-Castaño - October
For his performance in the Seve Trophy by Golf+

THE 2013 EUROPEAN TOUR SHOT OF THE MONTH AWARDS

The European Tour Shot of the Month Awards are presented throughout the year followed by an Annual Award

SHOT OF THE YEAR WINNERS

Year	Winner	
2012	Louis Oosthuizen	
2011	Rory McIlroy	
2010	Graeme McDowell	
2009	Rafa Echenique	
2008	Padraig Harrington	
2007	Angel Cabrera	
2006	Paul Casey	
2005	Paul McGinley	
2004	David Howell	
2003	Fredrik Jacobson	

Justin Rose - June
For his approach to the 18th during the US Open

Chris Wood - January
For his approach to the 18th during the Commercial Bank Qatar Masters

Charl Schwartzel - February
For his second shot to the 17th during the Joburg Open

Anders Hansen - March
For his eagle two at the second during the Maybank Malaysian Open

Maximilian Kieffer - April
For his birdie putt on the third extra hole during the Open de España

Ernie Els - May
For his eagle two at the eighth during the BMW PGA Championship

Francesco Molinari - July
For his eagle at the 12th during the Aberdeen Asset Management Scottish Open

Danny Willett - August
For his birdie at the sixth during the Johnnie Walker Championship

Peter Uihlein - September
For his eagle at the 18th at St Andrews during the Alfred Dunhill Links Championship

Craig Lee - October
For his eagle at the 16th during the BMW Masters

European Tour Properties –
A Swift and Structured Evolution

London Golf Club - 11th The Heritage

The expanding development of European Tour Properties, initiated when London Golf Club became the first Destination Venue in 2009, as an influential and internationally recognised network received increased momentum in 2013 with four new 'arrivals' taking the impressive collection of venues so far to 13 of which no fewer than six are currently hosting Tour competition.

Golf and Country Club Fleesensee in Germany, Diamond Country Club in Austria and PGA Catalunya Resort in Spain were all announced during the first half of the year as Destination Venues by David MacLaren, The European Tour's Director of Property and Venue Development, followed by the exciting news that Jumeirah Golf Estates (Dubai) had come on board.

So when the DP World Tour Championship, Dubai was played in November the powerful list of European Tour Properties Destination Venues staging Tour competition in 2013 rose to six following the playing of the Lyoness Open powered by Greenfinity (Diamond Country Club) and the Alstom Open de France (Le Golf National) on The European Tour International Schedule, the French Riviera Masters (Terre Blanche) on the European Senior Tour and, in addition

to a section of Stage One of the European Tour Qualifying School taking place at Golf and Country Club Fleesensee, the Qualifying School Finals returned to their traditional home at PGA Catalunya Resort.

Moreover, European Tour Properties now have their own "Magnificent Seven" in Golf World magazine's prestigious Top 100 Courses in Continental Europe with PGA Catalunya Resort (Stadium) rising from eighth to fifth, and notably becoming Number One in Spain, one place ahead of Le Golf National, Paris, France, with Terre Blanche Hotel Spa Golf Resort in the South of France climbing from 18th to 14th, Quinta do Lago (South) in Portugal from 57th to 53rd, Estonian Golf and Country Club (Sea) 84th to 83rd, The Dutch in The Netherlands entering for the first time at 86th and Linna Golf in Finland at 94th with Golf Club St.Leon-Rot, Germany, listed in a first-ever "Next 100."

There is no disguising the importance of this achievement with Golf World acknowledging: "The development of golf on the continent means trying to squeeze its elite courses into just 100 slots is proving increasingly difficult."

 MacLaren is enormously encouraged by the network's swift and structured evolution which he emphasises was given the ideal foundation by London Golf Club in Kent, one of South East England's premier golfing destinations, where two editions of The European Open were played in 2008 and 2009, becoming the first through a joint venture with The European Tour.

Moreover, he is equally gratified by the wide-ranging competition at European Tour Properties which sees players starting their careers, flourishing in the global

Linna Golf

arena and continuing to pursue their ambitions on the European Senior Tour.

Terre Blanche Hotel Spa Golf Resort, located in the foothills of the Southern Alps so combining the charm and character of Provence with the chic of the Côte d'Azur with Cannes, Nice and St Tropez only a short drive away, has become home to the French Riviera Masters. This was won in 2012 by England's David J Russell and then in 2013 by Australia's Peter Fowler with a simply stunning final round of 67 which matched the late September weather with the entire tournament played under blue skies and a hot sun.

Dave Thomas, the former Ryder Cup golfer, sadly passed away shortly before the 2013 edition unfolded on the Château course (6,616 metres; 7,235 yards; par 72) that is a superb legacy to his outstanding skills as an innovative course designer. Evidence of Thomas's huge respect of the landscape, its lakes and valleys, ravines and woodlands, is abundantly visible and his subtle use of spectacular water hazards combined with strategically placed bunkers makes for an invigorating examination in sumptuous surroundings.

Thomas was also responsible for designing the second of the two Championship courses set in the 750 acre resort and although Le Riou (6,005 metres; 6,567 yards; par 72) is shorter it nevertheless presents a thrilling test

featuring rolling fairways, wending their way through pine and oak-lined hills and valleys, inspirational views of Medieval Provençal villages and, of course, those Southern Alps with snow-capped peaks providing a breathtaking backdrop in the winter months.

 What further characterises Terre Blanche, where the opportunity exists to build a villa in the picturesque countryside and become a member of a quite unique resort, are the astonishing facilities. The 64-bay, two-tiered driving range, known as the Albatros Golf Performance Center, became in 2012 the very first European Tour Performance Institute and is also home to the 'Biomecaswing Performance Centre', managed by Jean-Jacques Rivet,

osteopath and accomplished athlete, where tailor-made programmes enable golfers of all levels to perfect their swings by combining a scientific knowledge of biomechanics with modern technology. The facility also includes a renowned David Leadbetter Academy.

Jean-Marie Casella, Director of Golf at Terre Blanche, says: "We offer a typical Provence experience with our five star Leading Hotel of the World facilities which perfectly complement the two golf courses and unique facilities. We will be celebrating ten years in 2014 and, of course, we are looking forward like everyone in our country to The 2018 Ryder Cup being played at Le Golf National, Paris, and as we host the French national amateur and Under-16 squads we hope that maybe one of those players will emerge to challenge for a place in Europe's Team."

Raphaël Jacquelin, who is seeking to follow in the footsteps of compatriots Jean Van de Velde and Thomas Levet by becoming a Ryder Cup player, is both European Tour Member and the Touring Professional at Terre Blanche, and not only does he use the facilities to hone his game but he is one of several golfers with attachments to European Tour Properties including Max Kieffer at Golf and Country Club Fleesensee. Coincidentally they met in an extraordinary play-off for the 2013 Open de España won by Jacquelin at the ninth extra hole!

Diamond Country Club

Holes 2 and 3, The Dutch

Jacquelin, like many of his compatriots, will be seeking European Team places in 2014 and 2016 but there can be absolutely no question that 2018 is firmly on all their agendas with Le Golf National, situated on the outskirts of Versailles near Paris, the host venue in addition to being the home on The European Tour International Schedule of the Alstom Open de France won in 2013 by 2010 US Open champion Graeme McDowell. He said: "We may have one of the greatest Ryder Cup venues in European golf hosting in 2018."

 L'Albatros Championship course (6,703 metres; 7,331 yards; par 71) is globally recognised as an impressive 'stadium' layout. It sits within the corn farmlands of Guyancourt which surround the historic Chateau of Versailles, once home to Louis XIV, and comprises vast undulating fairways dotted with large and small water hazards and innumerable links-style bunkers. Designed by Hubert

Chesneau in association with Robert von Hagge, L'Albatros is complemented by the classical 18-hole L'Aigle and nine hole L'Oiselet courses.

Meanwhile, Kieffer has become one of a number of exceptional German golfers, led by Martin Kaymer, the last green hero of 'The Miracle at Medinah', following in the footsteps of Bernhard Langer. He benefits from the opportunity to practice at Golf and Country Club Fleesensee which is an exceptional golf resort located less than 90 minutes from the German capital city of Berlin and boasting no fewer than five courses and four hotels.

Golf and Country Club Fleesensee had been part of The European Tour's portfolio of Tour Courses located across the continent providing golfers with a range of formidable playing opportunities. Each and every one is regarded as being among the highest quality venues in their

respective countries and includes Linna Golf in Finland, with which Mikko Ilonen, who claimed his third European Tour success by winning the Nordea Masters in neighbouring Sweden in 2013, has enjoyed a long association. Both Linna Golf, which has a spectacular Championship course in addition to the exquisite Vanajanlinna Hotel close by, and Estonian Golf and Country Club, featuring the stunning although daunting Championship Sea Course, which meanders through forest out to sea, and the nine-hole links-style Stone Course, extended their agreements in 2012.

 This special portfolio also includes Quinta do Lago with three 18 hole courses and a Paul McGinley Golf Academy set in the beautiful Algarve region of Portugal and Kungsängen Golf Club in Sweden with two 18-hole courses, the Kings, on which the Nordea (Scandinavian) Masters has been played four times, with Ryder Cup players Jesper Parnevik, Lee Westwood and McDowell among the winners, and the Queens.

Golf and Country Club Fleesensee became a Destination in March, 2013, and European Tour Properties provided the opportunity for significantly increased global awareness of the venue's outstanding facilities which include a Golf Academy, providing extensive practice and coaching facilities around a vast, circular driving range which is one of the largest in Europe.

The Tui Golf Course (6,301 metres; 6,891 yards, Par 72), set in the heart of the resort and the designated European Tour

Le Golf National 18th hole

Course, played host to a European Senior Tour event in 2000 and this stimulating test, with fast greens protected by clever bunkering and numerous water hazards, has since 2007 been a regular and much respected host of a First Stage European Tour Qualifying School event.

 Managing Director Thomas Döbber-Rüther said: "We are delighted to have become part of the distinguished network of European Tour Destinations which we fully believe will help to expand our brand internationally by developing the name and reputation of Fleesensee's leisure and golf facilities of which we are very proud."

Diamond Country Club in Atzenbrugg became in June, 2013, the recipient of the prestigious European Tour Destination Venue accolade and its expansion plans include a new, luxury hotel which will open its doors in the Spring of 2014 to realise the club's vision to offer a complete holiday experience combining golf, sightseeing, arts and culture to sit alongside The D G Academy which already provides superb practice facilities and is due to receive the prestigious European Tour Performance Institute endorsement.

The centrepiece of the venue, located less than one hour north west of the Austrian capital Vienna, is undoubtedly the Diamond Course (6,753 metres; 7,386 yards; par 72) designed by renowned English architect Jeremy Pern and opened in 2002. Miguel Angel Jiménez has been involved in redesigning a number of the holes on a course which provides a striking setting for the Lyoness Open powered by Greenfinity which was won in 2013 by Dutchman Joost Luiten.

Luiten would mark his finest season so far on The European Tour International Schedule by also winning on home soil by capturing the KLM Open at Kennemer Golf and Country Club, Zandvoort, on the same weekend in September that compatriot Daan Huizing won the Kharkov Superior Cup on the European Challenge Tour. That slice of 'Double Dutch Delight' was celebrated by everyone associated with The Dutch in Holland – future home to the KLM Open from 2016 to 2018 – where both Luiten and Huizing are members.

The Dutch (6,518 metres; 7,128 yards; par 71), a signature 18-hole Championship course designed by 2010 European Ryder Cup captain Colin Montgomerie in

conjunction with European Golf Design, is inland links in style with lightning-fast greens and many water features including lakes, canals and traditional Scottish 'burns.' Centrally located in the heart of The Netherlands, within easy access to the cities of Rotterdam, Amsterdam and Utrecht, officially opened in May, 2011, the course is recognised as both outstanding and challenging. It is complemented by a quite remarkable clubhouse, modelled on the best traditional Scottish clubhouses, and boasting many original golfing artefacts, and in April, 2013, hosted the fifth European Tour Properties Spring Conference which brought owners and executives from across the Tour's network of golf venues.

 Niek Molenaar, CEO of The Dutch, said: "We are happy to be part of this distinguished network. The Netherlands is the first country on the continent where golf was played and has the highest density of golfers in Europe, so it's more than fitting that one of our beautiful courses is a European Tour Destination."

Following the announcement in October, 2012, that the KLM Open, The Netherlands'

Hole 18, Estonian Golf and Country Club

A Network Of World Class Golf Venues

European Tour Properties comprises a network of world class golf venues, located in key golf markets.

European Tour Destinations and Courses all have the stamp of tournament quality and present a level of on and off-course facilities guaranteed to provide a memorable golfing experience for all members and visitors.

Visit www.europeantourproperties.com

Hole 1, PGA Catalunya Resort - Stadium Course

national Open, would be played at The Dutch for a minimum of three years, Alan Saddington, one of the founders of the course, said: "The Dutch was built with the quality of a European Tour event in mind. Now we have the opportunity to show some of the world's best players that we have been successful. We are very proud that KLM have put their trust in us."

 MacLaren added: "We have formed a special relationship with The Dutch, from its involvement in an excellent 2018 Ryder Cup Bid, to our appreciation of the industry-leading Made in Scotland corporate network, to its designation as a European Tour Destination. Staging the KLM Open is further proof of the outstanding quality that is evident throughout the venue, from the incredible playing surfaces to a quite beautiful clubhouse and standards of service which reflect a world class venue."

The announcement in July, 2013, that PGA Catalunya Resort had, from being part of the European Tour Courses portfolio, become a Destination Venue provided additional evidence of the growth and development of the network. PGA Catalunya Resort has enjoyed a multi-faceted relationship with The European Tour including hosting the Open de España in 2000 and 2009 and The European Tour Qualifying School Finals since 2008 on the Stadium and Tour Championship Courses, both of which were designed by Spanish golf legend Angel Gallardo and Ryder Cup player Neil Coles.

PGA Catalunya Resort has also opened the Sergio Garcia Junior Golf Academy, in collaboration with Fundación Sergio Garcia, to fulfil the twin objective of finding and coaching the best young talent and introducing golf to children with physical and learning disabilities through its 'Golf Adapted' programme. Garcia, who returned to PGA Catalunya Resort in October, 2013, to celebrate the first Anniversary of his Academy opening, said: "I'm very proud of this golfing initiative with PGA Catalunya Resort. For me, this is a dream come true. PGA Catalunya is a great complex, recognised throughout Europe, and it offers superb facilities on which to host an ambitious project such as this. The progress made by these youngsters in a year is impressive. With the highest quality of coaches and practice facilities available here there is great potential to develop stars of the future as well as introduce a

new generation to the joys of the game. Spain has a strong history of developing golfing talent, which I am proud to be a product of, and it is pleasing to be giving back to Spanish golf with this Junior Golf Academy."

In September, 2013, a high-calibre jury of international property experts identified PGA Catalunya Resort as the best example of a golf development from an extended list of entrants from across Europe with the outcome of being named the Best European Golf Development at the International Property Awards in London. The real estate project, located less than one hour north of Barcelona, will eventually consist of 368 properties combining contemporary architecture and subtle landscaping, ensuring complete privacy for both residents and golfers.

 Julio Delgado, CEO of PGA Catalunya Resort, said: "Our latest international recognitions – not least of which PGA Catalunya Resort's nomination as the eighth European Tour Destination – underline our commitment to providing our residents, golfers and guests with world class facilities and the highest levels of service and hospitality, which embodies our offering at PGA Catalunya Resort."

MacLaren also points out that the quality of the course not only provides dynamic and diverse challenges for players of all levels but also serves to showcase the game of golf globally, as will be the

The 2013 Allianz German Boys and Girls Open at Golf Club St. Leon-Rot

case at Golf Club St. Leon-Rot when The Solheim Cup is played there in 2015. The interest in this match was particularly heightened when in August, 2013, Europe returned home with the Cup following a rousing first ever win on American soil by the stunning margin of 18-10. In fact, a delegation from Golf Club St. Leon-Rot was in Colorado, Denver, to witness the win and experience the atmosphere and gather information.

Eicko Schulz-Hanssen, Managing Director of Golf Club St. Leon-Rot, said: "We felt it was essential to experience how The Solheim Cup was organised in Denver in order to be well prepared for hosting a smooth and outstanding event at our own Club where we will also stage The 2015 Junior Solheim Cup which emphasises the

importance we place on the development of junior golf."

The 2013 Allianz German Boys and Girls Open was once again held at Golf Club St. Leon-Rot which was founded in 1996 and is a sister venue of Terre Blanche. It is a stunning 45-hole complex situated near the scenic town of Heidelberg in the heart of Germany one hour's drive south of Frankfurt. The Club was four times the host venue to the Deutsche Bank-SAP TPC of Europe, won on three occasions by Tiger Woods, on The European Tour International Schedule.

St. Leon-Rot has a nine hole Academy course and a five hole 'bambini' course, demonstrating that junior golf is very much to the fore, to complement the Dave Thomas-designed St. Leon Course (6,541 metres; 7,153 yards; par 72) and the Hannes Schreiner-designed Rot Course (6,587 metres; 7,203 yards; par 72). It is the German Federation's national training centre and offers an innovative Allianz Indoor Short Game Centre of Excellence.

Dietmar Hopp, Founding President and Patron of Golf Club St. Leon-Rot, said: "Being part of European Tour Properties is an honour for us and I'm very happy that both Terre Blanche and St. Leon-Rot belong to the finest network of European courses in existence. We were delighted to become a European Tour Destination in 2012 and I

believe with this partnership we have a great chance to achieve our sporting and quality aims. Our vision is to see the golfers we support taking their place at the top of the world game, and at The Solheim Cup our athletes will get to see the world's best professional women golfers live, providing them with a unique and valuable experience for their careers."

The expansion of European Tour Properties continued in October, 2013, when it was announced that Jumeirah Golf Estates in the United Arab Emirates had joined the network so that the fifth edition of the DP World Tour Championship, Dubai was played on a Destination Venue in November with Henrik Stenson following in the footsteps of previous winners Lee Westwood, Robert Karlsson, Alvaro Quiros and Rory McIlroy.

MacLaren, explaining the reasoning behind the partnership with Jumeirah Golf Estates, said: "The Earth course at Jumeirah Golf Estates has proven itself to be a worthy challenge for many of the world's best golfers and a fitting host for The European Tour's season-ending finale. The strength of The European Tour in this part of the world makes it a logical expansion for our network of world class venues, and the recent announcement of substantial further development at Jumeirah Golf Estates makes the venue a worthy recipient of both the Destination and European Tour Performance Institute brands."

All of which with The Race to Dubai – a sequence of 46 tournaments played in 28 destinations in 2013 - now concluding at a European Tour Properties Destination demonstrates that the old adage that from small acorns do mighty oaks grow fits with the development of the network because unquestionably it was the initial link with the London Golf Club that was paramount to establishing the standards on which expansion and advancement could be implemented.

Without question London Golf Club enjoys a formidable bedrock with two courses both of which possess their own unique flavour. The Heritage (6,591 metres; 7,208 yards; par 72) on which both

Hole 13, Jumeirah Golf Estate - Earth Course

European Opens were played is a Jack Nicklaus signature design parkland layout with dramatic tee shots and daunting approaches to beautifully shaped, well protected greens. The International (6,405 metres; 7,005 yards; par 72), designed by Ron Kirby, is a downland course, more inland links in style, with undulating fairways and risk and rewards shots over water hazards.

 The relationship between European Tour Properties and London Golf Club progressed swiftly from those early days at The European Opens with the announcement at the beginning of 2010 that the wide-ranging partnership would initiate the new Venue and Property strategy of The European Tour. The terms of that partnership positioned London Golf Club as the flagship venue, being known as a European Tour Destination, with the focus on developing additional features to further enhance what was already recognised as one of the country's leading venues.

This has progressed with London Golf Club unveiling plans for a new five-star, 130-bedroomed hotel and spa development and the building of a European Tour Performance Institute (ETPI) complete with a state-of-the-art driving range, short game facility and an innovative nine-hole academy golf course which will be created by European Golf Design. The plans for these substantial developments encapsulate the club's vision of becoming a world class destination primed for hosting major golfing events.

MacLaren says: "The impact sparked by our original partnership with London Golf Club and the concept which we set out has seen European Tour Properties create a network of globally recognised venues located in key strategic golf markets. Now an integral part of The European Tour group, the venue portfolio is being selectively expanded with the clear objective to establish this as the world's premier golf and real estate brand with membership of this exclusive club offering significant and much desired benefits to venue owners.

 "There is already a wide range of high quality real estate opportunities at many of our Destination Venues ranging from expansive woodland plots at the exclusive resort of Terre Blanche; luxurious residences at Jumeirah Golf Estates in the vibrant city state of Dubai; contemporary villas and apartments at PGA Catalunya Resort; to charming and unique residences that harmonise with the landscape in Estonia. What remains key to the growth of the network, however, is the quality of the courses and we are very much delighted by our swift and structured evolution complemented by the high positioning of so many of our venues in Golf World's Top 100 Courses in Continental Europe."

Mitchell Platts

Hole 4, Le Chateau Course, Terre Blanche

Honorary Life Membership of The European Tour

Honorary Life Members of The European Tour

Year	Name	Year	Name
1978	John Jacobs OBE	2003	Bernard Gallacher OB
1978	Bernard Hunt MBE	2004	Neil Coles MBE
1978	Dai Rees CBE	2004	Christy O'Connor
1982	Peter Butler	2004	John Panton
1983	Seve Ballesteros	2005	Michael Campbell
1983	Tony Jacklin CBE	2007	Angel Cabrera
1985	Sir Henry Cotton MBE	2007	Padraig Harrington
1985	Fred Daly MBE	2008	Trevor Immelman
1985	Max Faulkner OBE	2010	Martin Kaymer
1985	Bernhard Langer	2010	Graeme McDowell M
1985	Sandy Lyle MBE	2010	Louis Oosthuizen
1987	Sir Nick Faldo MBE	2010	Tom Watson
1992	Ian Woosnam OBE	2011	Darren Clarke OBE
1994	José Maria Olazábal	2011	Rory McIlroy MBE
1995	Sir Bob Charles	2011	Charl Schwartzel
1995	Arnold Palmer	2011	Lee Westwood OBE
1995	Gary Player	2012	Roger Chapman
1997	Colin Montgomerie OBE	2012	Luke Donald MBE
1998	Ernie Els	2012	Brian Huggett MBE
1999	Paul Lawrie MBE	2012	Tommy Horton MBE
1999	Greg Norman	2012	Mark James
2001	Vijay Singh	2013	Dave Thomas
2002	Retief Goosen	2013	Justin Rose
2003	Peter Alliss		

Justin Rose and George O'Grady

Roger Chapman and George O'Grady

L-R: George O'Grady, Dave Thomas and John O'Leary

Roger Chapman, Justin Rose and Dave Thomas have all been added to a very special Roll of Honour by receiving one of the most coveted awards in sport – Honorary Life Membership of The European Tour. Happiness, however, too swiftly flies and little more than six months after graciously becoming the 46th recipient Thomas sadly passed away at the age of 79.

European Tour Chief Executive George O'Grady, who presented Thomas with his Silver Membership Card alongside European Tour Board Member John O'Leary at a special luncheon held in London in February, said: "Dave became a household name in the 1950s and 1960s when he helped to build the game in Britain and all over the world. He was a larger than life character, a truly great guy and wherever the Tour has travelled from Britain to the Continent to the Rest of the World we have played on courses designed by Dave. Both as a player and an architect he leaves a lasting legacy to the game he truly loved."

Thomas turned professional in 1949, twice finished runner-up in The Open Championship, played in four Ryder Cups, represented Wales 11 times in the World Cup and captured more than 20 titles including the Belgian Open (1955), the Dutch Open (1958), the French Open (1959) and the PGA Match Play (1963). He was also Captain of

The PGA in the Centenary Year of 2001.

Thomas's passing followed that of Bernard Hunt who, with John Jacobs and Dai Rees, became the first players in 1978 to be accorded Honorary Life Membership. Hunt, who died at the age of 83 in June, won more than 30 titles, played eight Ryder Cups and captained the team in 1973 and 1975, in addition to winning the Harry Vardon Trophy in 1958, 1960 and 1965.

O'Grady said: "Bernard was one of Britain's truly great champions and a steadfast ally to all involved in the growth of The European Tour. He was enormously respected by all his fellow players as was evidenced when he was appointed Ryder Cup Captain and also Captain of the PGA in 1966 and again from 1995 to 1997."

Chapman was awarded Honorary Life Membership in recognition of becoming in 2012 only the fourth player, following Gary Player, Jack Nicklaus and Hale Irwin, to win

both the US Senior PGA Championship and the US Senior Open in the same season in addition to the John Jacobs Trophy for finishing Number One on the European Senior Tour. Chapman turned professional in 1981, played 619 European Tour events and in his 472nd, after finishing runner-up six times, won the Brazil Rio de Janeiro 500 Years Open. He said: "I am extremely proud and grateful to George and everyone at The European Tour for their support and for this recognition."

Rose, who captured the first of his six European Tour titles in 2002, enjoyed a stellar year in 2012 winning the WGC-Cadillac Championship and helping Europe retain The Ryder Cup, then in June, 2013, won the US Open by two shots at Merion. He said: "It was a thrill to bring England its first US Open since Tony Jacklin in 1970 and an absolute delight to receive Honorary Life Membership of The European Tour."

Mitchell Platts

Honorary Life Vice Presidency of The European Tour

Gaston Barras
The Duke of Bedford
Sir Michael Bonallack OBE
Claude Cartier
Bernard Gallacher OBE
Ulf Laurin
Sir Neil Macfarlane
Akito Mizuno
Masato Mizuno
Padraig O'hUiginn
Len Owen
Johann Rupert
Emma Villacieros

His Grace The Duke of Bedford, owner of Woburn Golf Club, was presented by George O'Grady, Chief Executive of The European Tour, with Honorary Life Vice Presidency of The European Tour in recognition of his continued involvement with The European Tour, and golf in general, during a glittering staging of the European Senior Tour Annual Awards Dinner on the eve of the Travis Perkins plc Senior Masters, played in August 2013, for a 13th consecutive time on the Duke's Course. It was the 30th time that Tour competition had taken place at Woburn, which was home to the British Masters on 16 occasions, and the 53rd professional tournament to be contested there since its opening in 1976.

O'Grady said: "The game owes Woburn a great deal. They have always made us extremely welcome. We wanted to honour His Grace in making him a member of The European Tour family, making him one of the key people – led by Sir Michael Bonallack – and our other Honorary Life Presidents across the world of golf to who we can look to for advice."

Sadly Jaime Ortiz-Patiño, the man whose vision and commitment took The Ryder Cup to Continental Europe for the first time when it was played at his beloved Club de Golf Valderrama in Spain, and who was accorded Honorary Life Vice Presidency in May, 2010, passed away in January, 2013, at the age of 82.

O'Grady led the tributes when he said: "Jaime Ortiz-Patiño provided more than a few moments in the history of The European Tour and in many ways he changed the face of the game in Europe. His foresight and dedication through the Volvo Masters, played 16 times at Valderrama, and, of course, The Ryder Cup was legendary as was his dedication to excellence in terms of the preparation of the golf course. He raised the bar, he was a gentleman and he is sadly missed."

George O'Grady and His Grace, The Duke of Bedford

L-R: José Maria Olazábal, Jaime Ortiz-Patiño, George O'Grady and Angel Gallardo

PHOTOGRAPHERS

Nicolas Colsaerts

gettyimages®

David Cannon
Rob Carr
Tom Dulat
Mike Ehrmann
Stuart Franklin
Sam Greenwood
Scott Halleran
Richard Heathcote
Phil Inglis

Ross Kinnaird
Matt Lewis
Warren Little
Andy Lyons
Dean Mouhtaropoulos
Andrew Redington
Boris Streubel
Ian Walton

ADDITIONAL CONTRIBUTORS

P6	Jean-Lou Charon, Pascal Grizot, Valérie Fourneyron, and George O'Grady	FFgolf / Alexis Orloff
P9	Tony Jacklin, Sir Michael Parkinson, Peter Alliss, Bernard Gallacher and George O'Grady	Wentworth Club
P13	Henrik Stenson	Dagens Nyheter
P93	Gareth Shaw	Matt Browne, Sportsfile
	Jewel In The Glen by Ed Hodge (Arena Sport Books):	
P171	Jack Nicklaus, Dirk Bouts & Scott Fenwick Ian Marchbank	The Gleneagles Hotel The Gleneagles Hotel
P174	Peter Lederer & Jack Nicklaus	Jimmy Kidd
P175	Harold MacMillan & Sir Alec Douglas-Home	The Gleneagles Hotel
P 192-193	Bernd Wiesberger/Scott Hend/Wade Ormsby/ Liang Wen-chong/Thaworn Wiratchant	Asian Tour
	Michael McGeady	Fran Caffrey, Golffile
	Bernhard Langer	Gabe Roux, Gabe Roux Photography
	Mohd Siddikur	Hero
	Wu Ashun	Japan Golf Tour Organization
	Charl Schwartzel	OneAsia Tour
	Angel Cabrera	PGA Tour Latinoamérica
	Anirban Lahiri	PGTI
	Oliver Bekker/Anton Haig/Jean Hugo/ James Kingston	Sunshine Tour
	Jake Roos/Adilson da Silva/Jaco Van Zyl/ Tjaart Van der Walt	